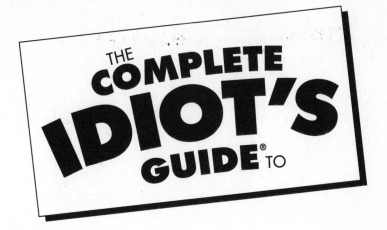

THE COMPLETE IDIOT'S GUIDE® TO

Freemasonry

by S. Brent Morris, Ph.D., 33°

ALPHA

A member of Penguin Group (USA) Inc.

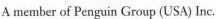

For Jacquelynn, my gentle butterfly, who supports me and brings joy and light to my life.

ALPHA BOOKS

Published by the Penguin Group

Penguin Group (USA) Inc., 375 Hudson Street, New York, New York 10014, U.S.A.

Penguin Group (Canada), 10 Alcorn Avenue, Toronto, Ontario, Canada M4V 3B2 (a division of Pearson Penguin Canada Inc.)

Penguin Books Ltd, 80 Strand, London WC2R 0RL, England

Penguin Ireland, 25 St Stephen's Green, Dublin 2, Ireland (a division of Penguin Books Ltd)

Penguin Group (Australia), 250 Camberwell Road, Camberwell, Victoria 3124, Australia (a division of Pearson Australia Group Pty Ltd)

Penguin Books India Pvt Ltd, 11 Community Centre, Panchsheel Park, New Delhi—110 017, India

Penguin Group (NZ), cnr Airborne and Rosedale Roads, Albany, Auckland 1310, New Zealand (a division of Pearson New Zealand Ltd)

Penguin Books (South Africa) (Pty) Ltd, 24 Sturdee Avenue, Rosebank, Johannesburg 2196, South Africa

Penguin Books Ltd, Registered Offices: 80 Strand, London WC2R 0RL, England

Copyright © 2006 by S. Brent Morris

International Standard Book Number: 1-59257-490-4
Library of Congress Catalog Card Number: 2005937486

08 07 06   8 7 6 5 4 3 2 1

Interpretation of the printing code: The rightmost number of the first series of numbers is the year of the book's printing; the rightmost number of the second series of numbers is the number of the book's printing. For example, a printing code of 06-1 shows that the first printing occurred in 2006.

Printed in the United States of America

Note: This publication contains the opinions and ideas of its author. It is intended to provide helpful and informative material on the subject matter covered. It is sold with the understanding that the author and publisher are not engaged in rendering professional services in the book. If the reader requires personal assistance or advice, a competent professional should be consulted.

The author and publisher specifically disclaim any responsibility for any liability, loss, or risk, personal or otherwise, which is incurred as a consequence, directly or indirectly, of the use and application of any of the contents of this book.

Most Alpha books are available at special quantity discounts for bulk purchases for sales promotions, premiums, fund-raising, or educational use. Special books, or book excerpts, can also be created to fit specific needs.

For details, write: Special Markets, Alpha Books, 375 Hudson Street, New York, NY 10014.

Publisher: *Marie Butler-Knight*
Editorial Director: *Mike Sanders*
Senior Managing Editor: *Jennifer Bowles*
Senior Acquisitions Editor: *Randy Ladenheim-Gil*
Development Editor: *Nancy D. Lewis.*
Production Editor: *Janette Lynn*
Copy Editor: *Jeff Rose*

Illustrator: *Shannon Wheeler*
Book Designer: *Trina Wurst*
Cover Designer: *Kurt Owens*
Indexer: *Brad Herriman*
Layout: *Ayanna Lacey*
Proofreading: *John Etchison*

Contents at a Glance

Contents

Foreword

The annual arrival of the Shrine Circus was a highlight of my boyhood. I loved the trapeze artists, the animal acts, and the special attractions. But I don't recall wondering what the Shrine was or ever making a connection with the Shriners until I grew older. And it took me even longer to realize that the group was made up of Masons. The fraternity was not hiding. It places its name on a circus. Its square-and-compasses symbol adorns numerous buildings. But I hardly noticed the fraternity.

Most people, I suspect, have a similarly limited awareness of Masonry. Some have some connection with the fraternity, often through a relative. Others, like me, vaguely recall seeing Masonic halls. But few outsiders understand much more about the Masons than that they are a secret society of men—a description that is largely true, but also misleading.

My own incomprehension continued until I began advanced study in early American history. Largely upon my mentor's suggestion, I started piecing together the Masonic past. This was a challenging task. Although its members included Benjamin Franklin, George Washington, and Paul Revere, Masonry's early development remained uncharted. I quickly found myself drowning in a sea of confusing terms that seemed just beyond my ability to grasp.

Even Masons themselves, I discovered, sometimes have difficulties with the complexities of their fraternity. Many members still know little about the Masonic past. And no one can be expected to know all the elements of the modern fraternity from the small Social Order of the Beauceant to the massive Scottish Rite.

Yet another group of people, small but vocal, fears the fraternity. With greater imagination than insight, they suggest that Masons worship the devil and seek to rule the world. The idea that the fraternity possesses deep secrets (whether for good or evil) inspired the best-selling author Dan Brown to create his wildly popular mysteries featuring Robert Langdon, an adventurous academic who specializes in the lore of groups such as the Masons.

The confusing, mysterious world of Masonry is difficult to enter alone. People starting on this journey need a guide, someone with the good sense and intelligence to distinguish fact from fiction and with the skill to explain both clearly. Allow me to introduce the perfect person for the job: S. Brent Morris. He has not (as far as I know) led the extraordinary life of the fictional Harvard symbologist Langdon, who attracts danger and dead bodies wherever he goes. But Morris knows more about Masonry. And he explains it with clarity, patience, and gentle good humor. He has written what I believe is the best short introduction to the fraternity available anywhere.

Morris expertly guides us through the maze of myths, symbols, and institutions that make up the fraternity. He introduces Masonry's extraordinary history—not surprisingly, the part of the book that I find most fascinating. But Morris does more than note such significant members as Theodore and Franklin D. Roosevelt and Henry and Gerald Ford. Morris also explores the myths that surround the Freemasons. He provides the straight dope on the design of Washington, D.C. He probes the mysterious "33" on the label of Rolling Rock beer. And he explains that strange eye that looks out at us from the back of the dollar bill.

I can think of no better guide to the odd, mystifying, and fascinating subject of Masonry than S. Brent Morris. I know you'll enjoy the tour.

Steven C. Bullock

Steven C. Bullock teaches history at Worcester Polytechnic Institute. His book *Revolutionary Brotherhood: Freemasonry and the Transformation of the American Social Order, 1730–1840,* served as the basis of a documentary aired on the History Channel. He has also commented on Masonry for CNN and National Public Radio.

Introduction

I became interested in Freemasonry almost forty years ago. The more I studied it, the more it fascinated me. Like any human institution, it's not perfect, but the scope of its successes more than makes up for its failings. This book concentrates on Freemasonry as it evolved in America. Not that the fraternity in other countries isn't important—it is, but there's only so much you can cover well in limited space.

I hope that you will find answers to your basic questions about the fraternity. Whether you're interested because a relative was a member, or because you've read or seen something, or perhaps because you're already a Mason and want to know more—I've tried to include something for you.

You can jump into almost any chapter and read just the information you need. But the chapters build on each other, and terminology or ideas may have been introduced and explained in earlier chapters. If you take the time to read through from the beginning, you'll have a better understanding of later chapters.

How This Book Is Organized

This book is presented in five sections:

Part 1, "The Basic Organization of Freemasonry," starts with what we know and have surmised about the formation of the Masonic fraternity. It appears that the British trade organization of stone workers or Freemasons transformed itself into a gentlemen's club. The fraternity migrated to the American colonies by 1730 and soon established itself as an organization of respect and honor. Many leading patriots were members, and the fraternity was a unifying force among officers in the Continental Army. Then modern American Freemasonry emerged from the aftermath of the abduction and disappearance of William Morgan in Batavia, New York. The part also ends with the story of Prince Hall Freemasonry, a branch of the fraternity that's predominantly African American and has a unique and proud heritage.

Part 2, "The Eastern Star, the York Rite, and the Scottish Rite," are organizations that give opportunities for Masons to be more involved in their fraternity. The Eastern Star is the largest of several organizations for Masons and their female relatives; others include the Amaranth and White Shrine of Jerusalem. You're likely to find an Eastern Star Chapter meeting in most Masonic halls. The York Rite expands on the lessons and legends of the lodge. There are thousands of York Rite bodies throughout America, often in small and mid-sized towns. There are about 400 Scottish Rite bodies in larger regional centers. The 33° of the Scottish Rite may be the best-known Masonic honor.

Part 3, "Building Higher, Having Fun, and Doing More," describes the dozens of additional Masonic organizations built on the foundation of the local lodge. There are several "honorary" groups whose membership is by invitation only, usually to those who have served in the York Rite. Other groups are for students of Masonic History. The Shrine is the best known of several groups that provide social activities for Freemasons as well as a wonderful philanthropy to support, the Shriners Hospitals for Children. The Grotto and Tall Cedars are the other two main social groups. Masons support several youth organizations, including the Order of DeMolay for boys, and Job's Daughters and Rainbow Girls for girls. Freemasonry supports an amazing number of philanthropies, spending over three quarters of a *billion* dollars a year on them!

Part 4, "Masonic Myths and Misunderstandings," looks at some of the issues people have had with Freemasonry. Anti-Masons have demonized Albert Pike as the epitome of everything that's wrong with the fraternity. You can read about some of the more flagrant misrepresentations. Lots of urban legends tell of "secret" Masonic symbols hidden everywhere—in the street plan of Washington, D.C., on the back of the dollar bill, and on beer bottles. Some objections to Freemasonry are serious, and usually stem from the fraternity's ecumenical nature. I've tried to summarize some of the more common concerns.

Part 5, "A Field Guide to Masonic Symbols and Jewelry," will help you identify fraternal jewelry, either among your family heirlooms, on a car, at a flea market, or on the lapel of a friend. We start with an overview of Masonic symbols and show how Masons have their own private language of ideas. Once you understand the basic symbols, it's an easy step to appreciate the many types of jewelry that incorporate these symbols.

Things to Help You Out Along the Way

There are notes throughout the book to help you better understand and enjoy this material.

A Good Rule

When studying the Masonic fraternity and its complicated lore, certain rules of thumb can help you avoid misunderstandings.

Hits and Myths

There's lots of misinformation about Freemasonry, and I've tried to steer you away from some of the most notorious examples. Take due notice thereof, and govern yourself accordingly.

def•i•ni•tion

Freemasonry, like any large organization, has developed its own specialized vocabulary, often common words but with particular meanings. I've tried to highlight words that might be new to you.

The Square Deal

There are so many good stories about Freemasonry that it's been hard to fit it all into the body of the text. From time to time, I've stuck in anecdotes and quotes about other Masons.

Acknowledgments

Many friends and Masonic brothers helped me with this book—so many that I fear overlooking someone. It would be a greater problem, however, to not try to acknowledge the generous assistance I have received. Arturo de Hoyos helped prepare the outline for this book and served as a sounding board for many sections. Alexandria-Washington Lodge No. 22 gave permission to use their image of George Washington's Masonic apron that they own. Bob Cooper explained about Scottish lodges operating without charters. Curtis Edic helped with information about the Royal Order of Jesters. Richard E. Fletcher, executive secretary of the Masonic Service Association of North America, helped with accurate statistics on their hospital visitation program. Sean Graystone and Reese Harrison helped with information about the Knights Beneficent of the Holy City. Pete Normand tried to keep me on the straight and narrow with my facts. Trevor McKeown, site administrator, Grand Lodge of British Columbia and Yukon A.F. & A.M., gave permission to use anything on their website. Wallace McLeod clarified the Old Charges for me. Art Pierson of Alexandria-Washington Lodge No. 22 took the photograph of George Washington's Masonic apron. Tom Savini, director of the Chancellor Robert R. Livingston Library of the Grand Lodge of New York, F.&A.M., gave permission to use their image of Daniel Tompkins's Masonic apron.

In addition to my Masonic brothers, I must acknowledge my family and friends who put up with me during the writing of this book. My wife, Jacquelynn, not only provided amazing support and wonderful dinners, but also was the first line of defense against confused ideas. Her most valuable guidance often came in the form of a question: "Why would anyone want to know about that?"

Thanks also to the following people and organizations for permission to use their photographs in the book:

Collection of Arturo de Hoyos

Jeremy L. Cross

Supreme Council, 33°, Washington, D.C.

www.freemasonry.bcy.ca

Trademarks

All terms mentioned in this book that are known to be or are suspected of being trademarks or service marks have been appropriately capitalized. Alpha Books and Penguin Group (USA) Inc. cannot attest to the accuracy of this information. Use of a term in this book should not be regarded as affecting the validity of any trademark or service mark.

Part 1

The Basic Organization of Freemasonry

Freemasonry is a complex organization that evolved gradually over several centuries. We can't point to a precise date or place of origin, like Philadelphia, July 4, 1776. Rather we need to examine documents, some going back over 600 years, and do some detective work to see what was happening. In this part of the book, you'll learn about those early records, how the fraternity operates without any central authority, American Freemasonry and its effect on Independence, and African American Freemasonry. Understanding Freemasonry is a lot like understanding the American Colleges system—there's a basic form that most schools follow—with lots and lots of variations.

What Is Freemasonry?

In This Chapter

- Freemasonry's organization and presence
- Masonic documentation from the 1300s
- Masonic secrets as symbols of fidelity and advancement within the fraternity
- Masonic ritual teaches morals and ethics through ceremonies and drama
- Freemason organizations in the United States

Freemasonry is the world's oldest and largest fraternity. Sometime in the late 1600s and very early 1700s (there are no records), London lodges apparently held quarterly meetings of lodge officers, but these were discontinued for reasons unknown. The modern fraternity began in 1717 when four old London lodges formed a *grand lodge* (a central governing organization) to revive the quarterly meetings and to hold an Annual Assembly and Feast. From these beginnings a worldwide fraternity grew and spread, attracting to itself a constellation of organizations such as the Scottish Rite (32° Masons), York Rite (Knights Templar), Shriners, Eastern Star (for ladies and men), DeMolay (for boys), and many more.

def•i•ni•tion

A **grand lodge** is the state or provincial or national organization that has final authority over all Freemasonry within its borders or jurisdiction. Most American grand lodges meet annually to conduct business.

A good model for thinking about the organization of Freemasonry is a university. There are a swarm of related organizations around a college campus—fraternities, sororities, academic honor societies, political clubs, the glee club, the ski club, the alumni association, and on and on. The university may directly control some of the groups, while others have varying degrees of independence. They are all, however, "university-related." In a like manner, autonomous "Masonic-related" organizations are connected with Freemasonry, all more or less working together. In this chapter, we'll concentrate on describing the organization of American Freemasonry while giving you a sense of how the fraternity operates elsewhere in the world.

The Fraternity's Real and Imagined Presence

Freemasons are members of the "Ancient, Honorable Fraternity of Free and Accepted Masons." The terms *Freemason* and *Mason* are interchangeable, as are *Freemasonry* and *Masonry*. The word is thought to refer originally to "freestone masons," skilled craftsmen who carved freestone (a soft, easily carved stone). Prof. Andrew Prescott, Director of the Center for Research into Freemasonry, University of Sheffield, discovered the earliest known use of the word in the London Coroners' Rolls for 1325–1326.

def•i•ni•tion

A **Masonic lodge** is a local chapter of the fraternity of Freemasons. Like the word *school*, the word *lodge* can refer to both the group of members and to the physical building. Other Masonic-related organizations use the words *chapter, council, commandery, consistory, priory, court,* and so on to refer to specific local organizations.

In 2005, 12,500 *Masonic lodges* and about 1.7 million Freemasons existed in America. Worldwide membership is probably a little less than double that in America, or about three million. Since lodges outside the United States tend to be much smaller than the American average of 135 members, there are an estimated 50,000–60,000 lodges worldwide. With an organization that large, it's not surprising to come across Masonic buildings almost everywhere.

In addition to their usually well-identified buildings, Masonic symbols are also common on other buildings. Since the Freemasons historically have performed the civic task of ceremonially laying cornerstones (most famously the U.S. Capitol, the

Washington Monument, and the White House), it's easy to find churches, court-houses, schools, and other buildings with the Masonic *square and compass* on their cornerstone.

The square and compass is the most universal symbol of Freemasonry (in America it usually has a "G" in the center). It reminds the Mason to square his actions by the square of virtue, to circumscribe his passions and desires with a symbolic compass, and to remember that as geometry was in the center of the Mason's trade, so should God be in the center of his life.

The square and compass (with "G" in America) is the most universal symbol of Freemasonry.

(Courtesy of the Grand Lodge of British Columbia and Yukon, www.freemasonry.bcy.ca)

Another symbol of the Masons is the all-seeing eye (see the figure that follows), a common eighteenth-century and earlier icon representing God watching humanity. ("Behold, the eye of the Lord is upon them that fear him, upon them that hope in his mercy …" Psalms 33:13)

It was not unique to Freemasonry, but it has become so strongly associated with the fraternity that any usage is generally thought to be Masonic related. Thus you hear the frequent claims that the Masons put "their" all-seeing eye on the back of the dollar for some reason, or that a church is a "secret Masonic church" because it uses the all-seeing eye in its decorations.

The All-Seeing Eye is a symbol of God watching over his people (see Psalms 33:13).

If the prevalence of the square and compass emblem and the all-seeing eye doesn't start you thinking, then perhaps a list of well-known Freemasons will get your attention: George Washington, Benjamin Franklin, John Hancock, Thurgood Marshall, Voltaire, Simon Bolivar, Bernardo O'Higgins, Benito Juarez, Mustapha Kemal Ataturk, Giuseppe Garibaldi, Robert Burns, Wolfgang Amadeus Mozart, Rudyard Kipling, John Philip Souza, Harry Truman, Edwin E. "Buzz" Aldrin, Reverend Jesse Jackson, and more.

Pretty soon it seems as if the Masons and their emblems are everywhere! Just what are they doing in their lodge halls, meeting behind closed doors? Do they secretly run the world or something?

Well, the reality isn't nearly that exciting. Freemasons and their lodges are indeed all over the place, especially in Middle America. They have attracted many prominent members to their ranks over the years, but that's not surprising for an organization that's had a formal existence of almost 300 years.

Freemasonry appeals to men who want to have fellowship with other men with high ethical and moral values and who acknowledge the importance of God in their lives. It is a popular fraternity that has as its tenets Brotherly Love, Relief, and Truth. And it is a complex organization with a long history that takes a little study to understand.

Documentary Evidence: 1390–1850

The oldest document connected with Freemasonry is the Regius Manuscript, dated to approximately 1390. It is one of the "Old Charges" or "Gothic Constitutions," the early governing documents of the Masons as a craft organization. The documents all probably trace back to one original document, with changes creeping in through copying errors and misunderstandings. Some 113 versions of the Gothic Constitutions, dated from 1390 to 1850 (the dates they were copied), have been identified, and doubtless hundreds of other copies have been lost through the years.

The Gothic Constitutions served the purpose of regulations for the organization, giving rules on how to conduct the trade, how Masters and Apprentices should interact, and how Masons should behave. Some old lodges treated their copy like a charter, believing they could not meet without the document being present. The Gothic Constitutions also contained some portions of Masonic ceremonies.

Here are some examples of rules and guidance found in some Old Charges:

♦ A Master Mason must be steadfast, trusty, and true.

♦ An apprentice must serve for seven years, and his Master must teach him the craft of masonry.

♦ A Master Mason must undertake no work that he cannot perform and finish.

♦ A craftsman must love God and His holy church, his master, and fellows.

♦ A craftsman must swear to be true to the king.

♦ Craftsmen must help one another by instructing those deficient in knowledge and skill.

♦ Craftsmen must obey the assembly of Masons on pain of forsaking the craft and being imprisoned.

♦ Do not talk with food in your mouth.

♦ Do not pick your teeth at the dinner table.

♦ Do not blow your nose in your napkin at the dinner table.

> ### The Square Deal
>
> An apprentice was usually a teenage boy bound by legal agreement to work for a Mason for a specific amount of time in return for instruction in the trade of freemasonry. Upon completing his apprenticeship, a young man could join the trade organization as a fellow or craftsman. A Master Mason was an employer of craftsmen, but within a lodge both were fully trained Masons.

The Constitutions also begin with a legendary history of the craft of masonry, tracing it back to Babylon, and then having the patriarch Abraham, his wife Sarah, and the Greek geometer Euclid together in Egypt at the same time! Historical events may be jumbled, but according to Wallace McLeod, retired Professor of Classics, University of Toronto, and expert on the Gothic Constitutions, the constitutions served an important psychological purpose. They showed Masons how Freemasonry "went back to the Sacred Writings, and how it could number among its votaries even monarchs themselves. This was no servile trade of recent devising, but an ancient and honorable institution."

The Square Deal

The Regius Manuscript ends with these words, "Amen! Amen! So mote it be! So say we all for charity." The phrase "So mote it be" can be translated as "So may it be" or "So might it happen." At Masonic gatherings today, after a prayer is given and the "Amen" said, the Masons present will all say, "So mote it be." This both affirms the prayer and continues a custom of over 600 years.

The Transition from "Operative" to "Speculative"

The oldest surviving lodge minutes are from the Lodge of Edinburgh for July 31, 1599. The minutes relate that the lodge reprimanded George Patoun for employing a *cowan*, a craftsman who didn't belong to a lodge or a "Mason without the Word," to work on a chimney. These and other early minutes clearly show the lodge's concern with the business of a trade union. There are many more records of Scottish lodges during the 1600s, but strangely there are virtually no records in England.

Significant Masonic events started to happen in Scotland in the 1600s, and by the 1630s non-operative Masons were being admitted to Scottish lodges as honorary members. On May 20, 1641, some members of the Lodge of Edinburgh initiated Sir Robert Moray, Quarter Master General of the Army in Scotland, while the army occupied Newcastle-on-Tyne, England. This is the first record of a non-*operative Mason* in England.

def•i•ni•tion

An **operative** Mason is a worker who constructs a building with stone. A **speculative** Mason is a member of the modern fraternity and one who "fits himself as a living stone for that house not made with hands, eternal in the heavens."

Five years later, Elias Ashmole, the famous English antiquary, recorded in his diary for October 16, 1646, "I was made a Free Mason at Warrington in Lancashire." His extensive diaries contain no further entries that deal with Freemasonry until March 10, 1682: "I received a summons to appear at a Lodge to be held the next day, at Mason's Hall, London." He wrote on the 11th, "Accordingly I went & about Noone were admitted into the Fellowship of Freemasons. ... I was the Senior Fellow among them (it being 35 years since I was admitted). ... We all dyned at the halfe Moone Taverne in Cheapside, at a noble dinner prepaired at the charge of the new-accepted Masons." Similar admissions of non-operatives or gentlemen Masons were also occurring in Scotland.

Something very interesting was happening to Freemasonry during the 1600s—and we're not quite sure what it was. In 1717 four old lodges of *speculative* Masons came together to form the Premier Grand Lodge in London. Apparently London lodges had discontinued their quarterly officers' meetings (there are no existing records), and these four lodges wanted to revive the meetings and to hold an Annual Assembly and Feast. The limited records show that in 1599 Freemasonry was a trade organization regulating the craft of masonry, and in 1717 it was almost entirely a gentlemen's club that retained the structure and terminology of the trade group.

During this century, lodges began accepting gentlemen as members, and after about a century the gentlemen dominated the organization. The trade union was now a fraternity. What happened and why? The basic answer that you'll hear time and again in this book is that we really don't know. This was during the Enlightenment when gentlemen pursued learning of all sorts, especially science. Freemasons obviously knew "secrets" of geometry and architecture that enabled them to build the soaring gothic cathedrals. If the legends of their Gothic Constitutions were correct, then they might have preserved knowledge from Abraham or King Solomon or from ancient times.

This was also the time of clubs and coffee houses in England, and gentlemen then needed few excuses to gather together. Being an ancient organization with a fabled history, known for mutual support, probably added a certain panache to Masonic gatherings. Further you couldn't just join—you had to go through the ancient ceremonies (possibly the same ones that King Solomon went through!).

This gradual transformation of the trade organization into a club is known as the "Transition Theory." I believe the evidence best supports this as the origin of the modern fraternity, representing a gradual evolution from 1390 to 1717. There is not unanimity about the Transition Theory, just as there isn't unanimity about most historical theories.

Historians worry about the big gaps that the Transition Theory leaps over, the absence of lodges in England, why gentlemen would have joined a trade organization, and the lack of evidence. (Of course, no theory of Masonic origins has much evidence; they all must fill in gaps between a few definite events.) The currently favorite romantic theory is that when Philip the Fair of France and Pope Clement V suppressed the Knights Templar, they went underground, continued their existence, and used the Freemasons as their "front" organization. (We'll discuss that theory in Chapter 15 of this book.)

Masonic Secrets

Freemasonry is sometimes called a "secret society." In America, however, its members advertise their membership with rings, pins, and car badges; lodge buildings usually have large signs out front and are decorated with the square and compass emblem; lodges and grand lodges have web pages and telephone directory listings; in some communities newspapers list lodge meetings. This isn't a very good way to run a "secret" organization!

Masons do hold private meetings; only members can attend. They do have "modes of recognition"—handshakes and passwords—that are important symbolic secrets, but they're hardly real secrets, as they've been in print for centuries. The first grand lodge was formed in 1717, and the first exposé of Masonic ritual secrets was in 1723 in the London newspaper *The Flying Post*—the grand lodge managed to keep its secrets for all of 6 years!

> **The Square Deal**
>
> There are real Masonic secrets, and there are symbolic Masonic secrets. Their value to Masons is as symbols of fidelity and of advancement within the fraternity. Masons make a solemn promise not to reveal the secrets to anyone. It doesn't matter to him that you can find the secrets in print; what matters to the Mason is that he keeps his promise.

It is thought that the secrets were originally a substitute for a membership certificate. At a time of general illiteracy, there was a practical problem of producing and reading documents of any sort. How could a Mason travel from one location to another and prove himself to be a member of the trade organization and to be eligible for employment or relief? The solution seems to have been the "Mason Word," in use since at least the early 1600s. It was a secret taught to new Masons upon completing an apprenticeship. The original simple and practical secret soon grew to symbolic passwords for every level of membership, along with special handshakes and hand signs.

Masonic Ritual

The thing that separates Freemasonry from most other civic organizations is its ritual: the formal ceremonies of initiation that both signify advancement in the organization and teach moral and ethical lessons. A ritual experience can be a transforming event for the participant. Ritual ceremonies can appear trivial when read or described, but when experienced they can be deeply moving. Consider the many small ceremonies that can be found in modern wedding rituals: the bride presents a flower to her mother, the father gives away the bride at the altar, the bride and groom exchange rings, the bride and groom say, "I do." Any of these simple actions can cause a tidal wave of emotion among the guests, all out of proportion to the event itself. Masonic ritual can be the same.

Early Masonic ceremonies described in some of the Gothic Constitutions are very primitive. When a man was to be made a Mason, the traditional history of the craft and regulations were read to him from the Gothic Constitutions. Then the initiate put his hands on "the Book" (the Bible) along with one of the elders and took the oath of a Mason.

Over the centuries the ceremonies grew by a gradual buildup. Symbolic tests, historical lessons, and penalties were added, the latter mostly derived from British penal codes. As gentlemen Masons came to predominate the membership, more highly refined symbolism was added. When the first grand lodge was formed in 1717, there were only two *degrees* or levels of membership. By 1730, a new third degree had been added, and Freemasonry then had three distinct levels of membership. (See Appendix C for two scripts of Masonic rituals.)

> ## def•i•ni•tion
>
> A Masonic **degree** is a level of membership or the ceremony required to attain that level of membership. The first three degrees correspond to membership levels in a trade union: 1° Apprentice; 2° Fellowcraft (or journeyman); 3° Master Mason. Hundreds of degrees have been invented over the years, both serious and humorous.

    1° Entered Apprentice

    2° Fellowcraft

    3° Master Mason

No one knows where the new Master Mason Degree came from. Was it a previously unmentioned ancient ceremony, or was it an invention of the new gentlemen Masons? Wherever it originated, it included the legend of Hiram Abiff, a character mentioned briefly in the Bible. "And king Solomon sent and fetched Hiram out of Tyre. He was a widow's son of the tribe of Naphtali, and his father was a man of Tyre, a worker in brass: and he was filled with wisdom, and understanding, and cunning to work all works in brass. And he came to King Solomon, and wrought all his work." (1 Kings 7:13–14) There's also a brief mention of Hiram Abiff in 2 Chronicles 2:13–14, where the King James Version refers to him as "Huram my father's." "My father's" in Hebrew is "abiv" or "Abiff." The Revised Standard Version (1901) and the New International Version (1984) translate "Huram my father's" as "Huram-Abi."

The legend varies from grand lodge to grand lodge, though most American versions are very similar. According to the story, Solomon, king of Israel, Hiram, king of Tyre, and Hiram Abiff were the three Grand Masters at the building of the Temple in Jerusalem. King Solomon organized the workers by skill for work efficiency. King Hiram furnished building supplies and workers for the Temple. Hiram Abiff was the master builder, responsible for all of the decorations of the Temple.

Three Fellowcraft Masons were impatient to receive the Master Mason word, and tried to extort it from Hiram Abiff. He refused to reveal the secret and was murdered. The murderers hastily buried the body of Hiram outside the city and tried to escape. They were captured, returned to Solomon for judgment, and punished. The body of Hiram was found and reburied in a more dignified grave.

This simple story of fidelity to a trust is the basis of most Masonic ritual legends. Other degrees elaborate on the Hiram Abiff story with sequels, prequels, elaborations, and spin-offs, each offering its own moral lesson. (See Chapters 8 and 9 on the York and Scottish Rites for examples.) The death and reburial of Hiram also teaches the importance of the individual Mason being prepared for his own death.

The Organization of American Freemasonry

This book concentrates on Freemasonry as it operates in the United States. American Freemasonry is not uniquely important, but its 50+ grand lodges and 1.7 million members are the largest contingent of Masons in the world. Understanding Freemasonry in America will give you a broad, general understanding of the fraternity elsewhere. The phrase "Family of Masonry" is often used to describe the large number of organizations that draw their members from Master Masons or their family. For example, the Eastern Star is a well-known group for Masons and their female relatives, while the Masonic Gathering is a less well-known group of Masons who are ham radio operators.

Regardless of which of the many Masonic organizations we talk about, there are certain points in common. Masons (and their relatives, in some cases) join these groups because they enjoy the fellowship, the ritual ceremonies, and the opportunity for community participation. As part of the community activity, all American Masonic groups combined give over $2 million a day to philanthropy—that's over three-quarters of a billion dollars a year.

Local Lodges and State Grand Lodges

The basic organizational unit of Freemasonry is the local Masonic Lodge. As mentioned earlier, in 2005, there were about 12,500 lodges in the United States with an average of 135 members each. Small, rural lodges might have only a few dozen members, while larger suburban lodges have hundreds. It is in these local lodges that all Masons begin their membership by *petitioning* to join the lodge.

def•i•ni•tion

A **membership petition** is what Masons call an application. The typical petition usually asks for name, age, residence, occupation, references, and the recommendations of two members of the lodge.

The presiding officer of a lodge is called the **Worshipful Master,** not because the members "worship" him, but because it's a traditional English title of respect. (English magistrates today are still addressed as "worshipful.") The Grand Master is **Most Worshipful,** and other officers may be Right Worshipful or Very Worshipful, depending on their rank. Other Masonic bodies use different superlatives to describe their local presiding officers: Excellent, Illustrious, Eminent, Venerable, and so on. When the word Most is used, that usually indicates the presiding officer of a state or national organization.

The lodges in a state constitute a grand lodge that governs all Masonry within their state or jurisdiction. It may sound backwards, but the 3° Masons of the grand lodge are the supreme authority over all Freemasonry in a state, even those with "higher" degrees. If other organizations that draw their members from Master Masons don't follow a grand lodge's rules and policies, then the grand lodge will not allow its members to participate in them, effectively closing down the other organization.

Local lodges elect their officers each year, headed by the *Worshipful Master* and Senior and Junior Wardens. (These are the equivalents of President and First and Second Vice-Presidents.) Lodge representatives meet each year at grand lodge and elect the *Most Worshipful* Grand Master to preside for a year. (A few Grand Masters have longer terms, up to three years.) A Master or Grand Master usually serves in several junior offices before being elected, so it can take up to seven or more years "going through the line" of offices before being elected to preside. Most grand lodges have District Deputy Grand Masters to oversee lodges within a district or region.

The Square Deal

Freemasonry has a long-standing custom of not soliciting members. This rule of nonsolicitation was codified as early as 1772 in William Preston's Illustrations of Masonry, a guidebook for lodge forms and ceremonies. In it, candidates are required to declare upon their honor "that unbiased by friends and uninfluenced by mercenary motives, [I] freely and voluntarily offer [myself] a candidate for the mysteries of Masonry." Some Masons have carried the nonsolicitation rule to the extreme that they will not even talk about the fraternity to a nonmember. In response to weakening community ties, when it's now difficult to know much about your neighbors, much less which are Masons, some grand lodges have loosened their restrictions on solicitation. It's now not uncommon to find "friendship nights" held by lodges where prospective members are told about the fraternity, but not directly asked to join. Part of this campaign of Masonic awareness is the bumper sticker, "2B1ASK1" = "To be one, ask one."

The York and Scottish Rites

Once a man becomes a Master Mason he is eligible to join one of the many Masonic-related organizations. (There are all sorts of these groups, including one for performing magicians who're Masons!) These groups might meet in the local lodge hall or be regional organizations. The two largest such groups are the York Rite and the Scottish Rite. (See Chapters 8 and 9 for detailed descriptions of these two rites.)

The York Rite is composed of three separate and loosely cooperating organizations: Chapters of Royal Arch Masons (about 4,300 in 2005), Councils of Cryptic Masons, and Commanderies of Knights Templar (about 1,300 in 2005). They all have local bodies and state grand bodies. Unlike American Freemasonry, the York Rite has national bodies that most state bodies belong to.

The Scottish Rite has fewer but larger regional bodies (about 300 in 2005). There are two Supreme Councils, the Southern Jurisdiction governing 35 states and the Northern Masonic Jurisdiction governing 15. An officer, appointed by his Supreme Council, governs each state.

Eastern Star, DeMolay, Rainbow, and Job's Daughters

Master Masons and their female relatives can together join several local organizations, including the Order of the Eastern Star, the Order of the Amaranth, and the White Shrine of Jerusalem. These groups have local, district, state, and national officers. There are also Masonic-sponsored organizations for young people. The largest such groups are the Order of DeMolay for boys, and for girls the Order of Job's Daughters and the Order of Rainbow for Girls.

Shriners and Other Fun Groups

In 1872, a group of Masons formed what would become one of the best known of any American organization: the Shriners. Their membership was initially limited to 32° Scottish Rite Masons or Knights Templar in the York Rite, but since 2000 any Master Mason can join. Shriners are immediately recognizable from their red fezzes and their various parade units. There are 177 regional Shrine Temples in America, and another 14 in Canada, Mexico, and the Philippines. Shriners are a social group of Masons that maintain an amazing network of 22 children's hospitals specializing in orthopedics and burns, with a budget of $625 million a year. There is never a charge for services at a Shriners hospital!

Master Masons have two other major "fun" groups—social groups that have fun and support philanthropies. Grotto members sport black fezzes and their humanitarian foundation supports a program that provides free dental care for severely handicapped children. The Tall Cedars of Lebanon have a unique green "pyramid" hat. They're also in the business of sponsoring social events, and their special philanthropy is Muscular Dystrophy research. (You can find the websites of the organizations mentioned here in Appendix B.)

The Least You Need to Know

◆ The oldest Masonic document is the Regius Manuscript from about 1390.

◆ In 1599, Freemasonry was a trade organization; by 1717 it had transformed itself into a gentlemen's fraternity.

◆ Masonic ritual gradually evolved over centuries and is used to teach moral and ethical lessons.

◆ Masonic secrets originally identified Masons who had completed their apprenticeship.

- The story of Hiram Abiff is the basic Masonic legend, on which most other ritual ceremonies are built.

- In the United States, Freemasonry is organized into state grand lodges with local lodges and district grand officers.

The Birth of the Masonic Fraternity

In This Chapter

- Four old lodges form a grand lodge in London in 1717
- Reverend James Anderson and his *Constitutions of the Free-Masons*
- The Third Degree emerges in 1730
- William Preston organizes ritual in his 1772 *Illustrations of Masonry*
- Irish Masons form a rival grand lodge in 1751
- The rivals reconciled and merged in 1813

As we covered in the last chapter, something very interesting happened to Freemasonry during the 1600s. In 1599, in Edinburgh it was a trade organization, then in 1717 in London, it had become a gentlemen's fraternity. But of equal interest, and importance, is the period roughly from 1717 to 1813, when the fraternity stabilized its governing structure and settled on its regular operations.

The Premier Grand Lodge codified its traditions in 1723 with the publication of Reverend James Anderson's *The Constitutions of the Free-Masons*.

Its first major crisis arose when a group of Irish Masons formed a rival grand lodge in London. The rivalry spilled over into the colonies, and affected the evolution of American Freemasonry. It was not until 1813 that the two factions merged to produce today's United Grand Lodge of England (though it took a little longer to patch things up in America).

The major difference between the two groups was the Royal Arch Degree. Was it an integral part of Freemasonry's degree structure, or was it just a nice, but optional, addition? There were other disagreements, and the debates, compromises, and solutions produced the modern fraternity.

In this chapter we'll cover the formation of the first grand lodge in London, the appearance of the Third Degree, the rivalry of the "Ancients" and "Moderns," and the creation of the United Grand Lodge of England.

The Creation of the Premier Grand Lodge, 1717

No minutes have survived from the first meeting of the first grand lodge in London (the first minutes available start in 1723). What we know of this important event in the history of the fraternity comes 21 years later in a summary published in the second edition of Reverend James Anderson's *The Constitutions of the Free-Masons* (1738). (The full title is typical of eighteenth-century books, *The New book of Constitutions of the Antient and Honourable Fraternity of Free and Accepted Masons.*)

> "On St. John Baptist's Day [June 24], in the 3d Year of King George I. A.D. 1717, the ASSEMBLY and Feast of the Free and accepted Masons was held at the foresaid Goose and Gridiron Alehouse.
>
> Before Dinner, the oldest Master Mason (now the Master of a Lodge) in the Chair, proposed a List of proper Candidates; and the Brethren by a Majority of Hands elected Mr. Antony Sayer Gentleman, Grand Master of Masons." (*The Constitutions of the Free-Masons* (1738), p. 109)

The Grand Lodge quickly attracted prominent men, including Dr. John T. Desaguliers, a preeminent scientist, who served as the third Grand Master, 1719–1720. It is thought that he was responsible for attracting the intellectual elite and nobility to the fraternity. In 1721, the fifth Grand Master was John, Duke of Montagu, and the Grand Masters since then have been from the nobility. The Grand Lodge did not do much during its first few years, but it soon started chartering new lodges, establishing regulations, appointing Provincial Grand Masters, and acting like a central authority. The Grand Lodge also set up a charity fund at the suggestion of Dr. Desaguliers.

The new grand lodge did not deal with operative masonry but with speculative masonry. Jeremy Ladd Cross provided one of the best explanations of the two types of masonry:

> "By operative masonry, we allude to a proper application of the useful rules of architecture, whence a structure will derive figure, strength and beauty, and whence will result a due proportion and a just correspondence in all its parts …

> By speculative masonry, we learn to subdue the passions, act upon the square, keep a tongue of good report, maintain secrecy, and practice charity … It leads the contemplative to view, with reverence and admiration, the glorious works of creation, and inspires him with the most exalted ideas of the perfection of his divine Creator …." (*The True Masonic Chart or Hieroglyphic Monitor* (2nd ed., 1820), pp. 25–26.)

The Codification of Masonic Tradition

The Grand Lodge of England took one of its most important steps on September 29, 1721. According to Anderson's second edition of his *Constitutions* (1738), which reconstructed the early minutes, "His Grace's worship and the Lodge finding Fault with all the Copies of the old Gothic Constitutions, order'd Brother James Anderson, A.M. to digest the same in a new and better Method." The result of compiling these old documents appeared in 1723 as the first official Masonic publication, *The Constitutions of the Free-Masons. Containing the History, Charges, Regulations &c. of that most Ancient and Right Worshipful Fraternity.*

The book is notable for codifying the rules and regulations of the fraternity, as well as combining the various legendary histories of Masonry. The resulting annals raise modern eyebrows, but they were as good as many other histories some 300 years ago. Here are some excerpts from the history in Anderson's 1723 *Constitutions of the Free-Masons*:

> "Adam, our first parent, created after the image of God, the *Great Architect of the Universe*, must have had the liberal sciences, particularly geometry [that is, masonry], written on his heart …"

> "Noah, and his three sons, Japhet, Shem, and Ham, all Masons true …"

> "The Grand Monarch Nebuchadnezar … set his heart on architecture, and became the Grand Master-Mason …"

"The said [King Athelstan's] youngest son, Prince Edwin, being taught Masonry, and taking upon him the charges of a Master-Mason ..."

"King James VI of Scotland succeeding to the crown of England, being a Mason King, reviv'd the English lodges ..."

"King Charles I, being also a Mason ..."

def•i•ni•tion

The **Great Architect of the Universe** is a title for God as Creator. Its first Masonic use was in Reverend James Anderson's 1723 *Constitutions of the Free-Masons.* Anderson, a Presbyterian minister, no doubt picked it up from John Calvin's *Institutes of Christian Religion.* Calvin, whose teachings formed the basis of theology for Presbyterian and Reformed Churches, refers to God as "the Architect of the Universe" and refers to His works as the "Architecture of the Universe." Masons sometimes abbreviate the phrase as G.A.O.T.U.

Anderson's *Constitutions* were distributed around the world, and formed a written foundation for consistent government of the fraternity. His unified history has faded from notice, but his six "Charges" still govern the behavior of regular Freemasons. They are as follows:

I. **OF GOD AND RELIGION:** A Mason is oblig'd, by his tenure, to obey the moral law; and if he rightly understands the Art, he will never be a stupid atheist ...

II. **OF THE CIVIL MAGISTRATE:** A Mason is a peaceable subject to the civil powers ...

III. **OF LODGES:** The persons admitted members of a lodge must good and true men ...

IV. **OF MASTERS, WARDENS, FELLOWS, AND APPRENTICES:** All preferment among Masons is grounded upon real worth and personal merit only ...

V. **OF THE MANAGEMENT OF THE CRAFT IN WORKING:** All Masons shall work honestly on working days, that they may live creditably on holy days ...

VI. **OF BEHAVIOR:** No private piques or quarrels must be brought within the door of the lodge, far less any quarrels about religion, or Nations, or State policy ...

Some grand lodges today reproduce his list as part of their constitution.

The Square Deal

Freemason Benjamin Franklin reprinted Anderson's *Constitutions* in 1734 in Philadelphia. His account book indicates about 120 were sold, and 17 can be accounted for today. This is one of the rarest American books ever published. It is the first Masonic book printed in America, Benjamin Franklin was the printer, and it is the first American songster (which is a "collection of three or more secular poems intended to be sung."). Keep your eyes out for another copy at used book sales!

The Evolution of Masonic Ritual

As far as we can tell, Masonic ritual and ceremony of the early 1700s was rather primitive. Lodge meetings were held in private rooms at taverns with dining and drinking as an important part of the proceedings. As far as we can reconstruct, a new member was presented to the lodge, asked a few questions about his motives for joining, sworn to loyalty on the Bible, and entered in the lodge's records as an apprentice. (The latter action is believed to be the origin of "Entered Apprentice" rather than just "Apprentice.") There also seems to have been a custom of a new Entered Apprentice buying gloves for all the members and their ladies.

Once the members were seated the Worshipful Master asked a series of questions around the table, for the instruction of both the new Apprentice and the current members. The first published exposé of Masonic ritual, known as "A Mason's Examination," was published in the April 11–13, 1723, issue of *The Flying-Post*, a London newspaper. (The first grand lodge managed to keep its secrets for all of six years!) Here are some of the questions and answers from that exposé to give you a flavor of early Masonic ceremonies:

> "Q: What makes a just and perfect Lodge?
> A: A master, two Wardens, four Fellows, five Apprentices, with Square, Compass, and Common Gudge.
> Q: Where was the first Lodge kept?
> A: In Solomon's Porch; the two Pillars were called Jachin and Boaz.
> Q: Is there a Key to your Lodge?
> A: Yes.
> Q: What is't?
> A: A well hung tongue [a good tongue that keeps secrets]."

These question-and-answer rituals are also called *catechisms*. One such, "The Mystery of Freemasonry," appeared in the *London Daily Journal*, August 15, 1730. Benjamin Franklin reprinted it in his *Pennsylvania Gazette*, December 5–8, 1730, so this is also the first exposé of Masonic ritual in America. It has been reprinted in its entirety in Appendix C.

The Appearance of the Third Degree

Changes in early Masonry are really not as sudden as they might appear, but it takes an alert student to detect the subtle hints that something new is going on. When the Grand Lodge was formed in 1717, there were only two degrees: the first for Entered Apprentices and the second for Masters or Fellowcrafts. Harry Carr, an expert on ritual evolution, commented on the distinction between a Master and a Fellowcraft, "Outside the lodge, one was an employer, the other an employee, but within the lodge, both were equal, both fully trained Masons, and they shared the same ceremony."

Even though the Grand Lodge functioned with only two degrees, something was going on. Two early manuscripts of 1711 and 1726 (*Trinity College, Dublin MS. and Graham MS.*), an exposé of 1723 (*A Mason's Examination*), and two minutes of 1725 meetings indicate that a Third Degree of Master Mason was being worked in some lodges. There are also some obscure references that could be interpreted as referring to a Third Degree.

Then in October 1730 the existence of the Third or Master Mason Degree in full form was absolutely established with Samuel Prichard's exposé, *Masonry Dissected*. It was a small 32-page pamphlet that gave the catechisms for three degrees: the Enter'd 'Prentice's Degree had 92 questions and answers, the Fellow-Craft's Degree had 33, and the Master's Degree had 30. Prichard's book was not a hint, nor an obscure reference; it was a detailed script that could have been used in a lodge to guide the proceedings.

Masonry Dissected was something of a bestseller. The first edition was advertised on October 20, 1730, the second edition on October 21 and 23, and the third edition on October 31. On top of these there was a pirated edition and a newspaper version—all within 14 days! There was surely some curiosity among the general public about Freemasonry, but probably not enough to drive sales like this. The best explanation is that the Masons themselves were eager for detailed information on their own rituals (the Grand Lodge had nothing in writing), and lodges working only two degrees wanted to know more about the new Third Degree. From this point on, Blue Lodge Freemasonry consisted of three degrees.

The introduction and rapid acceptance of the Third or Master Mason Degree by the Grand Lodge illustrates a curious phenomenon of Freemasonry: the openness to accepting new degrees as part of the Masonic tradition. It's not that every new degree was accepted or successful—there are plenty of defunct Masonic organizations to prove that, but rather that Masons were willing to try the new degrees and groups when they came along. The fraternity grew by layers, like an onion, with each new degree and rite expanding on core values and legends. When an older Masonic body didn't want to incorporate something new, the newcomers just formed a new organization and added another layer on the core.

Preston's *Illustrations of Masonry*, 1772

Freemasonry grew and expanded without a lot of central direction, especially in ritual matters. The extreme popularity of Prichard's *Masonry Dissected* and some later exposés has been interpreted as evidence of Freemasons wanting written guidance to help them with their ceremonies and procedures. It took until 1772, almost 60 years after the formation of the Grand Lodge, for some semi-official written guidance to be published.

William Preston was born in Scotland in 1742 and moved to London at age 18 to work for a publisher as an editor. Two years later, in 1762, he became a Mason and took a keen interest in the fraternity. He began a study of Masonic ritual, which varied dramatically from lodge to lodge. He acquired old Masonic documents and visited lodges to learn about different forms and ceremonies. He gradually arranged the materials into a systematic form and produced a series of lectures for the first three degrees. He published the nonsecret part of his material in 1772 in the book *Illustrations of Masonry*, and received the sanction of the Grand Master and other grand officers, "We having perused the said Book, and finding it to correspond with the ancient practices of this Society, do recommend the same." *Illustrations of Masonry* went through nine editions during Preston's lifetime.

Preston's lectures are rather long, as he seemed to accumulate everything and discard nothing in his research. Nonetheless, much that he committed to writing is still used today in Masonic lodges either in its original form or with minor variations. He also gave prayers for

> ## The Square Deal
>
> William Preston left a bequest in 1818 to fund "some well-informed Free-mason to deliver annually a Lecture on the First, Second, or Third Degree of the Order of Masonry." Each year the United Grand Lodge of England appoints a Mason to give the Prestonian Lecture. It is the only lecture given with the authority of the United Grand Lodge of England.

use during lodge and ceremonies for constituting a new lodge, installing its officers, and laying cornerstones.

Twenty-five years after the publication of Preston's *Illustrations*, in 1797 Thomas Smith Webb of Massachusetts published *The Freemason's Monitor* or *Illustrations of Masonry*. Webb said in his preface, "The observations upon the first three degrees, are principally taken from Preston's *Illustrations of Masonry*, with some necessary alterations. Mr. Preston's [lectures] not being agreeable to the present mode of working, they are arranged in this work according to the general practice." The variations that Webb produced formed the basis of American Masonic ritual in almost every state.

Webb's changes to Preston's work included language and arrangement of parts. He also made procedural changes that were more agreeable to a democratic republic. For example, in Preston's cornerstone ceremony he says, "This ceremony is conducted by the grand Master and his Officers, assisted by the members of the grand Lodge. No private member, or inferior officer of a private lodge is admitted to join in the ceremony." In contrast, Webb opens up the event. "This ceremony is conducted by the Grand Master and his officers, assisted by the members of the Grand Lodge, and such officers and members of private lodges as can conveniently attend."

The United Grand Lodge of England, 1813

The United Grand Lodge of England was formed in 1813 by the merger of two rival grand lodges. Their contentions for over 60 years had a profound effect on the fraternity in England and abroad, and their competition for members probably helped the fraternity grow. Because part of their rivalry was based on ritual differences, the Union of 1813 produced a new compromise ritual that was different in many ways from earlier practices. Earlier ritual exposés no longer reflected current ritual practices. It is curious that today American grand lodges generally have older rituals than England because they never discarded their earlier ceremonies.

The Appearance of the Ancient Grand Lodge, 1751

In 1751, a group of Irish Masons who had been denied admission to London lodges formed themselves into the "Grand Lodge of Free and Accepted Masons According to the Old Institutions." The Premier Grand Lodge not only was more bourgeois and aristocratic, but also had made some changes in the ritual.

In response to the growing number of published exposés that allowed a non-Mason to pass himself off as a visiting Mason at a lodge meeting (and probably be treated to dinner or a round of drinks!), the Grand Lodge switched the passwords of the First and Second Degrees. Only active Masons who attended lodge would hear the announcement of the change, and nonmembers would be caught when they gave the wrong passwords. This didn't sit well with conservative Masons who did not think any tradition of Masonry, but especially the ritual, could be changed.

The new grand lodge maintained the old traditions and started calling itself the "Ancients," because it didn't change traditions, and it called its older rival the "Moderns"—and the names stuck. This was a stroke of marketing genius! (And it can also easily confuse the casual historian who needs to remember that the "Ancients" were modern and the "Moderns" were ancient.) By 1753, the new grand lodge had a charity fund, and in 1756 the Earl of Blessington became Grand Master and gave noble leadership to the organization.

The Square Deal

Laurence Dermott prepared a book of constitutions for the Ancient Grand Lodge in 1754 titled *Ahiman Rezon: Or a Help to a Brother*. The words are thought to be Hebrew, and there have been arguments over the meaning of the title since then. It's generally believed to mean "a prepared brother" or "a prepared secretary." Some American grand lodges, especially those with strong Ancient backgrounds like Pennsylvania, called their book of constitutions and procedures Ahiman Rezon.

The Ancients were more aggressive than the Moderns in chartering lodges, and grew rapidly. In 1757, the Ancients instructed their lodges to admit no Modern Masons, thus creating the first case nonrecognition of Masonic grand lodges. (See Chapter 6 for details on recognition and regularity.) In 1757, they recognized the Grand Lodge of Ireland and in 1772 the Grand Lodge of Scotland. The Ancients may have been the "new kid on the block," but they quickly set about establishing themselves as a legitimate part of Freemasonry.

The Importance of the Royal Arch

About the time the Ancient Grand Lodge was being formed, the Royal Arch Degree was appearing as the next major degree after the Master Mason Degree. (See Chapter 8 for a detailed discussion of the Royal Arch Degree.) The Moderns worked the degree, but their grand lodge took slight official notice; the Ancients embraced the Royal Arch with much more fervor and worked it in their lodges.

In 1754, Laurence Dermott, Grand Secretary of the Ancients, said, "I firmly believe [the Royal Arch] to be the root, heart, and marrow of masonry." Despite this affirmation of the importance of the new degree, the Ancients didn't do much with the Royal Arch Degree until the 1770s. Then the degree took on increasing importance, with the Ancients declaring in 1794, "Ancient Masonry consists of Four Degrees—the three first of which are, that of the Apprentice, the Fellow Craft, and the Sublime Degree of Master; and a Brother being well versed in those Degrees ... is eligible, if found worthy, to be admitted to the Fourth Degree, the Holy Royal Arch." This Fourth Degree now was being used to distinguish the Ancients from the Moderns. (If you weren't sure which type of lodge to join, it might influence you that you got 33 percent more degrees with the Ancients!)

The Rivalry Spreads into the Colonies

The first lodges chartered in the American Colonies were Moderns, and they had no competition for about 30 years. Then in 1760 the Ancients chartered Lodge No. 69 in Philadelphia and appointed a Provincial Grand Master for Nova Scotia, and the next year they appointed a provincial Grand Master for Pennsylvania. In theory, the Ancient/Modern rivalry had now come to America, but it usually made little difference to American Masons. Regulations were passed that forbade one type of Mason visiting the lodges of the other, but the regulations were mostly honored in the breach.

The Square Deal

Joppa Lodge of Maryland gives a good example of the confusion of American lodges about the Ancient/Modern dispute. Chartered in 1765, Joppa Lodge had a bylaw that required all Modern Masons seeking membership to take the "obligations peculiar to Ancient Masons." Joppa Lodge certainly did not want any Moderns joining them, but they seem to have made an oversight when they obtained their charter: they received it from the Grand Lodge of Moderns, not the Ancients!

Professor Steven Bullock of Worcester Polytechnic Institute, an expert in colonial American Freemasonry, has shown that Modern American Masons tended to be wealthier property owners, while Ancient Masons were artisans and shopkeepers.

During the American Revolution, the former tended to support the king and the latter the revolutionaries. (As a broad generalization this is true, but you can find both types of Masons on both sides of the conflict.) When the revolution was over it was mostly the Ancient Masons left to establish American Masonry. American Lodges today retain many of the customs and practices of the Ancients.

Reconciliation and Union in 1813

The rivalry between Ancients and Moderns didn't seem to make a lot of sense to Masons in a local lodge. While their grand lodges were denouncing each other, individual Masons were visiting and in some cases joining lodges in the other camp. By the very early 1800s, the initial and most ardent supporters of the two camps were passing away, and tentative moves toward reconciliation were being made. Then in 1813 the Duke of Kent became the Ancient Grand Master and his brother, the Duke of Sussex, became the Modern Grand Master.

The two brothers (both familial and fraternal) wanted to end the rival grand lodges and achieve a union. Committees were appointed, and the various differences— procedural, ceremonial, and ritual—were ironed out. On St. John the Evangelist Day, December 27, 1813, nearly a century after the formation of the Premier Grand Lodge, the two rival grand lodges merged to form the United Grand Lodge of England with the Duke of Sussex as the Grand Master. This is the grand lodge that still governs Freemasonry in England.

Some careful language in the articles of union solved the issue of the Royal Arch Degree, which had become so important to the Ancients. "It is declared and pronounced that pure Ancient Masonry consists of three degrees, and no more, viz., those of the Entered Apprentice, the Fellow Craft, and the Master Mason (including the Supreme Order of the Holy Royal Arch)." Thus the Royal Arch was not a separate fourth degree, but recognized now as an integral part of the Master Mason Degree.

The Ancient/Modern rivalry thus died in 1813, except in South Carolina. There was an initial merger in 1808, but a dissident group sued to prevent the United Grand Lodge from collecting any money belonging to the Ancients. This reopened the wounds, and it was not until 1817 that the Ancients and Moderns merged in South Carolina and brought the conflict to an end.

The Least You Need to Know

- The first grand lodge was formed in London in 1717.

- Reverend James Anderson's 1723 book *Constitutions of the Free-Masons* established the basic operating rules of Freemasonry.

- The first Masonic lodges had only two degrees, but the Third or Master Mason Degree was introduced shortly before 1730.

- Irish Masons in London formed a rival grand lodge in London in 1751.

- The older, original grand lodge came to be called the "Moderns" while the newer rival was known as the "Ancients."

- The two grand lodges merged in 1813 to produce the United Grand Lodge of England.

3

The Beginnings of American Freemasonry

In This Chapter

- ◆ American Masonic lodges began meeting on their own
- ◆ Britain provided limited supervision
- ◆ Many revolutionary heroes were Masons
- ◆ There is no centralized American Masonic organization
- ◆ State grand lodges cooperate for charity

No one is quite sure when or where American Freemasonry began, but the available evidence points to 1730 in Philadelphia and probably in Tun Tavern (famous as the birthplace of the U.S. Marine Corps in 1775). The fraternity spread throughout the colonies as one of the few social institutions that transcended colonial boundaries. Even churches were largely regional—Anglicans to the south, Calvinists and Puritans to the north, Quakers in Pennsylvania, and a smattering of Catholics. The fraternity began with British immigrants bringing familiar institutions with them.

It soon attracted well-established and respectable colonists and, later, leading revolutionaries.

In this chapter you'll learn how Freemasonry evolved in the United States, which signers of the Declaration of Independence and the Constitution were Freemasons, which presidents were Freemasons, and what Freemasonry had to do with the Boston Tea Party.

The First Evidence of Freemasonry in America

Freemasonry in the American colonies came from England, Ireland, and Scotland. Each successive wave of immigrant Masons brought with them the then-current ceremonies and procedures of their home lodges. Without a strong central organization, however, the fraternity evolved without much order. We still don't know when and where the first lodge met or if it was a *chartered* or a *private lodge*.

def•i•ni•tion

A **chartered lodge** is a local lodge with a charter or warrant from a state or regional grand lodge. The lodge is obligated to obey the rules and regulations of the grand lodge that granted its charter. A **private lodge** is a local lodge usually held in a member's home without a charter or regular meetings. Found occasionally in the eighteenth century, such lodges are never seen today.

Jonathan Belcher was Governor of the colonies of Massachusetts and New Hampshire from 1730–1741 and the colony of New Jersey from 1747–1757. He was made a Mason in London around 1704 and founded Princeton University in 1748. It is entirely possible that he, or other Masons like him, held private lodges in their homes to enjoy Masonic fellowship, but we have no records of such meetings.

The First Written Records

The questions of when, where, or if early Masons met in the colonies was clearly answered with the discovery of an account book with "Liber B" marked on its cover. It contains the records of the earliest known Pennsylvania and American Lodge. The first record is for June 24, 1731. In that month, Benjamin Franklin is entered as paying dues five months back. Franklin's entry implies lodge activity from at least

December 1730. In fact, Franklin's *Gazette* for December 8, 1730, supports this: "There are several Lodges of Freemasons erected in this Province."

Within 13 years of the organization of the Premier Grand Lodge in London in 1717, a lodge was operating in the American colonies with enough formality that a ledger book was kept to record dues payments. We do not know the name of the lodge, where it met in Philadelphia, nor how it was organized, but we know it collected dues! It was likely a self-constituted *time immemorial lodge*.

There is strong circumstantial evidence that another self-constituted lodge was working in South Carolina in 1734. Benjamin Franklin sent 25 copies of his edition of James Anderson's *The Constitutions of the Free-Masons* to South Carolina in that year. It's hard to imagine that general readers in the Palmetto State were that curious about Freemasonry, and Franklin was too shrewd a businessman to send the books on a lark. It's more likely that members of an unrecorded lodge wanted the books to guide their operations. The next year, 1735, the Grand Lodge of England chartered Solomon's Lodge in Charleston, South Carolina, where it still meets today.

def•i•ni•tion

A **time immemorial lodge** is a local lodge that meets without a grand lodge charter. Before grand lodges established procedures, several Masons could come together and decide to create a lodge. There were very few such lodges, but two examples are Mother Kilwinning Lodge No. 0 of Scotland and Fredericksburg Lodge No. 4 of Virginia, George Washington's mother lodge. Fredericksburg Lodge has accepted a charter from the Grand Lodge of Virginia; Mother Kilwinning still operates without a charter.

Provincial Grand Masters

On June 5, 1730, about the same time the Philadelphia Masons were organizing themselves into a lodge, the Grand Lodge in London appointed Daniel Coxe Provincial Grand Master for New York, New Jersey, and Pennsylvania, giving the first official Masonic recognition to the English colonies. The idea was for Coxe to represent the Grand Lodge in his provinces, but he does not seem to have exercised his authority, even though he lived in New Jersey from 1731–1739.

The Premier Grand Lodge appointed twenty-five more Provincial Grand Masters who exercised various degrees of authority. Henry Price for New England, 1733, was the next and John Deas for South Carolina, 1781, was the last. In 1757, Scotland appointed the first of four Provincial Grand Masters, Captain John Young for North America. Finally, the Grand Lodge of Ancients, the youngest British grand lodge, appointed seven Provincial Grand Masters, starting with William Ball for Pennsylvania, 1761, and ending with General Mordecai Gist for South Carolina, 1787. The Grand Lodge of Ireland did not make any such provincial appointments.

Provincial Grand Masters were expected to charter and oversee lodges, settle disputes, and promote Freemasonry. In 1733, Provincial Grand Master Henry Price chartered "First Lodge" of Boston, which continues to work today as St. John's Lodge.

Loyalists vs. Patriots

In April 1775 at Concord, Massachusetts, "embattled farmers stood and fired the shot heard 'round the world." A little over a year later the thirteen United States of America issued their Declaration of Independence from Great Britain. Freemasons on both sides weren't quite sure how their fraternity should behave in the war. While many revolutionary leaders were Masons, the fraternity managed to stay aloof of the conflict. In fact, only four years after the Treaty of Paris in 1783, the formal end to the Revolutionary War, the Grand Lodge of Ancients in England appointed as their Provincial Grand Master in South Carolina the revolutionary leader General Mordecai Gist. And General Gist accepted the appointment!

Masonic Coordination of the American Revolution?

Myth: The American Revolution was organized and conducted by Masons.

It's easy to find exaggerated and unconfirmed statements about the scope of involvement of Freemasons in the American Revolution. This is because two groups promote such unsupportable statements: over-enthusiastic Masons who seek self-importance by hyper-inflating their fraternity and gullible conspiracists who want to show the hidden hand of a vast Masonic plot behind world events.

The truth is much less dramatic (though still a source of Masonic pride). Masons were active, sometimes influential, participants in the revolution, but they were just one of many groups involved.

Here are three examples of wild claims from the Internet:

- ◆ Of the fifty-six signers of the Declaration of Independence, between fifty-three to fifty-five were Freemasons.

- Of the fifty-five members of the Constitutional Convention, all but five were Masons.

- Twenty-four of George Washington's major generals were Masons and thirty of thirty-three brigadier generals were Masons.

Contemporary historians have established conservative guidelines for claiming that someone was a Mason. What lodge did he belong to? Are there records indicating he attended a lodge? Is there evidence showing he appeared in public and was accepted as a Mason? Earlier well-meaning Masonic writers made embarrassing and unsubstantiated claims of Masonic membership for almost any hero, and uncritical readers swallow these claims hook, line, and sinker.

A Good Rule

If someone is claimed to be a Mason, but his lodge is not identified, the claim is probably bogus.

Here are the facts. When Congress approved the Declaration of Independence on July 4, 1776, nine of its fifty-six signers were Masons:

- William Ellery, First Lodge, Boston, Massachusetts

- Benjamin Franklin, Grand Master of Pennsylvania

- John Hancock, St. Andrew's Lodge, Boston, Massachusetts

- Joseph Hewes, attended Unanimity Lodge No. 7, Edenton, North Carolina

- William Hooper, Hanover Lodge, Masonborough, North Carolina

- Robert Treat Paine, attended the Grand Lodge of Massachusetts

- Richard Stockton, St. John's Lodge, Princeton, New Jersey

- George Walton, Solomon's Lodge No. 1, Savannah, Georgia

- William Whipple, St. John's Lodge, Portsmouth, New Hampshire

Fifty-five delegates met in Philadelphia on May 14, 1787, to draft a Constitution. It was signed on September 17 by thirty-nine of the delegates, thirteen of whom were Masons:

- Gunning Bedford, Jr., Lodge No. 14, Christiana Ferry, Delaware

- John Blair, Williamsburg Lodge No. 6, Virginia

- David Brearley, Grand Master of New Jersey

- Jacob Broom, Lodge No. 14, Christiana Ferry, Delaware

- Daniel Carroll, St. John's Lodge No. 20, Baltimore, Maryland

- Jonathan Dayton, attended Grand Lodge of New Jersey

- John Dickinson, Lodge No. 18, Dover, Delaware

- Benjamin Franklin, Grand Master of Pennsylvania

- Nicholas Gilman, St. John's Lodge No. 1, Portsmouth, New Hampshire

- Rufus King, St. John's Lodge, Newburyport, Massachusetts

- James McHenry, Spiritual Lodge No. 23, Maryland

- William Patterson, Trenton Lodge No. 5, New Jersey

- George Washington, Fredericksburg Lodge, Virginia

Here are five Masons at the Constitutional Convention that did not sign the Constitution:

- Oliver Ellsworth, Lodge at Prince Town, New Jersey

- William Houston, Solomon's Lodge No. 1, South Carolina

- James McClurg, Williamsburg Lodge, Virginia

- William Pierce, Solomon's Lodge No. 1, South Carolina

- Edmund Randolph, Williamsburg Lodge, Virginia

Sixty-one general officers served the Continental Army (nineteen Major Generals and forty-two Brigadier Generals). Thirty-four were Masons, including Benedict Arnold. (Masons don't make as much to do over General Arnold as they do over General Washington and General Lafayette!)

Masonic Participation in the Boston Tea Party?

Myth: The Boston Tea Party was planned and executed by St. Andrew's Lodge at the Green Dragon Tavern.

St. Andrew's Lodge of Boston met in the Green Dragon Tavern, which the lodge owned. Its members included well-known revolutionary leaders such as Paul Revere, John Hancock, and Joseph Warren. On November 29, 1773, the tea ship *Dartmouth* arrived in Boston, and the Boston Committee of Correspondence, led by Joseph Warren, called for a mass town meeting to return the tea. The minutes of St. Andrew for the next night, November 30, read, "Lodge adjourned on account of the few Brothers present. N.B. Consignees of TEA took the Brethren's time." Some two weeks later on December 16 the minutes read, "Present [5 officers]. Lodge closed on account of the few members in attendance, until to-morrow evening." That evening after the lodge closed, a band of men appearing to be Native Americans emerged from the Green Dragon Tavern, boarded the *Dartmouth*, and threw its consignment of tea into Boston Harbor. This is probably the most famous Masonic lodge meeting that was never held!

The circumstantial evidence presented indeed seems to convict St. Andrew's Lodge. But there's more to the story. The Green Dragon Tavern was also home to truly revolutionary groups such as the North End Caucus, the Sons of Liberty, and the Boston Committee of Correspondence. Not all revolutionary firebrands, such as John and Sam Adams, were Freemasons. While it is certain that members of St. Andrew's Lodge participated in the Boston Tea Party—as probably did every able-bodied man in the tavern, there are no records to indicate that the politically neutral lodge planned the Boston Tea Party.

Hits and Myths

The Boston Tea Party as Masonic event is a wonderfully romantic story with just enough facts to make it believable, but there's not enough hard evidence to make it true.

Freemasonry in Action During the Revolution

The attitude of Freemasons during the Revolutionary War is epitomized by the story of Unity Lodge No. 18 of Pennsylvania. The lodge was a *military lodge* in the British Army's Seventeenth Regiment of Foot. The lodge's original Irish charter was replaced by a Scottish one, and this second charter was eventually lost at the Battle of Princeton, New Jersey. The lodge in 1778 requested another charter from the Grand Lodge of Pennsylvania, then controlled by loyalists. The lodge was chartered as Unity No. 18, but its charter was lost again in 1779 at the Battle of Stony Point, New York. This time, however, the lodge's charter and regalia fell into the hands of

def•i•ni•tion

A **military lodge** is one whose charter is granted to members of a military unit. The lodge is not limited to one city, but moves about with the unit. Freemasonry was spread throughout much of the world by traveling military lodges.

General Samuel H. Parsons, a member of American Union Lodge. The captured Masonic paraphernalia was returned to the British lodge with the following note.

West Jersey Highlands, July 23, 1779

Brethren: When the ambition of monarchs or jarring interest of contending states, call forth their subjects to war, ... and however our political sentiments may impel us in the public dispute, we are still Brethren, and (our professional duty apart) ought to promote the happiness and advance the weal of each other. Accept therefore, at the hands of a Brother, the Constitution of the Lodge Unity No. 18, to be held in the 17th British Regiment which your late misfortunes have put in my power to restore to you.

Samuel H. Parsons

The epilogue to this story is even more telling about the fraternal bonds that united warring enemies. By 1786, Unity Lodge had again lost its charter and wrote to the Grand Lodge of Pennsylvania, now controlled by Americans. This lodge of soldiers turned to their former enemies, requested another charter, and proposed to pay all back dues. The Grand Lodge of Pennsylvania welcomed back the lodge, but explained that their records were lost. The grand lodge allowed the lodge to use the "honor system" and pay whatever dues they thought they owed!

The Failure of a National Grand Lodge

Despite their political actions, American Masons weren't strongly inclined to independence from their mother grand lodges. But political events nudged them into that course. For example, the departure of the loyalist South Carolina Provincial Grand Master, Sir Egerton Leigh, for England in 1774 had the unintentional effect of launching South Carolina Masons into independence. Leigh's absence left a void of Masonic leadership in South Carolina that needed to be filled. In 1777, after the Declaration of Independence and armed conflict made requests to England impolitic if not impossible, South Carolina Modern Masons elected Barnard Elliot as "Grand Master of Masons," and an independently functioning grand lodge was born.

Virginia Masons held five conventions in 1777 and 1778, and elected John Blair their Grand Master. And so the pattern continued, with other states electing their own Grand Masters, either as an overt act of independence or as an administrative necessity. While the colonies had more or less political unity at this time, the Masons appeared to be satisfied with autonomous state grand lodges.

On March 6, 1780, the American Union Lodge and various lines of the Continental Army held a meeting. The Americans had done the unthinkable in separating from king and country. They had endured the bitter winter of 1777 in Valley Forge and the onslaughts of the world's greatest military machine. And yet they assumed a deferential posture in most things Masonic. The rebel soldiers, led by General Mordecai Gist, petitioned the grand lodges of the United States to create a General Grand Lodge, but only after obtaining "approbation and confirmation" from their "Grand Mother Lodge." The petition was as follows:

> *To the RIGHT WORSHIPFUL, the Grand Masters of the several Lodges in the Respective United States of America.*
>
>

UNION—FORCE—LOVE

>
> *… We beg leave to recommend the adopting and pursuing the most necessary measures for establishing one Grand Lodge in America, to preside over and govern all other lodges of whatsoever degree or denomination …*
>
> *Permit us to propose that you, the Right Worshipful Grand Masters of a majority of your number, may nominate as Most Worshipful Grand Master of said lodge, a brother whose merit and capacity may be adequate to a station so important and elevated, and transmitting the name and nomination of such brother, together with the name of the lodge to be established, to our Grand Mother Lodge in Europe for approbation and confirmation …*

The Grand Lodge of Pennsylvania had approved a similar resolution on January 13, 1780. They called for the creation of a national grand lodge by the election of George Washington as General Grand Master. Being in the midst of conducting a war against one of the greatest military forces in the world, General Washington had other things on his mind and declined the offer. Further, Massachusetts raised the issue of how state officers would be selected; they did not want to give up the right of electing their own Grand Master. The end result was that Americans who could agree on political independence and a unified government, backed into Masonic autonomy with no central authority.

The Emergence of State Grand Lodges

By the signing of the Treaty of Paris in 1783 (which ended the Revolutionary War), South Carolina, Virginia, and Massachusetts had independent grand lodges. Georgia,

def•i•ni•tion

A grand lodge or other Masonic body grants **recognition** to another body if it accepts it as a legitimate Masonic organization. Recognition usually allows inter-visitation by members and transfer of membership. It's similar to one college "recognizing" another by allowing the transfer of credits.

New Jersey, and Pennsylvania were next in 1786, and the last of the 13 colonies to form its own grand lodge was Delaware in 1806. There were several other attempts at creating a central Grand Lodge for the United States, but they all failed. The last serious effort was in 1855. This left the country with independent state grand lodges connected by a network of bilateral *recognition*.

The loose confederation of grand lodges worked well for over a century. There would be occasional disputes (typically over which state had control of a candidate or a territory) that would result in temporary suspension of recognition between the feuding grand lodges. Problems in providing relief to soldiers during World War I led to the formation of the Masonic Service Association of North America.

During World War I, the U.S. government was not willing to work with 49 independent state grand lodges plus the many other groups in the Family of Masonry. Much to the chagrin of American Masons, organizations with smaller memberships but central national governments were able to work with the federal government to provide relief to the Dough Boys. The Masonic Service Association was created in 1918 to avoid this problem in the future, to coordinate Masonic relief activities, and to publish educational materials.

A little more organization and coordination came about when the Conference of Grand Masters of North America started meeting in 1909. It held six meetings between 1909 and 1918, and has met annually since 1925 (except for 1945). The Conference has no authority over any grand lodge, but it does offer an opportunity for the discussion of common problems and solutions. The Conference's Commission on Information for Recognition gives recommendations on the recognition of new grand lodges. This advice results in a reasonably uniform position of American grand lodges toward Freemasonry elsewhere in the world.

Freemasonry and the Presidency

Myth: Most U.S. presidents were Masons.

Again we have two groups promoting this idea: Masons who want to inflate their self-importance, and conspiracists who want to "prove" the United States is controlled by sinister forces. It is ironic that both groups accomplish their ends by claiming every famous American is a Mason.

The truth is much more mundane. Fourteen of forty-three U.S. presidents can be confirmed as Master Masons. They are as follows:

- George Washington, Fredericksburg Lodge, Virginia
- James Monroe, Williamsburg Lodge No. 6, Virginia
- Andrew Jackson, Harmony Lodge No. 1, Nashville, Tennessee
- James K. Polk, Columbia Lodge No. 31, Columbia, Tennessee
- James Buchanan, Lodge No. 43, Lancaster, Pennsylvania
- Andrew Johnson, Greeneville Lodge No. 119, Greeneville, Tennessee
- James A. Garfield, Magnolia Lodge No. 20, Columbus, Ohio
- William McKinley, Hiram Lodge No. 21, Winchester, Virginia
- Theodore Roosevelt, Matinecock Lodge No. 806, Oyster Bay, New York
- William Howard Taft, Kilwinning Lodge No. 356, Cincinnati, Ohio
- Warren G. Harding, Marion Lodge No. 70, Marion, Ohio
- Franklin D. Roosevelt, Holland Lodge No. 8, New York
- Harry S. Truman, Belton Lodge No. 450, Belton, Missouri
- Gerald Ford, Malta Lodge No. 465, Grand Rapids, Michigan

Thomas Jefferson is often claimed to be a Mason, with his lodge given variously as Door to Virtue No. 44, Virginia, the Lodge of the Nine Sisters, Paris, or Charlottesville Lodge No. 90, Virginia. There is no contemporary evidence that he was a Mason.

Lyndon B. Johnson received the 1st or Entered Apprentice Degree in Johnson City Lodge No. 561, Johnson City, Texas, but did not advance any further and never became a full member of his lodge.

Andrew Jackson served as Grand Master of Tennessee, and Harry S. Truman served as Grand Master of Missouri.

Harry S. Truman and Gerald R. Ford received the 33rd Degree of the Scottish Rite.

Ronald W. Reagan was made an honorary Mason (which would be similar to him being an honorary astronaut).

William J. Clinton belonged to the Masonic-sponsored Order of DeMolay for boys, but he never became a Mason.

The Least You Need to Know

- ◆ The first American Masonic lodge met in Philadelphia by 1730.

- ◆ England and Scotland appointed Provincial Grand Masters from 1730 to 1781 to oversee American lodges.

- ◆ Masons were prominent in the American Revolution but it was not a Masonic event.

- ◆ State grand lodges declared their independence from Britain from 1777 to 1806.

- ◆ American Freemasonry has no central government but is a confederation of state grand lodges with bilateral agreements.

The Emergence of Modern American Masonry

In This Chapter

- ◆ William Morgan writes about Masonic rituals in 1826
- ◆ Morgan disappears after Masons abduct him
- ◆ The Anti-Masonic Party seeks to destroy the fraternity
- ◆ From 1826–1840, many lodges die or become dormant
- ◆ Freemasonry reestablishes itself in its current form

In September 1826, an itinerant worker named William Morgan announced a book "exposing" the rituals of Freemasonry. His abduction, disappearance, and presumed murder led to the creation of the Anti-Masonic Party and to the closure of hundreds of lodges. Once appreciated for its contributions to society and its respectable members, Freemasonry was branded as anti-Christian and un-American. It took some 15 years before Masonic lodges emerged from the aftermath of the "Morgan Affair." When they did, they were a more somber and formal organization with rituals and an organizational form that is much the same as today.

This chapter will discuss the abduction of William Morgan in 1826, how it affected the evolution of American Freemasonry, and what goes on in a Masonic Lodge.

The Morgan Affair

William Morgan, a brick mason (no, not another branch of the fraternity, it was his occupation), moved to Batavia, New York, with his wife Lucinda. The few available accounts seem to indicate that Morgan had problems with regular employment and personal finances. He claimed to be a Mason and visited lodges in Batavia and Rochester. No documentation of his membership has ever been found, however, and it is thought that he relied on bluster and printed exposés to gain admission. Once admitted as a visitor, his quick mind absorbed the ritual, and he soon became involved in lodge activities.

While his status as a Master Mason is questionable, there is no doubt that in Le Roy, New York, on the basis of his asserted membership, he became a Royal Arch Mason, the first body of the York Rite. He joined other Royal Arch Masons in applying for a charter for a new Royal Arch Chapter in Batavia, but his name was scratched out on the application. For reasons unknown, his fellow York Rite Masons no longer wanted him to be a charter member of the Batavia chapter.

Masonic Ritual and Morgan's Proposed Exposé

Masonic ritual is not static, but slowly evolving. It is a symbolic secret, not a real one. Masons promise not to tell anyone about it as a mark of honor, and no honorable Mason would break his promise. The fact that unprincipled men have broken their promises and have kept the "secrets" in constant print for over 275 years does not change the symbolic importance of Masonic secrecy.

> **A Good Rule**
>
> It would be difficult to use a published ritual to pass as a Mason and visit a lodge. The information available is often basically correct at the time of publication, but it doesn't always reflect the latest changes or the "working knowledge" a Mason would pick up from attending lodge.

Perhaps because of the snub in being dropped from the Royal Arch charter application, or perhaps because of financial problems, Morgan decided to make some money by publishing an exposé of Masonic rituals. It is ironic that neither Morgan nor the Batavia Masons seemed to be aware that Masonic rituals had been in continuous print since 1723, though Morgan did claim he would expose previously unpublished Royal Arch rituals.

In the spring of 1826, Morgan contracted with David Miller, a printer, to publish his book and bragged about his soon-to-be bestseller. Tensions rose between Morgan and Miller and the Masons, who feared that publication of their "secrets" would cause interest in the fraternity to die out. In September, Miller's printing office was discovered on fire, and the fraternity was accused of arson. The Masons replied that Miller probably set the fire for publicity. However the fire started, the controversy certainly provided lurid promotion for the book.

Masonic Secrecy

The two types of Masonic secrets are modes of recognition and ritual legends.

Masons can supposedly recognize a brother and his degree with handshakes, pass-words, and hand signs. No one is quite sure when or why these developed, but they are thought to have been inherited from the working origins of the fraternity. Because of the nature of their work, stonemasons needed to travel from job to job, unlike most other craftsmen. When a bridge or church was finished in a community, there might not be much more construction work for many years, certainly not enough for a large crew. Masons thus needed to travel to find employment. Arriving at a new job site, a Mason could identify himself to the master of the work by whispering the password in his ear. In a time of general illiteracy, documents would not have been of much use.

The gentlemen Masons of the eighteenth century took these practical trade proce-dures and elaborated their symbolic use and importance until there were "words," "passwords," "substitute words," "covered words," "hailing signs," "grips," "pass grips," and more. I don't know any Masons who remember all the grips and words of all their degrees. I certainly don't! Most Masonic words and signs have the same symbolic importance as a "key to a city."

The old trade organization legend, again part of the inheritance of the gentlemen Masons (or possibly their invention), has it that King Solomon organized the Free-masons into degrees of skill so they could work efficiently on the Temple in Jeru-salem. Other ritual legends have arisen, some completely fabricated and others inspired by biblical stories about the construction, destruction, and rebuilding of King Solomon's Temple. The exact details of the dramatic enactment of these morality tales are also secrets. They are a type of inspirational fiction like the opera *Amahl and the Night Visitors*, which is based on the biblical account of the wise men visiting the baby Jesus.

The Abduction, Trials, and Aftermath

On September 11, 1826, William Morgan was arrested and jailed for a debt of $2.68 assigned to Nicholas Chesebro, Master of the Lodge at Canandaigua, New York. The next day Chesebro obtained Morgan's release by discharging the debt against him. Chesebro and other Masons escorted Morgan from the jail and forced him into an awaiting carriage. There was a struggle, and Morgan's last words were said to have been, "Help! Murder!"

Morgan was driven through Rochester, Lockport, and Youngstown, eventually arriving at the old Powder Magazine at Ft. Niagara, where he was held for five days until September 19, after which he was never seen. It was presumed that the Masons murdered him, but a body was never found. A year later in 1827 a body washed up some 40 miles from Ft. Niagara and was declared to be that of William Morgan (even though the body had a full head of hair and Morgan was bald!). A Mrs. Timothy Munro eventually identified the body as that of her husband, but the sensational misidentification only increased the growing anti-Masonic sentiment.

Governor DeWitt Clinton, himself a Mason, offered a reward of $1,000 for the discovery of Morgan and $2,000 for the conviction of his abductors. In several trials spread over 1828–1831, six Masons were convicted of kidnapping (not then a felony in New York), conspiracy to kidnap, false imprisonment, assault, and battery. Nicholas Chesebro served a sentence of one year, and the others served from one to twenty-eight months.

These results weren't good for the fraternity. No one knew what happened to Morgan, the sentences appeared light, and Masons seemed to be everywhere in the procedures, from Clinton at the top to Sheriff Eli Bruce of Niagara County to the renegade brothers who abducted Morgan. Within months of Morgan's seizure, "Seceding Masons" held anti-Masonic conventions around Batavia. By 1828, the Anti-Masonic Party, the first "third party," was created to run candidates on their populist platform.

Freemasonry had gradually evolved from an exclusive mostly upper-class organization during the American Revolution to a broad-based middle-class one. Professor Steven Bullock, an expert on colonial American Freemasonry, has pointed out the irony that as the fraternity became larger and more broadly based, it generated greater suspicions. There was a general distrust of "secret" societies, for who knew what they plotted behind closed doors? There was also the Masons' custom of toasting and singing after meetings. The Puritans of New England disliked toasting (though they had no problem with drinking). According to Dorothy Ann Lipson, "An early Massachusetts law had forbidden 'that abominable practice' because it led to other sins." Thus, the population was ripe to believe the worst charges of the anti-Masons.

The Square Deal

Thurlow Weed was a prominent New York journalist and political boss, affiliated with the Anti-Masons, Whigs, and eventually the newly created Republicans. He usually worked behind the scenes and achieved his ends with favors for his friends and punishments for his enemies. He was known in New York politics as "The Dictator" and "My Lord Thurlow."

Weed commented on Morgan's disappearance in the Rochester, New York, *Telegraph* that those abducting him "must have been over-zealous members of the fraternity." Disturbed by the lack of action, Weed soon became an ardent anti-Mason. After Mrs. Timothy Munro identified her husband's body, Weed was asked by Ebenezer Griffin, a lawyer for some Masons, "Well, Weed, what will you do for a Morgan now?" To which Weed replied, "That is a good enough Morgan for us till you bring back the one you carried off." Weed's sarcastic response was distorted to have him say that the body "was a good enough Morgan until after the election." Weed may have engaged in classic back-room politics, but he never exploited Munro's body after its identification.

True Convictions or Political Expediency?

The Anti-Masonic Party succeeded in electing a governor in Vermont, eight congressmen in Pennsylvania, and scores of members of state legislatures. In 1831, they selected William Wirt of Baltimore, a former Mason, as their presidential candidate. Wirt garnered only 8 percent of the popular vote and the electoral votes from Vermont. Andrew Jackson won with 54 percent of the popular vote. His victory must have been particularly galling to the Anti-Masons since he was Past Grand Master of Masons in Tennessee. It must have been doubly galling that second-place Henry Clay with 37 percent of the vote was Past Grand Master of Masons in Kentucky.

Hits and Myths

The Anti-Masonic Party held the first political nominating convention in 1831 and nominated William Wirt as their candidate for president. All subsequent nominating conventions of any party have used the Anti-Masonic Party's method of selecting their candidates.

If the Anti-Masonic Party didn't attain its national political objective, it did accomplish its principal goal: the ruin of Freemasonry. The Grand Lodge of New York declined by about 85 percent; it dropped from 480 lodges and 20,000 members in 1826 to 75 lodges with 3,000 members in 1835. The Grand Lodge of Vermont and its lodges stopped meeting from about 1833 to 1846. Maryland lost all but 13 of its lodges. The farther away from New York you moved, the less effect the anti-Masonic movement had. By the time you got as far south as Virginia or west as Michigan, there was less impact (Alabama and Georgia were exceptions).

Because of public suspicion of all things secret, the college fraternity Phi Beta Kappa gave up its secret passwords and grip and became a strictly academic society. The Independent Order of Odd Fellows, another English fraternity similar to Freemasonry, was looked at with suspicion and sometimes attacked, but it largely survived the period unscarred.

The Anti-Masonic Party attracted enthusiastic reformers like abolitionist Thaddeus Stevens, who later became one of the principal architects of Reconstruction to punish the South. Eventually the Anti-Masonic Party became more of a vehicle for opponents of President Andrew Jackson than for any real reform. Political convenience and not any particular dislike of the Masonic fraternity attracted more and more members to the party. By 1836, the Anti-Masons were in decline, and they eventually merged into the new Whig Party.

Freemasonry Reemerges

Around 1840 American Masonry began to recover from the effects of the Morgan Affair. Lodges started meeting more regularly and openly. More and more representatives attended grand lodges, and the York and Scottish Rites revived themselves. As Freemasonry began the task of reconstruction—physical as well as organizational, it became much more cautious in its outlook. Where before boisterous toasting had been a standard part of after-meeting activities, the revived lodges were much more circumspect and pious.

The large number of ritual exposures published during the anti-Masonic period meant that it was easy for someone to pass himself off as a Mason. Grand lodges responded by creating annual dues cards or receipts that indicated the bearer was a paid-up member for the period shown on the card. It had been the previous custom that once initiated a man was a Mason forever, regardless of whether he remained active in his lodge or not. Now the idea evolved that a Mason had an obligation to be affiliated with and pay dues to a lodge to remain in good standing. This all had the effect of keeping a tighter control over members and preventing a non-Mason without a dues card (like possibly Morgan) from bluffing his way into a lodge.

Grand lodges expanded the administrative control of Freemasonry within their states, as seen by the adoption of the dues card system. It became more difficult for non-Masons to pretend to be a member, and with all Masons required to affiliate with a lodge, local lodges could insure that their members met high standards of behavior. The basic organizational structure of American grand lodges today is much the same as it was in 1840.

What Goes On in a Lodge?

The *Symbolic Lodge* or *Blue Lodge*, which confers the first three degrees, is the basic lodge to which all Masons belong. American lodge rituals, procedures, and layout have changed only a little since 1826, the time of the Morgan Affair. By 1843, American Masonry had recovered enough that a national convention was held in Baltimore to try to produce a uniform ritual. While the convention agreed on a standard, grand lodges supporting the standard started changing their minds shortly after adjournment. The result is that a uniform ritual does not exist in the United States. The ritual, however, has changed only very slowly since the Baltimore Convention of 1843, even though every state has its own variant.

def•i•ni•tion

A **Symbolic Lodge** or **Blue Lodge** confers the first three degrees: 1°, Entered Apprentice; 2°, Fellowcraft; and 3°, Master Mason. All Masons belong to a Blue Lodge. They may be "Blue" because their aprons are usually trimmed with blue, or because their symbolic covering "is no less than the clouded canopy, or starry-decked heavens" which is blue. In England and Europe, these are known as "Craft Lodges."

Most American grand lodges work some variation of the "Webb-Cross Work," the 1790-era ritual as taught by Thomas Smith Webb and Jeremy Ladd Cross. Pennsylvania is the notable exception. It never adopted the revised ceremonies of Webb and Cross, but stayed with the older forms they inherited from England.

Typical Layout of an American Masonic lodge

Outside the door to each lodge room is a small anteroom, the "Tyler's Room." The *Tyler* (or Tiler) is the officer that symbolically protects the lodge room door. The Tyler's Room will have *aprons* (see the image that follows) for the members and visitors to wear and a register for them to sign. The Tyler welcomes all attendees and arranges for a committee to examine visitors not known to other members of the lodge.

def•i•ni•tion

The **Tyler** (or Tiler) is the outer guard of a lodge room. The position is first referred to in James Anderson's *The New Book of Constitutions*, 1738. Its origin is unknown, but it likely originated from protecting a building by tiling its roof.

Operative Masons wore large leather **aprons** to protect their clothing. Speculative Masons wear small symbolic aprons as part of their trade inheritance, as shown in the following figure. These are usually 18–24" square with a triangular flap at the top, and are decorated to indicate rank. New Masons are presented with white lambskin aprons, symbolic of innocence and purity. American lodges provide white canvas aprons for meetings.

George Washington wore this apron (shown with the flap turned up) when he laid the cornerstone of the U.S. Capitol in 1793. It is now owned by his lodge, Alexandria-Washington No. 22 of Alexandria, Virginia.

(Copyright Alexandria-Washington Lodge No. 22, Alexandria, Virginia. All rights Reserved. Photography by Arthur W. Pierson.)

Most lodge rooms are rectangular with seating along the two long sides. At the far end, on a platform three steps above the floor, sits the Worshipful Master. Suspended over his head on the wall is a large "G" (symbolic of geometry and God) and on either side of him sit the Secretary and Treasurer. The Master's end of the room is called the "east" of the lodge room (regardless of the true compass orientation). On the opposite side of the lodge from the Master, the "west," sits the Senior Warden on a platform two steps above the lodge floor. In front of or to the side of the Senior Warden are two large pillars representing the pillars Boaz and Jachin in front of King Solomon's Temple (1 Kings 7:20, 2 Chronicles 3:17). On the symbolic "south" side of the lodge sits the Junior Warden on a platform one step above the floor. The Master and Wardens usually have podiums in front of them.

> **A Good Rule**
>
> The letter "G" has stood for both geometry and God since at least 1730. Geometry was central to the work of operative Masons, and God is central to the lives of speculative Masons.

In front right of the Master sits the Senior Deacon, and to the front left sits the Chaplain. The Secretary and Treasurer sit behind desks to the left and right of the Master. To the right of the Senior Warden, near the lodge door, sits the Junior Deacon, and to the left is the Marshal. On the left and right of the Junior Warden sit the Senior and Junior Stewards. The floor of a lodge is most often alternating black and white tiles, and in the center is an altar with a Volume of Sacred Law (usually a Bible in American lodges). Lodges use other layouts outside the United States, but they are similar to the American plan (see the figure that follows).

The Officers and "Going Through the Line"

Many organizations are governed by a President, a First Vice-President, and a Second Vice-President. When elections are held, the First Vice-President normally is elected President, and the Second Vice-President becomes First Vice-President, both without opposition. Any election competition occurs for the office of Second Vice-President. A system such as this provides training for the President and continuity of policies, since two thirds of the officers remain the same from year to year.

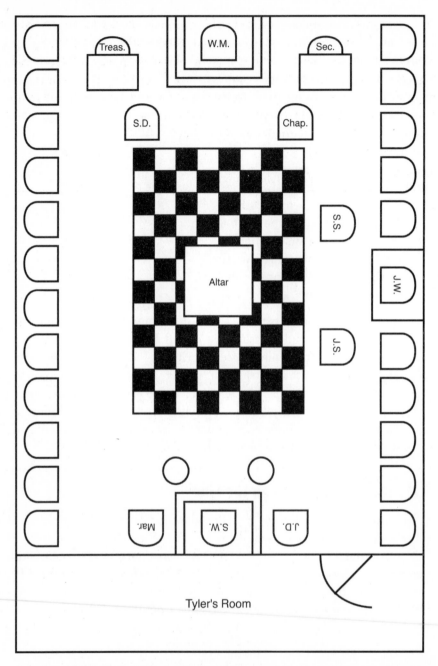

American Masonic Lodges follow this general layout, with wide variations in size and decoration. All locations of officers are approximate.

An American Masonic Lodge has seven officers that normally advance to become Master of the Lodge. Moving from office to office is called "going through the line" or "going through the chairs," and would take seven years if no offices are skipped. Some lodges may have additional officers in their line, while other, much smaller lodges may have only three or four officers in line with Past Masters filling in where needed. In most lodges, the members elect the Master, the two Wardens, the Secretary, and the Treasurer; the Master appoints the other officers.

Officers in an American Masonic Lodge

Line Officers	Duties
Worshipful Master	Presides over meetings, sets agenda, and manages lodge affairs (President)
Senior Warden	Serves in the absence of the Master (1st Vice-President)
Junior Warden	Serves if both senior officers are absent and is usually in charge of refreshments and entertainment (2nd Vice-President)
Senior Deacon	Assists the Master
Junior Deacon	Assists the Sr. Warden and guards the lodge room door from the inside
Senior Steward	Assists the Jr. Warden, especially with refreshments
Junior Steward	Assists the Jr. Warden, especially with refreshments (6th Vice-President!)

Other Officers	Duties
Secretary	Records minutes of meetings, handles correspondence, etc.
Treasurer	Manages the funds of the lodge
Chaplain	Opens and closes meetings with prayer, offers grace before meals
Marshal	Escorts officers and special guests around the lodge
Master of Ceremonies	Organizes procession and recession of officers and lodge ceremonies
Musician	Provides music for songs and entertainment
Tyler	Guards the lodge room door from the outside and examines visitors

Lodge Meetings: Degree Work, Philanthropy, Education, and Sociability

Freemasonry is distinguished from most other civic associations by its rituals and formalities. Becoming a Mason involves more than signing the lodge bylaws; it requires going through a prescribed initiation process before you can even attend a meeting. Experiencing and sharing those rituals are a central part of lodge meetings.

With over 10,000 Masonic lodges in the United States, it's hard to say what's "typical," but I can give you a pretty good idea. Most lodges hold regular meetings in the evening once or twice a month, with weekly or quarterly schedules occasionally seen. Most lodges don't meet in the summer. Members usually wear their "Sunday-go-to-meeting" clothes, typically a coat and tie. More formal urban lodges will have officers in tuxedoes and members in suits, while more informal rural lodges will see their members in slacks and casual shirts. The Master of an American lodge wears a hat as a symbol of his authority, often a top hat in more formal lodges. (Some Past Master rings incorporate a top hat and gavel in their design.)

The Square Deal

One of the cherished traditions of lodge meetings is the social period: usually dinner or a light meal before or after the meeting. It is while sharing a meal that Masonic friendships are established. Participating in the meal is sometimes jokingly called the "Knife and Fork Degree."

Each lodge meeting includes ceremonies intended to remind members of their initiation and to refresh that experience in their minds. When communities were smaller and most members lived within a few miles of the lodge hall, reports of sickness and distress led to immediate action from the lodge's charity fund. Today most lodge philanthropy takes the form of scholarships, support for medical research, and so on.

The following is the general format of an American Masonic lodge meeting:

- The Master announces the meeting is about to begin and the lodge door is closed.

- The Master determines that all present are Masons of the right degree, usually by having the deacons receive the password from members.

- Guards are symbolically placed inside and outside of the door (the Jr. Deacon and Tyler, respectively).

- The Master determines if his officers are prepared by asking them to recite their duties.

- God's blessings are asked for the meeting, and the members recite the Pledge of Allegiance.

- The Volume of Sacred Law is opened, and the Master declares the lodge opened.

- The minutes of the previous meeting are approved, correspondence is read, bills are paid, and business is conducted.

- The Master asks for reports of sickness and distress among the lodge members and the community.

- The evening's program is usually the initiation of a new member or a talk.

- The Master announces the meeting is about to close and invites final comments from the members.

- God's blessings are asked for the sick and distressed and for the members as they travel home.

- The Volume of Sacred Law is closed, and the Master declares the lodge closed.

Mark Tabbert did an excellent job in his book *American Freemasons: Three Centuries of Building Communities* of capturing the many dimensions of lodge meetings.

> "In the course of one lodge meeting, Freemasonry is a spiritual organization when the chaplain leads the brethren in prayer and asks for the blessing of Deity. It is a guild when the Master of the lodge teaches the new Mason the symbolic uses of stonemasons' tools. It becomes a school of instruction when the new brother learns about the importance of the seven liberal arts and sciences. At other moments, it is an amateur theater company when the ritual is performed. The lodge becomes a men's social club when meeting for dinner and fellowship. It becomes a charitable group when relief is provided to distressed brothers, their families or the local community. It is also a business association when members with similar interests share ideas. The lodge resembles a family when fathers and sons, strangers and friends bond as 'brothers,' and it is a community league when volunteers are needed for a project."

American Freemasons: Three Centuries of Building Communities (N.Y.: New York Univ. Press, 2005), p. 12.

The Least You Need to Know

- Masons abducted William Morgan in 1826 in Batavia, New York, because he wrote a book about the "secrets" of Masonry.

- Morgan's disappearance led to the creation of the Anti-Masonic Party, the first U.S. third party.

- Masonry was almost destroyed, but emerged about 1840 in its current organizational form.

- American Masonic lodges usually have seven officers that advance annually to become Worshipful Master.

African American Freemasonry

In This Chapter

♦ Fifteen African Americans become Masons in Boston in 1775

♦ The Grand Lodge of England issues a charter in 1784

♦ Independence is declared in 1827

♦ African American Masonry spread out from Boston

An unfortunate and persistent theme in American history is race relations. It pervades education, religion, law, and social organization, and Freemasonry has not been immune. In 1775, Prince Hall and 14 African Americans were initiated in a British military lodge, and the Moderns' Grand Lodge issued them a charter in 1784 as African Lodge No. 459 with Prince Hall as its first Worshipful Master. In 1827, African Lodge declared its independence from all Masonic authorities, constituted itself into African Grand Lodge No. 1, and started an independent path for African American Masons.

In the nearly two centuries since the creation of its first grand lodge, African American Freemasonry (broadly known as "Prince Hall Freemasonry") has paralleled its mainstream counterparts. There is a similar constellation of appendant bodies: Scottish Rite, York Rite, Eastern Star, and Shriners. There are also some unique organizations: Heroines of Jericho, Cyrene Crusaders, Order of the Golden Circle, Daughters of Isis, and Knights of Pythagoras.

Mainstream grand lodges have not recognized Prince Hall Freemasonry for most of its history. (See Chapter 6 for details on Masonic recognition.) This changed in 1989 when the two grand lodges in Connecticut—historically white and black—mutually recognized each other. Through 2005, there has been recognition in 38 states, and discussions are underway in several others.

This chapter will discuss the origin and growth of African American or Prince Hall Freemasonry.

Prince Hall of Boston

Little is known about Prince Hall, but then again little is known about most Americans who lived some 250 years ago. Complicating matters is the fact that at least four African Americans living in Massachusetts during the revolutionary period had the name Prince Hall. Further confusing matters is that one of the early and widely quoted books on Prince Hall, William H. Grimshaw's 1903 *Official History of Freemasonry Among the Colored People in North America*, created and perpetuated myths about Prince Hall without regard for documentation.

The Square Deal

Serious historians have abandoned William Grimshaw's *Official History*. Grimshaw was Grand Master of the Prince Hall Grand Lodge of the District of Columbia, but he had no authority to produce an "official" history. He claimed that Hall had been born in Bridgetown, Barbados, British West Indies, on September 12, 1748, to an English father and a French mother of African descent. No record of this exists, but the assertion makes Hall "free-born" and answers early objections about the legitimacy of his Masonic membership. The Gothic Constitutions, the early documents regulating the Masons' trade (see Chapter 1), required that apprentices be freeborn (not born in slavery) and not bondmen (bound to serve without wages). Grimshaw seems to have created dates that conveniently support various claims of Prince Hall Masonry, and he also promoted himself to the staff of the Library of Congress, when in fact he was the doorman.

It appears that the Freemason Prince Hall (Prince was his given name) was born about 1735 and was a slave in the service of William Hall of Boston. William was a "leather dresser" and taught the trade to Prince. In 1770, William freed Prince, as shown in the surviving certificate of manumission, and Prince continued working in the leather business. He also established himself as a caterer, as documented by Reverend William Bentley of Salem, Massachusetts, describing a turtle feast in his diary as "Our chief cook was Prince Hall, an African and a person of great influence among his color in great Boston, being Master of the African Lodge and a person to whom they refer with confidence their principal affairs."

Prince Hall exercised his right to vote, as indicated by multiple payments of the poll tax, and signed petitions to the Massachusetts Legislature in 1777 to abolish slavery and in 1788 against the slave trade and kidnapping. Dr. Charles H. Wesley, president of Wilberforce University and a biographer of Prince Hall, noted there were four men named Prince Hall listed in the *Massachusetts Sailors and Soldiers of the Revolutionary War*. He said, "These records support the evidence that a Prince Hall served in the American Revolutionary Army. It is not an easy task to select the exact one … However, Prince Hall was the name of the founder of Masonry for black Americans, and the tradition continues that he was one of the soldiers, supported by at least one of these documents." (*Prince Hall: Life and Legacy* [1977], pp. 40–41.)

Prince Hall married five times and had at least one son, Primus Hall, who received a pension for his service in the Continental Army. The church of Reverend Andrew Croswell, assembling in "the brick meeting house in School Street" accepted Prince Hall as a member in 1762. He died on December 4, 1807, and is buried in Copp's Hill Burying Ground in Boston. The *Boston Gazette* carried this obituary notice on December 7, 1807: "On Friday morning, Mr. Prince Hall, age 72, Master of the African Lodge. Funeral this afternoon at 3 o'clock from his dwelling-house in Lendell's Lane, which his friends and relations are requested to attend without a more formal invitation."

Sergeant Batt and Lodge No. 441, 1775

If Prince Hall did nothing more than overcome his enslavement and become a respected citizen of Boston he would deserve our admiration. But, indeed, he accomplished much more. On March 6, 1775, he and fourteen other free African American men were initiated by Sergeant John Batt, a member of Lodge No. 441, under the Grand Lodge of Ireland. Lodge No. 441 was attached to the 38th Regiment of Foot, British Army, in which Sergeant John Batt served. According to Henry Coil and John Sherman, authors of *A Documentary Account of Prince Hall and Other Black Fraternal*

Orders, after being discharged from the British Army in 1777, Batt served in the Revolutionary Army in Colonel David Henley's Regiment at Boston from February 20 to June 10, 1778.

The following are the fifteen African Americans initiated into Masonry on March 6, 1775 by Sergeant John Batt of Lodge No. 441, Ireland:

Prince Hall	Fortin Howard
Cyrus Johnbus	Prince Rees
Bueston Slinger	John Canton
Thomas Sanderson	Peter Freeman
Prince Payden	Benjamin Tiber
Cato Speain	Duff Buform
Boston Smith	Richard Tilley
Peter Best	

African Lodge No. 459, 1784

After being initiated, Prince Hall and his brothers formed a lodge and received, as Hall said, "a Permet from Grand Master Row to walk on *St. John's Day* and Bury our dead in form," apparently issued by John Rowe of Boston, the Moderns' Provincial Grand Master for North America. On June 30, 1784, after the Treaty of Paris ended the Revolutionary War, Prince Hall wrote to the Modern Grand Lodge in London and requested a warrant (another term for a charter) so they could fully function as a lodge. In particular, they could initiate new members.

The warrant for African Lodge No. 459 was issued on September 29, 1784, but it took another three years before it arrived in Boston on April 29, 1787. John Rowe's St. John's Grand Lodge, loyalist-leaning Modern Masons, has no records of meeting from 1775 to 1787, though newspaper and other accounts indicate some activity. This limited activity probably explains why they applied to the Modern Grand Lodge in London.

def•i•ni•tion

Saint John's Days are June 24, for St. John the Baptist, and December 27, for St. John the Evangelist. The Saints John are the patron saints of Freemasonry, dating back to at least the formation of the Premier Grand Lodge on June 24, St. John the Baptist's Day, 1717. It is a traditional day for feasting, parading, and attending worship.

While African Lodge was receiving its charter, interesting things were happening elsewhere in Massachusetts Masonry. The Ancient's Massachusetts Grand Lodge elected a Grand Master in 1777 to succeed Provincial Grand Master Joseph Warren, who was killed at the Battle of Bunker Hill. The change in title of their presiding officer from "Provincial Grand Master" to "Grand Master" was their declaration of independence from England, which they formally proclaimed in 1782. Massachusetts Grand Lodge, Ancients, and St. John's Grand Lodge, Moderns, finally merged in 1792. St. Andrew's Lodge, home of such revolutionary firebrands as John Hancock, Paul Revere, and Joseph Warren, decided not to affiliate with Massachusetts Grand Lodge, but remained with Scotland until 1809.

According to George Draffen of Newington, Depute Grand Master of Scotland and author of *Prince Hall Freemasonry*, African Lodge No. 459 was the last lodge formed in America by the Modern Grand Lodge. The Ancient Grand Lodge issued a warrant two years later to Lodge No. 326 in Charleston, South Carolina, in 1786. A Modern Grand Lodge had been formed in the state in 1777, but the Ancient Grand Lodge was not created until 1787.

Given the loose situation in Massachusetts, with an Ancient Grand Lodge, a weak Modern Provincial Grand Lodge, and the Scottish St. Andrew's Lodge, African Lodge may have preferred to remain loyal to the Modern Grand Lodge in London. And a London charter would have brought prestige to the small group of African Ameri-cans. Racism, however, was probably the main reason for African Lodge not affiliating with a Massachusetts grand lodge. Jeremy Belknap in his 1795 letter to St. George Tucker of Virginia observed, "The truth is, [white lodges] are ashamed of being on an equality with blacks."

African Lodge had several members from Providence, Rhode Island, who traveled to meetings in Boston. On June 25, 1797, Prince Hall granted the Rhode Island members (reported to be nine, but records are lost) a warrant to meet as African Lodge in Providence. In the early days of Masonry, before efficient communications and before grand lodges asserted their authority, individual lodges would charter other lodges. For example, Fredericksburg Lodge of Virginia, George Washington's lodge, chartered two other lodges in Virginia. Thus the request from the Philadelphia Masons to African Lodge was not that unusual for the time.

Also in 1797, eleven African American Masons in Philadelphia requested a dispensation for a lodge from Prince Hall and African Lodge. They said, "The white Masons have refused to grant us a Dispensation, fearing that black men living in Virginia would get to be Masons too." Prince Hall quickly replied and granted the request, establishing an African Lodge in Philadelphia. It's not clear whether this was intended to be an independent lodge with the same name or if it was a "branch" of No. 459. In any event, African Lodge was now exercising some of the powers that grand lodges were reserving to themselves.

The Square Deal

Two of the most prominent African American Masons in Philadelphia were Reverend Absalom Jones and Richard Allen. They worshipped together at St. George's Methodist Episcopal Church in Philadelphia one Sunday, and were asked by the ushers during prayers to move to the balcony reserved for African Americans. Rather than move to the balcony, they walked out of the church. Eventually they went on to form the African Methodist Episcopal church.

In at least 1802 and 1806, Prince Hall wrote to the Modern Grand Lodge of England and complained that his letters had been unanswered and charity contributions from African Lodge had been unacknowledged. International correspondence and funds transfers were uncertain activities at that time. What is important here is that African Lodge No. 459 of Boston acted as if it were still a subordinate of the Modern Grand Lodge of England.

After the Union of 1813 created the United Grand Lodge of England (UGLE), the new grand lodge removed all remaining American lodges from its rolls, assuming they had affiliated with one of the new American grand lodges. This information apparently never reached African Lodge, because in 1824 they wrote again to the Modern Grand Lodge (which merged into the UGLE in 1813) and asked for a renewed charter to confer the Royal Arch Degree. Thus as late as 1824 they considered themselves obedient to England in matters Masonic.

A Declaration of Independence, 1827

Shunned by the white Masons of Massachusetts and ignored by England, Prince Hall's fraternal descendents found themselves cut off from the Masonic world. On June 18, 1827, African Lodge took a bold step: they declared their independence of any other Masonic authority. This was the first step of a long and proud Masonic tradition of brotherly love, relief, and truth under a new banner.

These are the words that were published in the *Boston Advertiser*, June 18, 1827, to declare its independence:

> "Be it known to all whom it may concern,
>
> That we, the Master, Wardens, and members of the African Lodge No. 459, city of Boston, … have come to the conclusion that, with what knowledge we possess of masonry, and as people of color by ourselves, we are and ought by rights to be, free and independent of other Lodges.
>
> We do, therefore, with this belief, positively declare ourselves free and independent of any Lodge from this day …
>
> We agree solemnly to abide by all proper rules and regulations … resting in full hope, that this will enable us to transmit it in its purity to our posterity, for their enjoyment."

On the same day as they issued their declaration of independence, African lodge created a committee of three Past Masters to travel to New York City to grant a charter to Boyer Lodge No. 1, an African American lodge that had been established earlier but did not have a charter. There seem to have been some problems with Boyer Lodge accepting a charter from African Lodge of Boston. What is important, however, is that African Lodge was beginning to act like a grand lodge and chartering other lodges of African Americans. Eventually three grand lodges descended directly from African Lodge No. 459: Prince Hall Grand Lodge of Boston, Massachusetts; First Independent African Grand Lodge of North America of Pennsylvania; and Boyer Grand Lodge of New York.

The National Compact Grand Lodge

The history of African American Freemasonry is very difficult to write because so few primary documents remain. This is not surprising considering the difficulties that faced African American Masons. It's really not known how the Anti-Masonic period affected African American lodges. We can imagine that men who faced general hostility when meeting in private were doubly cautious when meeting during the time of a strong movement for the total destruction of their organization.

Mainstream Freemasonry began to emerge from the Anti-Masonic period in the early 1840s, and evidently so did African American lodges. In 1847, African American grand lodges created a National Grand Lodge, something their mainstream counterparts had never achieved.

At a convention in Boston in 1847, representatives of Prince Hall Grand Lodge of Boston, Hiram Grand Lodge of Pennsylvania, First African Grand Lodge of Pennsylvania, and Boyer Grand Lodge of New York established the National "Compact Grand Lodge" of Free and Accepted Ancient York Masons. It was ratified the next year at a convention in New York by Massachusetts and Pennsylvania, but New York did not approve. (These details, and many others about the national grand lodge, come from Alton Roundtree's 2005 book *Out of the Shadows: The Emergence of Prince Hall Freemasonry in American, 1775–2005*.)

The presence of two grand lodges from Pennsylvania was foreshadowing of the problems of irregularity and schisms that have plagued African American Freemasonry. Hiram Grand Lodge was irregular, but the delegates at the 1847 convention *healed* them.

def•i•ni•tion

Healing is the process of making an irregular Mason or Masonic lodge regular, usually authorized and under the supervision of a Grand Master. The Mason or lodge to be healed must acknowledge that they have deviated from accepted Masonic norms. The healing process usually involves at least repeating the solemn obligation of membership.

The National Compact Grand Lodge was to meet triennially, but there are only four published proceedings prior to 1888 (1856, 1862, 1865, and 1874). It established subordinate grand lodges in at least twenty more states: Arkansas, California, Colorado and Wyoming Territory, Florida, Georgia, Illinois, Indiana, Kentucky, Louisiana, Maryland, Michigan, Mississippi, Nebraska, New Jersey, North Carolina, Ohio, South Carolina, Tennessee, Texas, and Virginia. The expansion of African American Freemasonry is due almost entirely to the National Compact Grand Lodge, though this fine record did not prevent significant problems from developing.

New York did not approve and did not join the National Compact Grand Lodge, and Pennsylvania withdrew in 1849, only two years after voting in convention for its creation. There were three reasons for Pennsylvania's withdrawal: 1) states could no longer form grand lodges without the permission of the National Compact Grand Lodge; 2) decisions by state grand lodges were no longer final, but could be appealed to the National Compact Grand Lodge; 3) the National Compact Grand Lodge imposed excessive taxation on the state grand lodges.

Resistance to the national grand lodge seemed to grow. In 1850, the "Eastern Independent Grand Lodges," consisting of Delaware, Maryland, New York, Pennsylvania, and New Jersey, declared their opposition. The objections seemed to center on the issue of sovereignty: the state grand lodges and Grand Masters did not want their decisions appealed to or overturned by the national grand lodge. In 1868, the National Grand Master, Richard Howell Gleaves, suspended the Grand Lodge of Ohio because it wouldn't follow national regulations.

Records are scant, but it appears the state grand lodges began withdrawing in force from the National Compact Grand Lodge about 1860. After they withdrew, if they refused to return to the central organization, the national grand lodge would find men to create new lodges and a new grand lodge in the seceding state. By 1878, the National Compact Grand Lodge seemed to be so weakened that it was thought by many to be out of existence. In fact, it has continued in operation as originally organized with a national grand lodge and subordinate state grand lodges.

The Current State of Prince Hall Masonry

The "states rights" or independent grand lodges are today the strongest and largest of the African American Masonic bodies, with 42 state grand lodges. The National Compact Grand Lodge has 25 state grand lodges. The two organizations, both tracing their lineage to Prince Hall and African Lodge No. 459 of Boston, do not recognize each other nor do they consider the other's members to be Masons. (See Chapter 6 for more on "recognition.")

In 1944 at a conference of Prince Hall Grand Masters meeting in Hot Springs, Arkansas, the recommendation was made that their grand lodges incorporate the words "Prince Hall" into their titles. It took about twenty years, but by the 1960s most of the independent African American grand lodges descended from African Lodge No. 459 had changed their names to "Most Worshipful Prince Hall Grand Lodge, Free and Accepted Masons, State of [Name]." These grand lodges and their lodges usually identify themselves with the initials "P.H.A." for "Prince Hall Affiliation." National Compact grand lodges and lodges use "P.H.O." for "Prince Hall Organization."

The constellation of Masonic organizations that grew around mainstream Masonry also grew around African American Freemasonry. In 1797 when the African American Masons in Philadelphia wrote to Prince Hall and African Lodge No. 459 asking for a warrant, they stated, "We have all been try'd by five Royal Arch Masons," which seems to imply they were Royal Arch Masons. The letter goes on to say that their

Worshipful Master, Peter Mantore, "was arched and Royal Arched Knight Templar of Ireland, Carrickfurgus Lodge, True Blue, No. 253." This shows that African American Masons were Knights Templar at about the time the degree was established in Philadelphia (1794).

> ## Hits and Myths
>
> All Prince Hall Masons are "three-letter Masons"—F.&A.M., Free and Accepted Masons. Mainstream Masons are "four-letter Masons"—A.F.&A.M., Ancient, Free, and Accepted Masons. About half of the mainstream grand lodges are F.&A.M., about half are A.F.&A.M., and all Prince Hall grand lodges are F.&A.M. The mainstream Grand Lodge of South Carolina is A.F.M.—Ancient Free Masons, and that of the District of Columbia uses four letters where everyone else uses three, F.A.A.M.—Free and Accepted Masons.

African American Masons worked the fundamental parts of the York Rite, the Royal Arch, and Knight Templar, at an early date, and established all of the bodies of the York Rite. Similarly there is evidence of African American Scottish Rite Masons by the 1830s. Today both Northern and Southern Prince Hall Supreme Councils exist as well as well-established Prince Hall bodies of the York and Scottish Rites, (see Chapter 8 for details on the York Rite and Chapter 9 for the Scottish Rite.) There are also a Prince Hall Shriners, the Ancient Egyptian Arabic Order Nobles of the Mystic Shrine.

For African American women, there are Prince Hall Eastern Star Chapters, but the women's groups took an interesting turn in their development. In about 1873, Robert Macoy developed a "Rite of Adoption" that consisted of three degrees: Eastern Star, Queen of the South, and Amaranth. Eventually among mainstream Masons the rite fell apart, with the Queen of the South disappearing and the Amaranth becoming an independent group. According to Professor Paul Rich, a prolific author on Freemasonry and fraternalism, Prince Hall Masonry has preserved the Rite of Adoption with its three degrees. (See Chapter 7 for details on women and Freemasonry.)

Prince Hall Royal Arch Masons have also preserved the Heroines of Jericho for their female relatives. The Heroines only exist in mainstream Masonry in the Order of True Kindred, a small group for Master Masons and their female relatives. In addition to these degrees found in mainstream Masonry, Prince Hall Masons have developed several unique organizations for their female relatives: Ladies of the Circle of

Perfection for Royal & Select Masters; Cyrene Crusaders for Knights Templar; Order of the Golden Circle for Scottish Rite Masons; and Daughters of Isis for Shriners. Where mainstream Masonry supports the Order of DeMolay for boys, Prince Hall Masons support the Order of the Knights of Pythagoras. The Eastern Star has the OES Youth Fraternity, for boys and girls. Some Prince Hall organizations are devoted to Masonic history. The foremost is the Phylaxis Society, formed in 1973 to publish papers about Prince Hall Freemasonry. (See Chapter 10 for more details on the Phylaxis Society.)

The Least You Need to Know

- Sergeant John Batt of Irish Lodge No. 441 initiated Prince Hall and 14 other African Americans in 1775.

- The Modern Grand Lodge granted a charter to African Lodge No. 459 of Boston in 1784; African Lodge remained affiliated with England even though a Grand Lodge of Boston had been formed.

- In 1827, because of neglect by England and shunning by Massachusetts, African Lodge declared its independence.

- In 1847, the Prince Hall Grand Lodges of Massachusetts and Pennsylvania formed the National Compact Grand Lodge; this established at least 20 state grand lodges, and then the state grand lodges withdrew.

- Today the strongest Prince Hall organizations are the independent state groups, though the national grand lodge is still in existence.

- Prince Hall Masonry has a full panoply of appendant bodies, including York Rite, Scottish Rite, and Eastern Star.

Chapter 6

Masonic Regularity

In This Chapter

- Anyone can say they're a Mason
- Grand lodges decide on whom they'll recognize based on various principles
- Fundamental Principle: Legitimacy of Origin
- Fundamental Principle: Exclusive Territorial Jurisdiction
- Fundamental Principle: Adherence to the Ancient Landmarks
- Withdrawal of recognition is the only enforcement tool

Masonic regularity is one of those topics that might seem too detailed for the nonspecialist. But it is the very basis of what makes a Mason. If you don't understand what makes a lodge regular, then you won't understand why you can find nine Masonic grand lodges with a New York City phone listing (and probably several more in the city with unlisted phones) or why "Prince Hall Affiliation" and "Prince Hall Organization" Masons—both descended from African Lodge No. 459—don't consider each other legitimate Masons.

In this chapter we'll look at Masonic recognition, the basic principles of recognition, and some examples of the consequences of non-recognition.

The Importance of Recognition

Freemasons value the traditions of the fraternity, and this includes strict rules on who is—and isn't—a Mason. You can't just buy a *Boy Scout Handbook* and some uniforms and create a scout troop; you must meet the standards of and be approved by the Boy Scouts of America. By the same token, you can't just get a copy of some Masonic ritual exposé, buy some aprons, and start calling yourself a Masonic lodge. (Well, you actually can since there's no trademark on the name "Masonic lodge," but you'd be considered *clandestine*—working without a valid charter or warrant from a recognized grand lodge—and wouldn't be recognized by other Masonic lodges.) It's not even enough to have been regularly chartered at one time; you must maintain constant regularity of practices.

The Conference of Grand Masters of Masons of North America has a Commission on Information and Recognition that investigates requests from grand lodges for recognition. The commission's findings, which are purely advisory for members of the conference, are based on carefully developed standards summarized as follows:

◆ Legitimacy of Origin

◆ Exclusive Territorial Jurisdiction, except by mutual consent and/or treaty

◆ Adherence to the *Ancient Landmarks*—specifically, a Belief in God, the *Volume of Sacred Law* as an indispensable part of the lodge, and the prohibition of the discussion of politics and religion

---

The Square Deal

The **Ancient Landmarks** are those fundamental principles of Masonry that cannot be changed. Any deviation from them results in an organization that is not Freemasonry. There is no universally agreed-upon list of landmarks; groups of grand lodges that recognize each other rely upon consensus. In a Masonic lodge, the **Volume of Sacred Law** is the book or books held sacred by the members. In British and American lodges, it is nearly always the Holy Bible. The Volume of Sacred Law represents God's revelation to mankind. The **jurisdiction** of a Masonic body is the geographic area over which it has Masonic control.

Before considering the components of Masonic regularity, you need to understand the only enforcement tool of grand lodges: recognition. Recognition is a bilateral "treaty" between two grand lodges. Both grand lodges agree to respect each other's *jurisdiction*, not chartering lodges in or taking members from the other's territory. The grand lodges appoint representatives—"ambassadors" if you will—to keep track of each other's affairs. Grand lodges that recognize each other work together on charitable and educational projects and share in leadership and program activities.

Perhaps the greatest advantage of recognition is that Masons from one grand lodge can visit lodges of the other. It is a warm experience to visit a Masonic lodge in a strange town. The fraternal reception of a visitor is best summed up by the sign seen outside many lodge rooms: "There are no strangers within these doors, only friends you have not met." A more practical advantage to recognition, especially years ago, was financial assistance, burial, or admission to the state Masonic retirement home or orphanage.

Because there is no central governing organization for Freemasonry, recognition is maintained through thousands of bilateral mutual agreements. The web of recognition is somewhat archaic and a bit inefficient, but it does serve the purpose of eventually keeping everyone in line with the generally accepted principles of Freemasonry. There is not complete unanimity, there are occasional squabbles, but the system is fairly stable and seems to work. Mutual recognition can be compared to frequent flyer programs, where some airlines have mutual agreements that allow the miles earned in one program to be redeemed in another.

Denial of recognition ostracizes a grand lodge and leaves its members "stranded," unable to participate in the larger "Family of Masonry." Of course, some grand lodges don't care about recognition and, in some cases, don't want it. They may have separated themselves because they don't agree with a particular mainstream Masonic principle, for example that all Masons must believe in God. Or they may not want to associate with a male-only organization like traditional Masonry. Some self-created grand lodges (these are the ones that get started by finding a ritual exposé and buying some aprons) exist to sell insurance or to promote their own religious ideas.

Legitimacy of Origin

A regular lodge has a valid charter or warrant from a regular grand lodge. That grand lodge was formed by at least three regular lodges, each with charters from other regular grand lodges, and so on. It's not certain why Masons are so concerned about legitimacy of origin, but it probably dates back to the trade organization. Then it wasn't enough that you were a skilled craftsman; you had to be apprenticed and tested before you could join a lodge. Any other method of joining would have destroyed the ability of the organization to regulate its members and its trade.

Once the Grand Lodge of England was formed in 1717, no further lodges could be properly formed there without a charter. (Okay, maybe the rule didn't go into effect immediately, but the Grand Lodge moved quickly to assert its authority as the only source of Masonic legitimacy.) We can infer from James Anderson's 1723 *Constitutions of the Free-Masons* that some Masons were forming unauthorized lodges by 1723, perhaps with an eye toward profiting from initiation fees. Anderson's General Regulation 8 says:

> "If any Set or Number of Masons shall take upon themselves to form a Lodge without the Grand-Master's Warrant, the regular Lodges are not to countenance them, nor own them as fair Brethren and duly form'd, nor approve of their Acts and Deeds; but must treat them as Rebels, until they humble themselves, as the Grand Master shall in his Prudence direct, and until he approve of them by his Warrant ...."

Except for the handful of Time Immemorial Lodges (like Kilwinning No. 0 of Scotland, which works without a charter), every lodge must have a charter from a grand lodge authorizing it to work. It must follow the regulations of its grand lodge or its charter can be cancelled. A new grand lodge must be formed by at least three regular lodges within a state, province, or country. When a new grand lodge is formed, all of its new lodges must return their old charters to their mother grand lodges and receive new charters from the new grand lodge. Any lodge choosing not to join the new grand lodge may continue its allegiance to its mother grand lodge, but no new lodges can be formed in the new grand lodge's territory or jurisdiction.

Those lodges that might continue their connections with their mother grand lodges do so by mutual consent with the new grand lodge. So well established is this principle that a new grand lodge would fail to gain recognition from other grand lodges if it didn't allow the original lodges within its jurisdiction to opt out of joining the new grand lodge.

The Square Deal

A grand lodge has legitimate origin if it was formed in a regular fashion and if it can trace its genealogy back to one of the three original British grand lodges in an unbroken succession of regular charters or warrants. The British grand lodges—England (1717), Ireland (1725), and Scotland (1736)—are "grandfathered" in as being of legitimate origin, since the first grand lodges there were self-created.

Exclusive Territorial Jurisdiction

A grand lodge must be the sovereign Masonic authority within its jurisdiction; its decisions are final. There have been situations where a Scottish Rite Supreme Council of 33° Masons controlled a grand lodge, electing or appointing the Grand Master and grand officers. This is strictly irregular. Traditional Masonic law requires the 3° Master Masons to control the grand lodge; all other Masonic organizations are subordinate to the grand lodge—period.

Freemasonry, being a human institution, is beset with all the frailties of the human race. From time to time there have been splits within a grand lodge—over an election or finances or some policy. An aggrieved minority may then withdraw and start a new grand lodge, but other grand lodges usually will not recognize such a breakaway because it is within the jurisdiction of an existing grand lodge.

After failing to gain recognition from the community of grand lodge, the secessionists may reconsider their departure and reconcile with the grand lodge they left. Some-times such splits will divide the larger Masonic community, with some grand lodges supporting one faction and some supporting the other faction. Such divisions are rare, but they are usually settled in a spirit of brotherly love (once tempers have cooled down).

"Invasion of territory" is what happens when a grand lodge charters a lodge within or accepts a member from the territory of another grand lodge. This doesn't happen among long-established grand lodges, but sometimes a new grand lodge will look to a neighboring jurisdiction as a good source of members, or it might feel that the language or form of its rituals would better serve its neighbors. Thus are born disputes between grand lodges.

Since there is no central Masonic authority, resolutions of problems are reached slowly through withdrawal of recognition, the only enforcement mechanism available in Freemasonry. A consensus is usually eventually reached by a majority of grand lodges withdrawing recognition from an offending grand lodge. The logical conclusion of nonrecognition is for the jurisdiction to be declared "open territory," that is without any recognized grand lodge. Then new lodges will be formed there and eventually a new grand lodge, in direct competition with the now-abandoned grand lodge. This is the extreme case, much more likely to happen with a violation of the ancient landmarks than with an invasion of territory.

Adherence to the Ancient Landmarks

Regular lodges must maintain certain standards: they must adhere to the Ancient Landmarks. Their members must believe in God and be men. Regular lodges must display a Volume of Sacred Law at their meetings, and they cannot discuss nor be involved in partisan politics or sectarian religion.

We turn again to Anderson's 1723 Constitutions for the first Masonic use of the term. General Regulation 39, the last one, says in part, "Every Annual GRAND-LODGE has an inherent Power and Authority to make new Regulations, … Provided always that the old LANDMARKS be carefully preserv'd …" This all sounds good, except Anderson didn't define the landmarks. This has led to countless disagreements and rifts within the fraternity.

In the late 1800s, American Masonic scholars started a fad of producing lists of "landmarks." Each researcher engaged in the mental exercise of trying to come up with the smallest list that still covered what he considered fundamental. Albert G. Mackey, a prolific and mostly reliable author, came up with an impressive list of 25 landmarks. About half the American grand lodges have adopted Mackey's list, while the other half either have different lists or none at all. Most grand lodges outside of America have simply ignored the issue. They know a landmark when they see one, and they don't need a list to help them.

Hits and Myths

It is a myth that Mackey's 25 Landmarks are the universally recognized underpinnings of Masonry. Mackey's list starts with "1. The modes of recognition"; "2. The division of symbolic Masonry into three degrees"; and ends with "25. These Landmarks can never be changed." The list provides a guideline of what is generally considered fundamental in American Masonry, but too many grand lodges ignore it for it to be considered universal or even very good. Further, some of Mackey's "landmarks" are simply wrong. Take number 2, for instance. We know that when the Premier Grand Lodge was formed in 1717 there were only two degrees; the third degree was added a little before 1730. How can "the division of Symbolic Masonry into three degrees" be a landmark if that division didn't happen until after Symbolic Masonry was formed?

The largest divide between grand lodges has occurred over what, if anything, a Mason must believe about God. Anderson's First Charge, "Concerning God and Religion," from his 1723 Constitutions provides the starting point of all discussions:

> "A Mason is oblig'd by his Tenure, to obey the moral Law; and if he rightly understands the Art, he will never be a stupid Atheist, nor an irreligious Libertine. But though in ancient Times Masons were charg'd in every Country to be of the Religion of that Country or Nation, whatever it was, yet 'tis now thought more expedient only to oblige them to that Religion in which all Men agree, leaving their particular Opinions to themselves; that is, to be good Men and true, or Men of Honour and Honesty, by whatever Denominations or persuasions they may distinguish'd …."

Once again Anderson is imprecise. What is "that Religion in which all Men agree"? Some have suggested that Anderson, as a Presbyterian Minister, might have meant that all men agree on Christianity. In this interpretation, Anderson was trying to create a common ground for Catholics and Protestants to fellowship together. The generally accepted Masonic interpretation of the phrase is that a beneficent God created the universe. In other words, all men (who are not "stupid atheists") agree that God exists (and religious discussions stop there in Masonry). It is thought the imprecision was intentional so as to not build barriers; the goal of the grand lodge was inclusiveness. This inclusiveness is demonstrated by the acceptance of Jewish Masons in London by at least 1721, only four years after the formation of the Premier Grand Lodge.

French Masonry

In 1877, the *Grand Orient* of France fundamentally altered its membership requirements. Its members were given complete liberty in their beliefs about God; they could believe or not believe. Atheists could now belong to lodges in the Grand Orient of France. This idea of absolute freedom of conscience spread in European lodges, but was contrary to the Ancient Landmarks as understood by British and American grand lodges. Once the full affect of the Grant Orient's change was understood, British, American, and other regular grand lodges withdrew recognition.

def•i•ni•tion

Grand Orient is another name for a grand lodge. It means "Grand East," and refers to the location of the seat of the Grand Master in the grand lodge. While the Grand Orient of France will admit atheists, the name "Grand Orient" itself says nothing about an organization. For example, the Grand Orient of Haiti is a regular grand lodge formed in 1822.

Not all French and European lodges agreed that a belief in God could be dropped from their membership requirements, and they in turn formed new grand lodges that retained the belief in God. Because the network of regular grand lodges had withdrawn recognition from the original grand lodges, thus making those countries "open territory," the new grand lodges were quickly recognized. The result is that there are often at least two grand lodges in most European countries, one requiring a belief in God by its members (generally recognized by British and American grand lodges) and one with no religious requirements on its members (generally recognized by the Grand Orient of France).

Belgian Masonry

The situation in Belgium illustrates the complexities of Masonic recognition, especially in Europe.

Following the lead of France, the Grand Orient of Belgium gave its members complete freedom of conscience in religious matters and admitted atheists. They also allowed and even encouraged the debate of religious and political matters. In 1959, a group of Belgian Masons, dissatisfied with these deviations from traditional Freemasonry, established the Grand Lodge of Belgium. Over the years, however, members of the new grand lodge began to want fellowship with the Grand Orient, involvement in political issues, and no restrictions on religious beliefs.

Finally in 1979 another break-off occurred, and the Regular Grand Lodge of Belgium was created, with an absolute requirement in the belief in God and a total prohibition of political and religious discussions. Thus today in Belgium there are several grand lodges: the original Grand Orient, the Grand Lodge formed in 1959, the Regular Grand Lodge formed in 1979, the Women's Grand Lodge formed in 1981, and the Belgian Federation of "Le Droit Humain" (men and women or "mixed" Freemasonry). Only the Regular Grand Lodge of Belgium is recognized by traditional British and American grand lodges.

Everyone's Regular to Someone

Every grand lodge is regular to someone—if only itself. British-American grand lodges do not recognize the Grand Orient of France, but the Grand Orient of France has its own network of bilateral mutual recognitions. Starting in 1985 we saw the historic recognition of Prince Hall Affiliation grand lodges by British-American grand lodges. This amounted to a gradual merger of two previously independent recognition networks.

Scores of Masonic recognition networks exist around the world today. Think of it like the networks of colleges that accept transfer courses from each other, or even allow the other's students to freely enroll in their courses. There are also colleges that would never be acceptable by mainstream schools. (I'm thinking of those that offer a "Ph.D." for "life experience" and a few thousand dollars.)

It's important to remember there's no central governing body for Masonry. Each grand lodge decides for itself what other grand lodges it will recognize as regular, and each grand lodge chooses its own landmarks for determining regularity. This independence may appear to verge on chaos. In fact, there is reasonable stability and agreement among those grand lodges that are descended from the British grand lodges and that have maintained mutual recognition. These are the Masons whose lodges you are most likely to see in your community. They are the ones who place God in the center of their lives, who separate politics and religion from their lodges, and who contribute over $2 million a day to philanthropy.

The Least You Need to Know

- There is no central governing organization for Freemasonry.

- Regularity is determined by a network of bilateral mutual treaties of recognition.

- There are many independent recognition networks.

- Traditional Freemasonry demands a belief in God, territorial sovereignty, and adherence to the Landmarks.

Part 2

The Eastern Star, the York Rite, and the Scottish Rite

When you get to this part, you should understand the basic organization of Freemasonry into lodges, district or provincial grand lodges, and state or national grand lodges. You're ready to look into other organizations built onto the foundation of Masonic lodges: the Eastern Star for Masons and their female relatives; the British-origin York Rite; and the French-origin Scottish Rite. Many people think that 33° Masons run everything, but you'll get the straight story here.

7

Women and Freemasonry

In This Chapter

- ◆ Women becoming Freemasons
- ◆ Organizations for female relatives of Masons
- ◆ Co-Masonry for men and women starts in France in 1882
- ◆ Masonry for women only starts in France in 1945

Because there were no women stonemasons, the historical foundation of the fraternity was predisposed against women members. Reverend James Anderson formalized this in his 1723 *Constitutions of the Free-Masons*, in which it says in Charge III, "The persons admitted members of a lodge must be good and true men, free-born, and of mature and discreet age, no Bondmen, no women, no immoral or scandalous men, but of good report." (We note without comment that women were lumped together with immoral and scandalous men!) While that tradition has continued in mainstream lodges, women have been involved in the fraternity in many ways.

Early traditions, though difficult to detail, tell of women overhearing a Masonic initiation and themselves being initiated to insure secrecy. Better documented are the early organizations for Masons' female relatives, both in Europe and America. The most successful of these organizations for female relatives was the Order of the Eastern Star created in the 1850s, followed closely by other, similar groups for Master Masons' female relatives. Comparable groups were later started for women associated with Shriners, Knights Templar, Grottos, and so on.

In 1882, a French lodge formally initiated a woman, Marie Deraismes, and started a new chapter in Masonic history. The Symbolic Grand Lodge of France disbanded the lodge. Eleven years later Marie and others started Co-Masonry, Freemasonry for men and women, which has spread around the world. In 1952, the Feminine Grand Lodge of France was created with lodges for women, and it, too, has spread around the world. Today there are lodges for women only, men and women, and men only, though traditional men-only lodges predominate.

This chapter will discuss the few women who have been initiated in regular lodges, organizations for female relatives of Masons, Co-Masonry, and Female Masonry.

Early Examples of Women Freemasons

From 1717 onward, the modern fraternity of Freemasons has followed the traditions of their trade predecessors: the Masonic lodge was for men. But just as sure as you put up a "Men Only" sign, you will attract the curious. There is a body of stories of women being initiated into Masonic lodges that have a similar plot. A woman accidentally (or perhaps on purpose) overhears the secret initiation ceremonies of a lodge. She is discovered, much to the consternation of the brothers. After some discussion, the woman is formally initiated up to the degree she overheard in order to guarantee her silence.

Most of the stories do not hold up well under scrutiny, but they form an interesting body of Masonic folklore. There are so few of these stories that they are constantly repeated, so we'll briefly go over some of the more frequently repeated ones.

Elizabeth St. Leger Aldworth, Ireland, Around 1710

The prototype of the "Woman Freemason" is Elizabeth St. Leger, daughter of Arthur St. Leger, Viscount Doneraile of Ireland. The evidence points to her story being true. Elizabeth was born in 1693, and the events occurred when she was a "young girl," generally agreed to be around 1710 when she was about 17. This was before the Grand Lodge of Ireland was formed and formal regulations for Masonic lodges were established.

Her father was an enthusiastic Mason and held lodge meetings in his home. The time of the events was before the formation of any grand lodge, so the lodge couldn't have a charter and probably met irregularly, when it was convenient for the members. One evening the lodge was initiating a new member and Elizabeth was in the adjacent room. Because of uncompleted construction on the separating wall, she was able to remove a brick and witness the ceremonies. When she tried to slip away she was discovered, and the Masons pondered what to do to preserve their secrets. Their solution was to initiate Elizabeth and thus impose on her the obligation of Masonic secrecy.

Over the years various details have been embroidered on the story, but the details here are common to all versions. Supporting the story are some interesting facts. Elizabeth, later Mrs. Richard Aldworth, is listed as the second subscriber, after the Grand Master of Ireland, to Fifield Dassigny's 1744 *Serious and Impartial Enquiry into the Causes of the Present Decay of Freemasonry in the Kingdom of Ireland*. When the local Masons held benefits for the poor, she attended in Masonic regalia (see the figure that follows). There is a painting of her wearing a Masonic apron, and her apron is on display at the Masonic Hall, Tuckey Street, Cork, Ireland.

Elizabeth St. Leger Aldworth, the Lady Freemason, was initiated into Freemasonry in Doneraile, Ireland, around 1710.

(From Mackey's Revised Encyclopedia of Freemasonry, 1929)

Mrs. Bell, England, 1770

The story of Mrs. Bell is quite different and strictly speaking doesn't involve a woman becoming a Mason. It is similar to the St. Leger episode in that Mrs. Bell listens to Masonic ceremonies through a wall. The story is completely contained in an excerpt of the Newcastle, England, *Weekly Chronicle* for January 6, 1770, from Coil's *Masonic Encyclopedia*:

> "This is to acquaint the public that, on Monday, 1st inst., being the Lodge of Monthly meeting-night of the Free and Accepted Masons of the 22nd Regiment, held at the Crown, new Newgate, Mrs. Bell, the landlady of the house, broke open a door with a poker, by which means she got into an adjacent room, made two holes through the wall, and by that stratagem, discovered the secrets of Masonry, and knowing herself to be the first woman in the world that ever found out the secret is willing to make it known to all her sex. So that any lady that is desirous of learning the secrets of Freemasonry by applying to that well-learned woman, Mrs. Bell, who has lived fifteen years in and about Newgate, may be instructed in all secrets of Masonry."

Mrs. Havard and Mrs. Beaton, Hereford, England, 1770

The tradition of Palladian Lodge No. 120, Hereford, England, is that they initiated a Mrs. Havard in 1770. There are no records of the event, and it seems to be apocryphal. John Stacy's 1829 book, *A General History of the County of Norfolk*, reported that a Mrs. Beaton discovered the secrets of Masonry by hiding in the wainscoting of a lodge room. Mrs. Beaton, whose given name is undiscovered, died in 1802 at age 82 without anything ever being said about her adventure during her lifetime. Her story is unlikely.

Hannah Mather Crocker, Boston, 1778

Women Freemasons appear to have had a lodge in Boston in 1778, though it's unknown where they originally joined. The scant information comes from an 1815 book by Hannah Mather Crocker, *A Series of letters on Free Masonry*. In the book, Crocker defends the fraternity against charges of excessive revelry, questionable members, and irreligion, and she refers to a St. Anne's Lodge of Boston in 1778. The quote that follows is from Kent Walgren's 2003 bibliography, *Freemasonry, Anti-Masonry and Illuminism in the United States, 1734–1850:*

"I had the honour some years ago to preside as Mistress of a similar institution, consisting of females only; we held a regular lodge [including tokens, words, and signs], founded on the original principles of true ancient masonry, so far as was consistent for the female character. We recognized the Brotherhood as preeminent, as may be seen from several Addresses and Songs that were printed in the *Centinel* … The prime inducement for forming the lodge, was a desire for cultivating the mind …."

The Square Deal

Hannah Mather Crocker, granddaughter of Cotton Mather and daughter of Increase Mather, published a book in 1918 titled *Observations on the Real Rights of Women*. She was an early feminist and said God had "endowed the female mind with equal powers and faculties." The American Antiquarian Society acquired the Mather library from Hannah and thus began their preservation of the papers of important early New Englanders.

Catherine Babington, North Carolina, 1815

An American variation of the eavesdropping female Freemason is Mrs. Catherine Babington. Her initiation is supposed to have occurred in Princess, Kentucky, when she was a girl, and her obituary gives the summary of the story:

"BABINGTON. An aged and estimable lady, Mrs. Catherine (Sweet) Babington died in Shelby, on Monday evening, June the 28th, 1886 … At her death she was the only female Mason in the United States, and was well versed in the mysterious workings of the Blue Lodge. Having overheard the secrets of Masonry when she was a girl of sixteen years, it was thought best to initiate her as a member and thus prevent any disclosure."

Her son, J. P. Babington, a member of Cleveland Lodge No. 202, Shelby, North Carolina, published *Biography of Mrs. Catherine Babington, the Only Woman Mason in the World, and How She Became a Blue Lodge Mason.* According to her son's account, she hid in a lectern in her uncles' lodge and listened to Masonic ceremonies for more than a year before she was caught. Her uncles examined her and were astonished to discover that she had memorized most of the Masonic ritual—and better than they had!

The book goes on to relate several incidents when Mrs. Babington used her knowledge of Freemasonry to save herself from embarrassment and danger. Some of the events happened in the presence of her son, which adds a note of authenticity. But the story has some problems. There was no Masonic lodge anywhere near her grandfather's home, as the book says, so it would have been difficult for her to sneak into meetings for a year. Masonic records indicate that her grandfather was a Mason, but no evidence proves her uncles were Masons.

Was Catherine Babington made a Mason to preserve the secrets of Masonry? Her son thought so, and it's hard to discount that family tradition. The distance to the lodge and the absence of membership records for her uncles, however, raises doubts. It does seem clear that she knew enough about Freemasonry to impress other Masons, but she could have picked up that much information from the many available exposés. I think this falls into the category of "might be true," but the evidence is weak.

The French Rite of Adoption

Freemasonry was introduced into France in the 1720s, and the high degrees became particularly popular there. Organizations of men and women associated—sometimes tenuously—with Freemasonry grew after mid-century among the upper classes. It is difficult to know which groups were widespread, and which existed as little more than paper exercises. The groups included the Order of Felicity, Knights and Ladies of the Dove, and the French Rite of Adoption. (Think of "adoption" as the lodge "adopting" the women as sisters.)

The latter body seemed to be one of the most popular in France, and its date of formation is often given as 1774. It eventually developed a four-degree system of 1° Apprentice, 2° Craftswoman, 3° Mistress Mason, and 4° Perfect Mason. The French Rite of Adoption never got established in America, but knowledge of it probably inspired many of the late-nineteenth-century American groups for female relatives of Masons.

The Eastern Star and Sister Organizations

If the exposés of the American Anti-Masonic period (1826–1841) are to be believed, there were several degrees available to the female relatives of Masons, including Mason's Daughter, Heroines of Jericho, and True Kindred. These early American ladies' degrees seemed to exist to give a Mason's lady a way to identify herself to another Mason if she needed assistance. This was done with secret signs and passwords that presumably would become known to all Masons. Apparently any Mason who had received one of the degrees could assemble a group of Masons and their ladies and in turn confer the degrees on them. There was no central organization.

These are secret signs used by Heroines of Jericho to identify themselves to each other and to Masons. Sign 3 is their "Grand Hailing Sign of Distress."

(From Avery Allyn's 1831 exposé A Ritual of Freemasonry*)*

The Square Deal

Exposés of Masonic "secrets" have been around since 1723. Their goals seem to be to embarrass or destroy Masonry or to make some money for the author. The Masonic fraternity flourishes nonetheless. It is ironic that much of our knowledge of early Masonic practices comes from such publications, though it requires a trained eye to separate accurate descriptions from bogus sensationalism. The biggest irony is that American Anti-Masons wanted to forever eradicate all "secret societies" and expected the exposés to be the final nails in their coffins. What happened is that during the Golden Age of Fraternalism (1870–1920), their exposés served as convenient templates for the creation of scores of new fraternal organizations!

As Freemasonry recovered from the Anti-Masonic Period, the women's degrees don't seem to have received much attention. Around 1850 Rob Morris of Kentucky created the Order of the Eastern Star for Freemasons and their female relatives. The ritual ceremony consisted of a recitation of the stories of five women in the Bible who exemplified the virtues taught by the ceremonies.

The Five Women of the Eastern Star, Their Symbols and Virtues

Woman	Emblem	Virtue
Adah, the daughter	Sword and Veil	Fidelity
Ruth, the widow	Sheaf of Wheat	Constancy
Esther, the wife	Crown and Scepter	Loyalty
Martha, the sister	Broken Column	Faith
Electa, the mother	Cup	Love

The five points of the Eastern Star emblem refer to these five women. (The Eastern Star has given the name "Adah" to Jephthah's daughter, in Judges 11, and has created the name "Electa" for the "elect lady" in 2 John 1:1.)

The five "star points" of the Eastern Star Emblem contain the emblems that refer to five women in the Bible: Adah, Ruth, Esther, Martha, and Electa.

The Eastern Star Degree initially was conferred without any central authority or local chapters. Morris tried to organize the ladies into local "Stars" governed by state "Constellations," but his strength was writing impressive ritual ceremonies, not creating efficient administrative organizations. In the late 1860s, Morris turned over the Eastern Star to Robert Macoy of New York, who had the organizational skills that Morris lacked.

Macoy organized the Eastern Star into the structure it has today: local Chapters, state Grand Chapters, and a national General Grand Chapter. All state Grand Chapters belong to the General Grand Chapter, except for New York and New Jersey. Membership is open to Master Masons and their female relatives who believe in the existence of God. New York does not require women members to have a Masonic relative, and New Jersey requires its members to be Christian. The Eastern Star has also spread to Canada, Scotland, Australia, and Germany. The United Grand Lodge of England will not allow its members to join the Eastern Star.

> **The Square Deal**
>
> The presiding officer of an Eastern Star Chapter is the Worthy Matron assisted by the Worthy Patron, and all of the principal officers are women. Yet Eastern Star regulations require that a Mason be present before a meeting can open.

The Eastern Star is certainly not an "auxiliary" of Freemasonry. It is an independent organization that sometimes works hand-in-hand with Masons, especially at the local level. In some states, the Masonic retirement home is jointly run with the Eastern Star. Total membership (men and women) in the Eastern Star was about 25 percent at the beginning of the twentieth century and had risen to 50 percent by 1916. Membership varied between 50 percent and 60 percent of the Masons for the rest of the century.

Order of the Amaranth

After the Order of the Eastern Star spread and became established, a new movement pushed to create a Rite for women, with a series of organizations and degrees, like the York or Scottish Rites. James B. Taylor wrote the original Amaranth Degree about 1860, and Robert Macoy rewrote it in 1873 when a Supreme Council for the Order was created. Macoy's vision was for a Rite of Adoption with three degrees: Eastern Star, Queen of the South, and Amaranth.

Originally members in the Amaranth had to belong to the Eastern Star. The Eastern Star, however, objected to becoming merely an introductory step in a larger system, and eventually the Amaranth dropped the requirement of Eastern Star membership and became an independent organization for Master Masons and their female relatives. While the Rite of Adoption generally fell apart, and the Queen of the South Degree disappeared, Prince Hall Masons have kept the system going.

White Shrine of Jerusalem

The Order of the White Shrine of Jerusalem was formed in 1894 for Christian Master Masons and their female relatives. Like the Amaranth, it initially required its members to belong to the Eastern Star and looked upon itself as a "higher degree" for Christian Eastern Star members, much like the Knights Templar are for Master Masons. Once again the Eastern Star objected to being the introductory degree for any order, and the White Shrine eventually dropped the requirement. It is now an independent organization with local shrines in the United States and Canada.

Female Organizations for Other Masonic Groups

If an organization for female relatives of Master Masons is a good idea, then it should work for all Masonic organizations, right? In theory, yes, but in practice the Eastern Star and Amaranth have been the two most successful such organizations. There are some other success stories, especially for female relatives of Shriners.

The Square Deal

The first nationally organized American fraternal organization for female relatives of male members was the Rebekah Degree of the Independent Order of Odd Fellows. While there was initial opposition from some of the men, the Rebekah spread more rapidly than the Eastern Star. This was because the Odd Fellows had a national grand lodge that accepted the Rebekah as an official part of its organization.

One of the oldest Masonic groups for women is the Heroines of Jericho, limited to female relatives of Royal Arch Masons. We're not sure when it started, but its ceremonies were exposed in Avery Allyn's 1831 book, *A Ritual of Freemasonry*, one of the anti-Masonic publications that followed the Morgan Affair. *Coil's Masonic Encyclopedia* suggests that David Vinton formed the Heroines around 1815–1820. They died out during the Anti-Masonic Period and experienced a slight rebirth before the Civil War. Female relatives of Prince Hall Royal Arch Masons still practice the Heroines of Jericho in its original form.

The Social Order of Beauceant was formed in 1890 for Knights Templar and their ladies. The Shriners' ladies have the Ladies Oriental Shrine of North America, formed in 1903, the Daughters of the Nile, 1914, and the Daughters of Isis for Prince Hall Shriners. The women related to the Prophets in the Grottos of North America can join the Daughters of Mokanna formed in 1919. These organizations provide social activities for their members, and take pride in their charitable activities. For example, the Daughters of the Nile have given over $35 million since 1924 to the Shriners Hospitals for Children.

Marie Deraismes and Co-Masonry

As the Order of the Eastern Star was spreading and gaining recognition in America, women and French Freemasonry moved in a different direction. "Adoptive Masonry" seems to have first appeared in France and gained popularity there. This perhaps set the stage for in 1882 for the initiation of Marie Adelaide Deraismes, a humanitarian and feminist writer, into the Free Thinkers Lodge in Pecq, France. The Symbolic Grand Lodge of France immediately disbanded the lodge.

Eleven years later Marie and French Senator and Mason Georges Martin started the lodge Le Droit Humain (Human Rights) in Paris, and eventually a grand lodge and a supreme council. The idea of Masonic Lodges for men and women became popular and gradually spread throughout Europe. The organization is known by several names: Co-Masonry, Droit Humain, and Mixed Masonry. The first Co-Masonic lodge was formed in America in 1903, and its national organization is known as the American Federation of Human rights. Traditional men's Freemasonry does not have any formal ties with Co-Masonry, nor are its members allowed to visit Co-Masonic lodges. The situation in France and Europe is much more complicated, and varies from grand lodge to grand lodge.

It is interesting to think what would have happened in 1903 when the first American Co-Masonic lodge was formed if the Eastern Star, Amaranth, and others were not already well established. American women by 1903 had expended large amounts of human capital in creating organizations which they ran (a radical idea for women at that time) and in which their Masonic relatives could participate. Co-Masonry has had the same difficulties as men's Masonry, with disagreements on higher degrees, belief in God, ritual details, and so on. This sort of conflict is not unique to Free-masonry, but seems to be part of the human condition.

Female Grand Lodges

Co-Masonry came to England in 1902, but some of the lodges soon became dissatis-fied with a grand lodge in France. They broke away and formed their own group in 1908. They soon decided that it would be better to have a grand lodge for women, and they transformed themselves into the Order of Women Freemasons, allowing the few male members to remain until their deaths. In 1913, the issue of allowing lodges to work the Royal Arch Degree caused a group to break away and form the Honourable Fraternity of Ancient Freemasons. It is ironic that one of the causes of the English Ancients/Moderns rivalry, the Royal Arch, would cause the same problem in English women's Freemasonry.

In 1901, the Grand Lodge of France, one of several French grand lodges, reactivated Adoptive Masonry. Then in 1945 the men's Grand Lodge of France helped transform the Adoptive Lodges into an independent group that is known today as the Feminine Grand Lodge of France. This grand lodge has chartered women's lodges around the world including the Feminine Grand Lodge of Belgium, which in 1981 chartered several women's lodges in America.

This brief overview just touches the high points of a complex story. Other Co-Masonic and female grand lodges exist, some requiring a belief in God and some not, some working the York Rite, some the Scottish Rite, and some following mystical and spiritual paths unknown in their mainstream counterparts. Today those interested in Freemasonry can find a lodge for men only, women only, or men and women and choose the one that suits them best.

The Least You Need to Know

- Many, mostly apocryphal, stories tell of women being initiated after overhearing lodge ceremonies.

- There appears to have been a women's lodge in Boston in 1778.

- The Eastern Star was started in America in 1850 for female relatives of Masons.

- America has many organizations for female relatives of Masons.

- Marie Deraismes was initiated into a men's lodge in 1882 and went on to found Co-Masonry for men and women.

- The Order of Women Freemasons was formed in England in 1908, and was the first of several similar groups.

Chapter 8

The York Rite

In This Chapter

- ◆ The York is the oldest American "high degree" rite
- ◆ The York Rite is a confederation of independent organizations
- ◆ Royal Arch Masons Chapters, the sequel
- ◆ Cryptic Masons Councils, the prequel
- ◆ Knights Templar Commanderies, the spin-off
- ◆ Knight Templar uniforms look sharp in parades

You will probably not be surprised to learn that no one is quite sure when, where, or how the York Rite started. Like so many Masonic groups, it coalesced into its current form over several years rather than being created with its existing organization.

The York Rite is best thought of as a confederation of autonomous and cooperating Masonic *bodies*—Chapters of Royal Arch Masons, Councils of Cryptic Masons, and Commanderies of Knights Templar—that rests on common membership in Blue Lodges. Like all Masonic rites, the York Rite expands on and develops the basic legends of the Blue Lodge.

The component Masonic organizations of the York Rite exist all around the world, but they're known as the "York Rite" mostly in America. In England, you might get a blank look if you ask about the York Rite. Just as America has a two-party political system, American Freemasonry evolved into a "two-rite" system: York and Scottish. The York Rite tends to have smaller local groups in contrast with the larger regional groups of the Scottish Rite. The York Rite is governed by a patchwork of autonomous or semi-autonomous grand bodies, while there are two national supreme bodies for the Scottish Rite. The Knights Templar, the "pinnacle" of the York Rite, limit their membership to Christian Masons, effectively creating a Christian Rite, even though the lodge, chapter, and council are open to Masons of all faiths.

def•i•ni•tion

Body is the generic term used to refer to Masonic organizations rather than lodge, chapter, council, commandery, consistory, preceptory, priory, conclave, and so on. Thus Masons would say, "The York Rite is composed of four bodies," rather than, "The York Rite is composed of lodges, chapters, councils, and commanderies."

This chapter will discuss the three independent but cooperating bodies that make up the York Rite, their organizations, and how they expand on Blue Lodge ritual legends.

A Good Rule

The York Rite doesn't come from York, England; it is an American creation. Most of the individual pieces came from England, but the Rite was assembled in America. The Scottish Rite doesn't come from Scotland; it is a French export. (And Philadelphia Brand Cream Cheese doesn't come from Philadelphia!)

Capitular Masonry: Royal Arch Masons

The Royal Arch Degree appeared a few decades after the Master Mason Degree and has become the most widespread "high degree." There are about 2,500 Royal Arch Mason Chapters in the United States alone, and they confer a total of four degrees.

def•i•ni•tion

Royal Arch Masonry is called Capitular Masonry because its bodies are called chapters, and *capitulum* is Latin for *chapter.*

The Royal Arch Degree

The *Royal Arch* Degree is often called the "completion of the Master Mason Degree," because it's the second act of a two-act play, with the Master Mason Degree the first act. The oldest reference to the

Royal Arch is a vague report in *Faulkner's Dublin Journal* for January 10–14, 1743, that Youghall Lodge No. 21 celebrated St. John's Day with a parade in which there was "the Royal Arch carried by two excellent Masons." Was this a reference to a new "high degree," or was it simply part of the parade, perhaps an arch that the Worshipful Master or other senior officers walked under? No one knows.

The second oldest reference came when Fifield D'Assigny published in *Dublin: A Serious and Impartial Enquiry into the Cause of the Present Decay of Freemasonry in the Kingdom of Ireland* (1744), "I am informed in that city [York] is held an assembly of Master Masons under the title of Royal Arch Masons, who, as their qualifications and excellencies are superior to others they receive a larger pay than working masons …" This seems to refer clearly to a new type of Mason and connects the degree's legend to York, England. Tantalizing connections to York, such as this, influenced the adoption of the name "York Rite."

The third and most important reference to the Royal Arch is December 22, 1753. That's when the lodge in Fredericksburg, Virginia, conferred the degree of Royal Arch Mason on three Master Masons. This new degree had now leapt across the Atlantic and emerged fully formed in Virginia. The previous references had been just hints that something was going on, but here is the first full-blown record anywhere that a new ceremony existed. The first English record of a degree conferral is five years later on August 7, 1758, in Bristol. After this, the Royal Arch gained popularity and spread throughout Britain and America

The legend of the Master Mason Degree is a simple story of fidelity to a trust. At the end of the tale, however, the great secret—the Master Mason's Word—is lost and only a substitute remains. At the allegorical level, this is a wonderful ending, as the Mason's search for "that which is lost" must continue, perhaps forever and outside the lodge. On another level, it's like seeing only the first act of a two-act play—you want to know how the story ends! The Royal Arch Degree is the second act: it tells how the lost word of a Master Mason is recovered.

Thus Royal Arch Masons felt their Masonic knowledge had been completed or fulfilled, and that they were perhaps superior to "mere" Master Masons who didn't know how the story ended. Early records indicate that the Royal Arch Degree was conferred on the authority of a lodge charter. The lodge would transform itself into a Royal Arch Mason Chapter as needed, in the same way it converted itself from an Entered Apprentice Lodge and into a Fellowcraft Lodge. Eventually the Royal Arch Degree was "spun off" from lodges and operated in Royal Arch Chapters under the administration of a state or national Grand Chapter.

The Royal Arch legend most used in America tells the story of rebuilding the Temple in Jerusalem after the Babylonian Captivity. The principal officers represent Jeshua, the high priest, Zerubbabel, the king (prince of Judea), and Haggai, the scribe (Haggai 1:12, 14). In English chapters, the presiding officer is the king, Zerubbabel. American Royal Arch Masonry developed around the time of the American Revolution, and perhaps not liking the idea of a king presiding over them, they adopted a version of the legend with the high priest as presiding officer.

The Square Deal

The Royal Arch legend is an elaboration and completion of the Master Mason narrative. Several variations exist in different Masonic traditions, so it's not possible to speak of the Royal Arch legend. *Coil's Masonic Encyclopedia* says the Royal Arch Degree is "related to the removal of rubbish of the first Temple to lay the foundations for the Second, in the course of which the Mason-Knights, working with trowel in one hand and sword and buckler in the other, came to an aperture leading to an underground vault or crypt, usually under the Ninth Arch wherein was discovered a cubical or white stone or metal plate or triangle upon which appeared the ultimate great Masonic secret, the possession of which by [Royal Arch Masons] rendered them superior to other Master Masons ..."

The Other Degrees in an American Royal Arch Chapter

Four degrees are conferred on candidates in an American Royal Arch Mason Chapter with the Order of High Priesthood for Past High Priests.

- Mark Master Mason
- Past Master
- Most Excellent Master
- Royal Arch Mason
- Order of High Priesthood (for Past High Priests)

The first of the series of degrees in a Royal Arch Chapter is that of Mark Master Mason. It is built upon the ancient custom of Masons selecting their mark to cut into the stones they dressed in the quarry to identify the craftsman for quality control and payment. Originally marks were composed of a few straight chisel cuts and occasionally a curve, though there are no such restrictions on speculative Mark Master Masons. The side of the stone with the mark usually faced inside the wall, so that most marks are now hidden, though hundreds and hundreds have been identified in European cathedrals and other buildings. During the ceremonies, the candidate enters his mark in the Mark Book, and it is then his personal "brand."

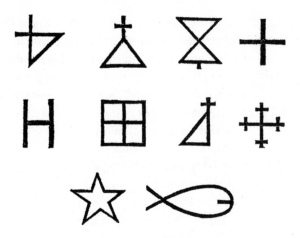

These marks were cut on stones in European buildings and served to identify the Mason who prepared the stone.

Evidence shows that early Scottish operative masons used their marks in place of a signature. William Schaw, Master of Work to the King, visited the Lodge of Edinburgh on June 8, 1600, and the Masons in attendance signed the minutes using their Marks.

The Mark Master Degree also has a legend about producing the keystone that went in the principal arch of King Solomon's Temple. A keystone with the letters "H T W S S T K S" in a circle is the emblem of the degree. It is often used in America as a symbol for the Royal Arch Chapter.

This keystone is the principal emblem of the Mark Master Mason Degree. When used in jewelry, the central circle of the keystone is often engraved with the member's personal mark.

The Royal Arch followed the same paths as Blue Lodge Masonry in spreading around the world, though it never reached 100 percent of the Masons, only the most

def•i•ni•tion

In many Masonic organizations, the presiding officer goes through a special installation ceremony, another degree in fact, where he receives the **chair degree**. A chair degree, with passwords, signs, and grips, is called such because it's only given to those who sit in the presiding officer's chair.

enthusiastic and active. It was originally limited to Past Masters, those who had presided over a Master Mason Lodge and had received the *chair degree*. As the attraction of the Royal Arch grew, however, increased demand encouraged some way around the requirement that candidates had to preside over a lodge for a year. The result was a "virtual" Past Master Degree where the candidate symbolically presided over a lodge and received the secrets necessary to become a Royal Arch Mason. In America, the Past Master Degree is still part of the sequence of degrees leading to the Royal Arch, while in England it's no longer required.

The next-to-the-last degree in the Royal Arch Chapter, Most Excellent Master, is a combination of elements of existing degrees from the late 1700s that created this American original. Its legend is about the completion of King Solomon's Temple and centers on the placement of the keystone in the principal arch of the Temple. Like all Masonic degrees, the Most Excellent Master legend is not literally true; it is an allegory intended to teach moral lessons. In fact, no evidence shows that the Temple even had arches with keystones, though it could have. The principal symbolism revolves around putting the final stone in place and completing the Temple, whatever and wherever that stone may have been.

This is a symbolic representation of placing the keystone in the principal arch of King Solomon's Temple.

Cryptic Masonry: Royal and Select Masters

In Hollywood, a successful movie quickly generates sequels and prequels; Freemasonry seems to operate on the same principal. The Master Mason Degree was a smash hit, soon followed by a very successful sequel, the Royal Arch Mason Degree. It wasn't long before a prequel was needed, and the degrees of Royal Master and Select Master filled the bill. In the Master Mason Degree, the word is lost, in the Royal Arch it is recovered, and in the Royal and Select Master Degrees, a Mason learns why, where, and how the word was preserved inside nine arches below King Solomon's Temple.

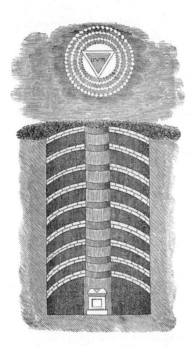 

These depictions of the nine arches below King Solomon's Temple are taken from Amos Doolittle's 1819 engravings in Jeremy Cross's book, The True Masonic Chart. *Sometimes the arches are shown vertically, and other times horizontally.*

The Degree of Select Master was originally a *side degree* of the Scottish Rite, having appeared in Charleston, South Carolina, as early as 1783. It was spread either by the Inspectors General of the Rite or by itinerant Masonic lecturers. As an example of the latter, consider Jeremy Ladd Cross (1783–1861), one of the leading traveling lecturers of his day. In 1817, he chartered councils of Select Masters for $20 (about $275 in 2005). (Note that these councils only conferred one degree, that of Select Master.) During a six-week, 635-mile trip from Haverhill, New Hampshire, to Richmond, Virginia, Cross chartered at least six councils.

def•i•ni•tion _____

> A **side degree** is a Masonic degree that's not under the control of any central governing organization. Generally anyone who has received the degree can give it to someone else. Some side degrees created their own governing body, but most died out for lack of interest. Modern side degrees tend to be humorous fundraisers with the fees going to a designated charity.

The Degree of Royal Master appeared in New York City around 1805 and spread from there. The self-creation in 1810 of Columbian Council in New York City formalized the existence of the degree, and in 1821 the council took the important step of absorbing a Select Master Council. In 1818, while New York was organizing itself, Jeremy Cross received the Royal Master Degree and started conferring the Royal and Select Masters Degrees together in Connecticut. The first council in that state formed in New Haven in 1818, the same year the grand council for the state was formed.

def•i•ni•tion _____

> The Degrees of Royal and Select Masters are called **Cryptic Masonry** because they deal with the legend of a crypt hidden under King Solomon's Temple to preserve Masonic secrets.

The degrees of *Cryptic Masonry* were popular, but their government was unsettled. In some states, independent grand councils controlled the degrees, while in other states the Grand Chapter of Royal Arch Masons exercised control. Eventually most states created independent grand councils, though the Grand Royal Arch Chapters of Virginia and West Virginia continue to control the cryptic degrees.

One other degree is associated with Cryptic Masonry, that of Super Excellent Master (a blush-inducing combination of superlatives!), even though it has nothing to do with the crypt under Solomon's Temple. The history of this degree is even more obscure than most degrees, and it has the odd distinction of being an optional degree. Both the Royal and Select Masters Degrees are required for full membership in a council; the Super Excellent is not required at all. It is conferred only occasionally, often as part of a statewide gathering. Its legend deals with the fall and destruction of Jerusalem while Zedekiah was king and with the exile of the Jews to Babylon.

Thus these three degrees in Cryptic Masonry, like any good prequel, fill in the gaps in the legends of Symbolic and Royal Arch Masonry. There is no chair degree.

- Royal Master
- Select Master
- Super Excellent Master (optional)

Chivalric Masonry: Knights Templar

Thus far in the York Rite we've seen an original story, a sequel, and a prequel. When Hollywood wrings everything it can out of a story line, it also turns to spin-offs. The Knights Templar can be thought of as a spin-off of the basic Masonic theme. The Templars take up new legends quite different from the themes of loss, recovery, and preservation found in lodge, chapter, and council.

As with the 1753 Royal Arch records from Fredericksburg, Virginia, America has the oldest records of Masonic Knights Templar. On August 28, 1769, in St. Andrew's Royal Arch Chapter in Boston, William Davis received "the four steps, that of Excellent, Super-excellent, Royal Arch, and Knight Templar." We're really not sure about the meaning of the steps of "Excellent" and "Super-excellent," except that the latter had nothing to do with the present Super Excellent Master Degree of the Cryptic Masons. The Royal Arch and Knight Templar, however, are known, and the sequence of Royal Arch followed by Knight Templar continues today (with a few other degrees thrown in). It is generally accepted that the Masonic Knight Templar ceremonies developed in England or the continent and most likely were brought to America by a military lodge. The second and third recorded Knights Templar were also in St. Andrew's Royal Arch Chapter: Paul Revere on December 11, 1769, and Joseph Warren on March 14, 1770.

The first English Masonic Knight Templar record is a certificate from York (again reinforcing the legendary origins of the rite) that a Brother was "Raised (4th degree or R.A.M.) 27th October 1779, Knight Templar (5th degree) 29th November 1779." (The first three degrees here were those of the Symbolic Lodge, Apprentice, Fellow-craft, and Master.) After this, Masonic Templarism blossomed. Local American chapters of Templars, called "Encampments" (today, "Commanderies") existed in Charleston, South Carolina, in 1780, Baltimore in 1782, Long Island in 1783, and Philadelphia in 1794.

Encampments of Knights Templar were mostly located in larger cities, and the organization became truly the summit of American Masonic activity. Only the most active and dedicated Masons could become involved; the expense was also not insignificant. First a man was elected and paid the initiation fees and annual dues to a Blue Lodge. Then he underwent another ballot and paid more fees and dues to become a Royal Arch Mason. Finally, after those steps and expenses, he was ready to go through it a third time to become a Knight Templar.

The lodge and chapter are open to any man who believes in God, but only Christians are eligible to become Knights Templar, effectively making the York Rite a Christian rite. The ceremonies of the Order of the Temple (the formal name of the Knights Templar) have the candidate take a symbolic pilgrimage to the Holy Sepulcher and then receive a Christian interpretation of the Master Mason's word. The interpretation is based on chapter 1, verse 1 of the Gospel of John, "In the beginning was the Word, and the Word was with God, and the Word was God."

The Degrees of the Knights Templar

The first degree conferred in a Commandery of Knights is the Illustrious Order of the Red Cross. Its legend has nothing whatsoever to do with medieval knights, but rather is a prequel to the story of Zerubbabel returning from Babylon to Jerusalem and rebuilding the Temple. Of course, historical accuracy has never been a requirement for an allegorical story, and Masonic legends are no different. The degree does provide a good connection to the Royal Arch.

The legend of the Illustrious Order of the Red Cross in the Encampment of Knights Templar is one of the most widespread in Freemasonry. According to *Coil's Masonic Encyclopedia*, all versions of the degree "tell almost the same story in the same way, that is the preparations for building the Second Temple and Zerubabbel's embassy to Persia to procure the repatriation of the Jews for that purpose." When in the court of Darius, king of Persia, Zerubbabel participates in a debate on the question, "Which is greater: Wine, the King, or Women?" This episode is based on 1 Esdras 3, 4 from the Apocrypha. Zerubbabel wins the debate by arguing for women, but trumps everyone with the argument, "Great is Truth, and mighty above all things" (see the figure that follows). Darius declares Zerubbabel the winner and grants his wish to rebuild the Temple in Jerusalem.

This legend is found in the Scottish Rite, divided into two "acts": 15°, Knight of the East or Sword, and 16°, Prince of Jerusalem. The story is divided into three "acts" in the Knight Masons U.S.A. (an invitational body): Knight of the Sword Degree, Knight of the East Degree, and Knight of the East and West Degree.

The second degree conferred by the Knights Templar is technically not a degree but an order: the Order of St. John of Jerusalem, Palestine, Rhodes, and Malta—better known as the Knights of Malta. It has no connection with the Catholic or other orders of similar names. The ceremony includes brief lectures on the Birth, Life, Death, Resurrection, and Ascension of Jesus. The letters "B.L.D.R.A." become a reminder to Knights of Malta of the story of Jesus.

The motto on the banner of the Order of the Red Cross comes from the debate in the court of King Darius: Magna est Veritas et Prevalebit (Truth is Mighty and Will Prevail).

It is somewhat incongruous to have Knights of Malta subordinate to Knights Templar since the Order of St. John was the Templars' rival in the Holy Land and inherited all of the Templars' property when the latter were disbanded in 1312. Yet again we see that good allegory does not depend on historical faithfulness. Originally the Masonic Order of Malta was conferred after the Order of the Temple, but this was eventually changed because it didn't make sense for the ultimate ceremony to be next to last.

The last step in the Commandery and in the York Rite is the Order of the Temple. Having allegorically time-traveled from the construction of King Solomon's Temple (about 950 B.C.E.) to the rebuilding of the Temple by Zerubbabel (about 515 B.C.E.), a Mason has no problem symbolically joining a medieval order of crusading knights (1118–1312 C.E.). A candidate journeys symbolically as a pilgrim penitent and then as a pilgrim warrior, eventually arriving at the Holy Sepulcher where Jesus was buried.

He is reminded that death is the final destination of this world and that his only preparation for the world to come is faith in Jesus Christ. After promising to defend the Christian religion he is knighted and becomes a member of the Order of the Temple.

The pilgrim warrior symbolically visits the Holy Sepulcher in the Knight Templar Degree.

Like Cryptic Masonry, there is no chair degree for the Knights Templar. A Commandery confers only three degrees.

- Order of the Red Cross

- Order of Malta

- Order of the Temple

The Knights Templar Uniform

As popular and as exclusive as the Knights Templar may have been, they were almost destroyed during the Anti-Masonic Period (1826–1840) following the Morgan Affair in New York. When they emerged from their forced hibernation, part of their tradition thrust them into unexpected popularity: their uniforms. The original uniform of American Knights Templar was rather simple: a black triangular apron with skull and bones (a "Memento Mori," a reminder to remember death), a shoulder-to-hip sash, and a sword, all worn over street clothes. Following the American Civil War came the "Golden Age of Fraternalism," when there was a popular obsession with joining fraternal organizations, as much for their social benefits as for the insurance that many offered. The Knights Templar updated their uniforms, added military drills to their ceremonies, and became featured units in many civic parades around the country. They even had drill manuals for mounted platoons!

The new Knights Templar Uniform was based on a black uniform frock coat, similar to Civil War–era uniforms with full trimmings. The modern uniforms had no connection with those of the historic Knights Templar, though they certainly met Victorian standards of dashing taste! These elaborate uniforms looked stunning coming down the street in a parade, both on foot and horseback, and were supplied by a growing industry of regalia manufacturers that also outfitted the Knights of Pythias, Patriarchs Militant of the Odd Fellows, Knights of the Maccabees, and many more. If expense is a widely held (if inappropriate) measure of prestige, then Knights Templar topped the popular scale with their uniforms (unsuitable for anything but Templar meetings) and their exclusive memberships in and fees for Lodge, Chapter, and Commandery.

These images give a good comparison of the Knights Templar historic garb and Victorian Masonic uniforms.

The Knights Templar uniform was defined as follows, "Full Dress: Black Frock Coat, Black Pantaloons, Scarf [sash], Sword, Belt, Shoulder Straps, Gauntlets and Chapeau, with appropriate trimmings." ("Edict of 1862," from H. B. Grant, *Tactics and Manual for Knights Templar*, Louisville, KY, 1882)

The Creation of the York Rite

In Britain, the Royal Arch Masons are one of several organizations a Master Mason can join, and the Knights Templar is one of a number for Royal Arch Masons. The sequence of Master Mason, Royal Arch Mason, Knight Templar is common in Freemasonry, but it's mostly in America that it's known as the "York Rite." The Cryptic Masons, between the Royal Arch Masons and Knights Templar, are an optional step in some states.

The term "York Rite" probably started as convenient shorthand to distinguish a Knight Templar from a 32° Scottish Rite Mason. ("Oh, you're in the Scottish Rite? I'm in the York Rite.") Also most American lodges are descended from the Grand Lodge of Ancients in England, who were very liberal about letting their lodges work additional, new degrees under authority of their charters. American Ancient lodges and grand lodges often called themselves "Ancient York Masons" because of an old legend appearing around 1500 that the first general assembly of Masons in England was held at York in the 900s. Robert Plot quoted the legend from a parchment scroll in his *The Natural History of Stafford-shire* (1686):

> "Edwyn loved well masonry, took upon him the charges and learned the manners, and obtained for them of his Father [king Athelstan (924–940 C.E.)] a free-Charter. Whereupon he caused them to assemble at York, and to bring all the old Books of their craft, and out of them ordained such charges and manners, as they then thought fit … Thus was the craft of masonry grounded and confirmed in England."

An important organizational distinction of the York Rite is that it has mostly small, local, sometimes rural bodies, in contrast with the larger regional Scottish Rite bodies usually located in large cities. The rural to urban migration of the twentieth century has hurt the York Rite while benefiting the Scottish Rite.

When the Shriners (Ancient Arabic Order Nobles of the Mystic Shrine) were created in 1872, they required their candidates to be either Knights Templar or 32° Scottish Rite Masons. As the Shrine became popular and prestigious, their "dual entry" created a competition between the rites and presented those interested in the Shrine with a clear choice: York or Scottish?

The three bodies of the York Rite work together, but they are still only loosely confederated in many states. Some state Grand Commanderies require their candidates to be both Royal Arch and Cryptic Masons, while other states follow the older requirement of only requiring that candidates be Royal Arch Masons. As in all organizations, one of the issues is, "Who's in charge?" Is it the larger Royal Arch Masonry, with autonomous state grand chapters and some non-Christian members, or is it the Christian-only Knights Templar with a strong national control? The American York Rite can be best understood on a state-by-state basis, where in some states the three organizations have virtually merged, and in others they continue their independent ways.

The Least You Need to Know

- The York Rite is a confederation of three autonomous organizations building on membership in a Blue Lodge.

- The Royal Arch Mason legend tells the story of the recovery of the lost Master Mason word.

- The Royal and Select Masters legend explains the preservation of the word.

- The Knights Templar, limited to Christian Masons, reinterpret the word and give it a Christian explanation.

- The Knights Templar uniform and military drill were very popular during the Golden Era of Fraternalism.

- York Rite unity varies from state to state, mostly because of the issue of "Who's in charge?"

Chapter

The Scottish Rite

In This Chapter

- ◆ High degrees blossom in France
- ◆ They move to America via the Caribbean
- ◆ The Scottish Rite is born in Charleston
- ◆ Scottish Rite Degrees are produced like plays

The Scottish Rite is the best-known branch of Freemasonry in America, if not the world. It seems like almost everyone with a Masonic relative has one that was a Thirty-Second Degree Mason, the highest membership level normally attained in the Scottish Rite. (In the old *Dennis the Menace* TV show, there's even an episode in which Dennis brags at school that his dad is a "32° Mason.")

The Scottish Rite functions in many ways like the York Rite. Membership in the Scottish Rite is open to Master Masons (but unlike the York Rite, without any religious restrictions), it elaborates on the Blue Lodge legends, and it gives Masons another way to get involved in their fraternity. There are several organizational differences between the Scottish and York Rites. The Scottish Rite tends to have large, centralized bodies in contrast to the smaller, more dispersed, local bodies of the York Rite. The Scottish rite from top to bottom is governed by a strong central organization, the

Supreme Council. (America has two Supreme Councils, each independently governing different groups of states.) The presentation of Scottish Rite Degrees (allegorical plays teaching moral and ethical lessons) has evolved into theatrical events performed on large stages with sophisticated scenery, costumes, and lighting.

The Thirty-Third Degree is possibly the most widely recognized Masonic honor, and also the most misunderstood. If anyone knows anything about Freemasonry, they're probably vaguely aware that the Thirty-Third Degree is limited to some elite, inner group of Masons. They might have read that the 33° Masons not only control Freemasonry but also the government, the media, and most commerce. The first part is true; the Thirty-Third Degree is indeed an honor awarded for exceptional service to the Rite or humanity and is given to only a little more than one percent of the members. The second part represents urban legends and outlandish conspiracy theories about hidden powers controlling the world.

This chapter will discuss the "high degrees" in France, their transformation into the Scottish Rite, how the American Scottish Rite functions, and the Thirty-Third Degree.

High Degrees in France

Like so much early Masonic history, the origins of the Scottish Rite are hidden in mist. There's evidence in the early 1730s in England of "Scotch Masons" or "Scots Master Masons," a step after the Master Mason Degree (and apparently unrelated to Scotland). By 1742, in Berlin, there was talk of "higher or so-called Scottish Masonry." In 1743, the Grand Lodge of France adopted a regulation limiting the privileges of "Scots Masters" in lodges. It's clear from these few mentions that something was going on behind the scenes with "Scottish Masonry," but we're not quite sure what. These developments happened at the same time the Royal Arch was gestating before its birth in 1754. It's even possible that the Royal Arch and Scottish Masonry came from the same sources. We just don't know.

def•i•ni•tion

A **high degree** is any Masonic degree after 3° Master Mason, for example the Royal Arch Degree of the York Rite or the 32° Master of the Royal Secret of the Scottish Rite. "High Degree Masons" only have authority in the organization that gave them the high degree. The Grand Master is the highest Mason in any grand lodge.

What we do know is that the *high degrees* found fertile ground when introduced to French Masonry. In 1745, two years after restricting Scotch Masons, the Grand Lodge of France gave them special privileges, and more privileges and authority followed in 1747 and 1755. In contrast, the Royal Arch appears in lodge minutes in America in 1753 and England in 1758 with little official notice. By 1766, we know that an elaborate sequence of High Degree or "Scottish" Masonry is being worked in France. There's much activity prior to 1766 that we'll cover later, but we want to take a look now at that sequence of high degrees.

The Most Secret Mysteries

In 1766, an important Masonic ritual exposé appeared in France, *The Most Secret Mysteries of the High Degrees of Masonry Unveiled (Les Plus Secrets Mystères des Hauts Grades de la Maçonnerie Dévoilés)*. Just as Prichard's *Masonry Dissected* absolutely confirmed the existence of the Third Degree, *The Most Secret Mysteries* confirmed that a sequence of degrees beyond the Master Mason Degree was being worked. The degrees exposed were not necessarily the oldest or most popular or even the largest system, but they were the first in print. They formed a cohesive series of dramatic episodes and moral lessons centered around building or rebuilding King Solomon's Temple.

The Square Deal

Masonic degrees are initiatory steps and short allegorical plays that teach ethical and moral lessons. An initiatory step usually leads the candidate into self-reflection and contemplation of universal principles. When an allegorical play is presented, its plot usually builds upon the legends of the Blue Lodge, sometimes introducing new legends. (See Appendix C for examples.) An initiatory step and an allegorical play can be combined in one degree. A Masonic "rite" is a collection of degrees that co-herently expand on the Blue Lodge legends while teaching a cohesive set of ethical and moral lessons.

Here's a quick summary of the seven degrees from *The Most Secret Mysteries*. (The first six degrees have been translated in full and published in *Heredom*, the transactions of the Scottish Rite Research Society: 1°–5°, vols. 1–5, 1992–96; 6°, vol. 11, 2003.)

The Seven Degrees from the *Most Secret Mysteries of the High Degrees of Masonry Unveiled* (1766)

Degree Name	Legend Plot Summary
Perfect Elect Mason	King Solomon permits a zealous Mason to help find Hiram Abiff's murderers; one is found and slain.
Elect of Pérignan	A farmer, Pérignan, helped discover the murderer slain in the preceding degree.
Elect of the Fifteen	An elite group of fifteen Masons capture the remaining two murderers and return them to King Solomon for judgment.
Junior Architect	King Solomon selects a replacement for Hiram Abiff to serve as Intendant of the Works.
Senior Architect	King Solomon selects a skilled architect to complete the Temple.
Knight of the Sword	Zerubbabel receives permission to return from Babylon to Jerusalem to rebuild the Temple.
Prussian Knight	Prussian Knights are descendents of Phaleg, architect of the Tower of Babel (older than King Solomon's Temple). They let "descendents of Hiram" (ordinary Masons) join them during the Crusades.

This is the first Masonic "rite" complete with a knightly legend, though it was not called a rite in 1766. This sequence of morality plays, like the sequels, prequels, and spin-offs of the York Rite, expands on the basic Masonic legends surrounding King Solomon's Temple and conclude with a legend about crusading knights. These degrees and themes formed the skeleton on which the Scottish Rite and other rites were eventually built. Note that the 6°, Knight of the Sword, has the same plot outline as the Illustrious Order of the Red Cross in the U.S. Knight Templar's Commandery. The only element missing is the debate on the power of wine, women, or kings that had not yet been added to the ceremony as it appeared in *The Most Secret Mysteries*.

Emperors and Knights in France

Competition is the force that drives the world's economies, and it also seems to have driven Scottish Masonry in France. Years before *The Most Secret Mysteries* was published in 1766, there was jockeying for power within the Grand Lodge of France. The Council of the Knights of the East, Sovereign Prince Masons, was organized in

1756, and included in its government middle-class Masons who had been excluded in previous high-degree ventures. It is not known how many degrees the Knights worked, but they seem to have faded out around 1768–1779.

Coming on the heels of the Knights of the East in 1758 was the Sovereign Council of Emperors of the East and of the West, Sublime Scottish Mother Lodge. The Emperors attracted the upper class and nobility and competed with the knights in the number of degrees they offered. (Just from a marketing point of view the newer group bested the older: "Emperors" are more powerful than "Knights," and "East and West" is twice as extensive as only "East.")

The Square Deal

As Freemasonry became a popular or fashionable activity, interest in the high degrees grew everywhere. Masons must have thought to themselves, "How can I learn more about and advance in the fraternity?" Entrepreneurs soon offered quick advancement to any "level" desired in return for the proper consideration—which could be a good meal! In other words, "customers" could purchase any Masonic degree without being elected to membership or going through the initiatory steps. In March 1752, the minutes of the Grand Committee of the English Grand Lodge of Ancients had an interesting report on this sort of purchase:

> "A formal complaint was made by several Brethren against Thos. Phealon and John Macky, better known as 'leg of mutton Masons' for clandestinely making Masons for the mean consideration of a leg of mutton for dinner or supper … The Grand Secretary had examined Macky, and stated that he had not the least idea or knowledge of Royal Arch Masonry but instead thereof he had told the people he had deceived a long story about twelve white marble stones, &c., &c., and that the rainbow was the Royal arch …."

Rather than discover ancient Masonic knowledge, the gullible purchasers rediscovered some ancient wisdom: "A fool and his money are soon parted."

The Invention of Stephen Morin

In August 1761, Stephen Morin received a *patent* from the Grand Lodge of France "authorizing and empowering him to establish perfect and sublime Masonry in all parts of the world, etc., etc." Morin was a wine merchant from Bordeaux and set up business in Santo Domingo in what is now the Dominican Republic in the Caribbean. Morin is little remembered for his wine business, but his Masonic activities have gained him lasting fame.

def•i•ni•tion

A **patent** is an official document conferring a right or privilege. In Masonry, it nearly always refers to a Scottish Rite document either certifying membership or granting authority and power. Modern patents almost only certify membership.

It took Morin about 15 months to make it from France to Santo Domingo, arriving in January 1763, because his ship was captured by the English and he was taken to England. While we know that he arrived with a patent of authority over the high degrees, we don't know how many or which high degrees he controlled! What we do know is that he met a Dutch merchant, Henry Andrew Francken, and made him a Deputy Inspector General sometime between 1763 and 1767. Francken in turn traveled to Albany, New York, and created there a Lodge of Perfection (4°–14°) in 1767.

In addition to creating the Albany Lodge of Perfection, Francken at least three times copied all of his degrees into books: 1771, 1783, and an undated version. The "Francken Manuscripts" contain the earliest English versions of 21 degrees from 4°, "Secret Master," to 25°, "The Royal Secret or Knights of St. Andrew's—the faithful guardians of the Sacred Treasure," a 25-degree system with the first three degrees conferred in Blue Lodges. This should establish conclusively that Morin worked a system of 25 degrees, right? Well, only if the degrees that Morin gave to Francken are the same ones that he received in France!

Growing evidence suggests that Morin took whatever high degrees he received in France and refashioned them into the Order of the Royal Secret (often called the "Rite of Perfection" by earlier historians, creating additional degrees as needed. The governing document, the "Constitutions of 1762," has been discovered by Masonic scholar Alain Bernheim to be a slightly modified version of the constitution of the Grand Lodge of France. Morin apparently acted to create a new Masonic body with himself as the only "Grand Inspector."

The First Supreme Council: Charleston, 1801

However the 25-Degree Order of the Royal Secret came into being, it proved popular. These French high degrees, unlike the English York Rite, were spread by traveling Inspectors who conferred them for a fee. It wasn't necessary to wait for enough Masons in a town to receive the high degrees somewhere else and for them to apply for a charter; the itinerant Inspector could take care of everything as soon as he arrived. Eight bodies of the Royal Secret were formed in America before 1800, from New Orleans to Albany. The weakness of the Order proved to be the unchecked system of Inspectors General.

Each Inspector General could confer the degrees on Master Masons, establish local bodies, and create new Inspectors—all for an appropriate fee. There were no guidelines on cost, no limitation on numbers, and no restriction on how many more Inspectors an Inspector could create. By 1800, there were over 80 Inspectors General, and the system was moving toward chaos.

Then on May 31, 1801, the first Supreme Council of the Thirty-Third Degree, the Mother Council of the World, declared its existence with a motto of "Ordo ab Chao" (Order from Chaos). It announced a new 33-degree system of high degrees that incorporated all 25 of the Order of the Royal Secret, and added eight more, including that of 33°, Sovereign Grand Inspector General. This new organization declared control of High Degree Masonry in America.

Hits and Myths

It is a myth that the Scottish Rite with 33 degrees controls all Freemasonry and the Mother Supreme Council controls the Scottish Rite.

This makes a certain naive sense: the number "33" is bigger than "3," so the Supreme Council with 33 degrees must be more powerful than a Grand Lodge with only 3 degrees. Right? No—wrong!

In the first place, the Scottish Rite is just one of many other Masonic rites—in America there's the York Rite, and in Europe there's the Swedish Rite, the Rectified Scottish Rite, and the French Modern Rite, just to name a few. The relationship of the Scottish Rite to grand lodges is more like that of the Phi Beta Kappa honor society to a university board of trustees. The Scottish Rite or Phi Beta Kappa may be respected because its leaders are chosen from exceptional Masons or students, but the control of the grand lodge rests with its members and elected officers just as the control of the university rests with its trustees.

Every legitimate Supreme Council can trace its genealogy to the "Mother Supreme Council"—the first in the world. Once a Supreme Council has been created, however, it is sovereign and independent from all others. The Mother Supreme Council has no authority over its "daughters"; it is merely the first among equals.

The new Supreme Council had a written constitution and a plan for organizing and managing the bodies under its control. The problem it faced was how to rein in the roving Inspectors General. The solution was shrewd and depended upon convincing the Inspectors to voluntarily yield allegiance to the Supreme Council. Any Inspector of the 25° would be given authority to confer up to the 32° (the extra seven degrees would make his product more attractive), if he turned in his old patent and agreed to follow the rules of the Supreme Council. This strategy was reasonably successful, and independent Inspectors General soon disappeared.

The Second American Supreme Council: New York, 1806

The Charleston Supreme Council had organized itself according to the "Grand Constitution of the Thirty-Third Degree," purportedly written by Frederick the Great of Prussia in 1786. The Constitution provided for one Supreme Council in each country, except that the United States of America could have up to two. (This is an odd provision for a document supposedly originating from Prussia in 1786!) The decision to create a second American Supreme Council was unexpectedly thrust upon the Supreme Council in Charleston.

The second Supreme Council in the world was established in Santo Domingo in 1802, a fitting return to Stephen Morin's home. This Supreme Council died with the slave revolt on the island, but one of its members, Antoine Bideaud, fled to New York. While there, he came across five Frenchmen who were interested in the high degrees. For a fee of $46 in 1806 (about $565 in 2000), Bideaud conferred the degrees upon his customers and formed them into a "Consistory" of the 32°—all without the knowledge of the Charleston Supreme Council.

The same year that Bideaud was creating his Consistory, Joseph Cerneau, a French jeweler, moved from Cuba to New York City. He had a patent from an Inspector of the Order of the Royal Secret that gave him limited powers in Cuba, but that didn't stop him from setting up his own Consistory in New York City. Cerneau operated without saying much about whether he had a 25-degree or 32-degree Consistory.

Emmanuel de la Motta, the Grand Treasurer from the Charleston Supreme Council, arrived in New York City in 1813, examined the two competing factions, and decided against Cerneau. De la Motta regularized Bideaud's group and transformed them into the second Supreme Council for America. Also in 1813, Cerneau transformed his group into a Supreme Council of the 33rd Degree for the United States. This action was probably a marketing strategy to let his 25-degree system compete with the 33-degree Supreme Council operating elsewhere in the city. The Cerneau Supreme Council continued as a competitor until it united with its northern rival in 1867.

The Innovation of Fraternal Theater

In the early to mid-1800s, the Scottish Rite did not have the wide popularity of the York Rite, which may have explained the small number of regional bodies for the Scottish Rite. As Freemasonry emerged from the Anti-Masonic Period in the 1840s and as men once again joined the Masons and the rites, the American Scottish Rite made a bold innovation in the presentation of its degrees: they started conferring degrees—the allegorical dramas teaching ethical and moral lessons—as theatrical events before candidates as an audience rather than as an intimate participatory ceremony.

We don't know why this innovation was made. Perhaps the increasing number of candidates was more than a single body in a large town could handle. Perhaps members wanted to enhance the initiatory experience with scenery and costumes. We do know that rather than increase the number of bodies in a city, the Scottish Rite chose to increase the number of men who could receive the degree at one time. The result was an explosion of Scottish Rite theaters that allowed their thespian members to participate in theatrical spectaculars.

An 1859 report claims the Scottish Rite Degrees were presented in a theatrical setting. By 1864, the Cincinnati Scottish Rite had installed a raised stage and boasted of "rooms, painting, scenery, wardrobe, properties, &c., &c., necessary for conferring the … degrees." This change in performance venues came at the beginning of and continued through the "Golden Age of Fraternalism" when Americans were interested in all things fraternal.

Theatrical staging spread faster in the north than in the south, but it was a movement that couldn't be stopped. American Scottish Rite bodies erected stages, painted and purchased scenery, and bought costumes to put on their degrees. They became repertory theater companies with a repertoire of 29 plays. Now when King Solomon stepped forward to speak, it wasn't necessary to imagine his exotic dress or magnificent throne room—he stood there in purple robes with a crown, surrounded by his guards and advisors in an oriental palace of stunning opulence. (And the members got to take turns playing Solomon!)

Success bred success, and Scottish Rite bodies tried to outdo each other in putting together lavish stages and extravagant productions. Theatrical supply companies competed to provide scenery, costumes, makeup, and lighting (see the figure that follows). Larger cities might have stages with 100 or more drops, full lighting, a wardrobe room, a property room, and crews to keep everything running. The single center of

Scottish Rite per city now became an advantage with plenty of members available to fill all of the supporting jobs in a major production, including kitchen crews, orchestras, and choirs. The conferral of Scottish Rite Degrees two to four times a year became major events, with hundreds of members and candidates gathering together. After witnessing the degrees, new members eagerly signed up to take part themselves, and the cycle continued.

This ad for costumes appeared in the Southern Jurisdiction's The New Age *magazine for December 1904.*

Scottish Rite Operations Today

Reviewing the first few dozen years of Scottish Rite in America, it's easy to forget that its motto was "Ordo ab Chao." Today the two Supreme Councils provide stable government for their branch of the Masonic fraternity. The Northern Masonic Jurisdiction consists of 15 midwestern and northeastern states from Wisconsin and Illinois northeast to Maine. The Southern Jurisdiction is composed of the other 35 states plus the District of Columbia and Puerto Rico.

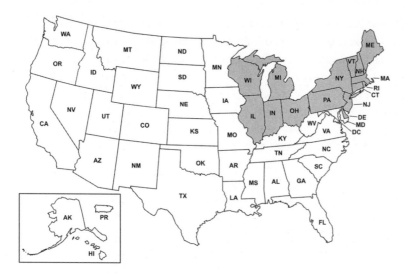

The Northern Masonic Jurisdiction is composed of 15 midwestern and northeastern states (gray); the Southern Jurisdiction is the remaining 35 states, the District of Columbia, and Puerto Rico (white).

Each Supreme Council has a limited number of voting or active members: 33 in the S.J. and 67 in the N.M.J. (The current N.M.J. is the result of the union in 1867 with the rival "Cerneau" Supreme Council. The union was achieved by combining two Supreme Councils of 33 members each and having the Grand Commander serve as the tie breaker.) All of the other Thirty-Third Degree Masons are nonvoting or "honorary" members of the Supreme Council.

A Good Rule _____

The two American Supreme Councils have similar, but distinct ways of identifying themselves. The older is the Supreme Council, 33°, Southern Jurisdiction (S.J.), and the younger is the Supreme Council, 33°, Northern Masonic Jurisdiction (N.M.J.). Don't get confused and write incorrectly, "NJ" or "SMJ."

In the Southern Jurisdiction, an active member or Sovereign Grand Inspector General (SGIG) serves until age 80. Upon his resignation or death, the Grand Commander appoints a "Deputy" to replace him. A Deputy serves at the pleasure of the Grand Commander in a trial capacity. If the trial is successful for a few years, the Supreme Council will elect the Deputy to full voting membership on the Council.

A Deputy or SGIG administers the Scottish Rite *Valleys* in his *Orient* with the same powers as a Grand Master of a Grand Lodge. At any given time the S.J. Supreme Council usually has 5–10 Deputies.

def•i•ni•tion

The Scottish Rite refers to states as **Orients** and the cities or regions where Scottish Rite bodies are located as **Valleys**. Thus, I belong to the Valley of Baltimore in the Orient of Maryland.

A **reunion** is a Scottish Rite event when a Valley gathers to confer the degrees on new members. A reunion may be a long weekend or it could be spread out over several weeks. While all 29 degrees are rarely conferred during one reunion, members can usually see all of the degrees over a few years in a region.

The Northern Masonic Jurisdiction has 67 voting members for 15 states; there must be at least two, and sometimes several more, active members in each Orient. One of the active members is the "Deputy" and administers the state. Active members in the N.M.J. serve until age 75.

Both American Supreme Councils have "Deputies," but the positions are quite different. In the N.M.J., a Deputy is the senior Active Member in any state, administrating the Scottish Rite in that state. In the S.J., a Deputy is administrating a state, but he's in a trial position before possibly being elected to be an Active member.

In the N.M.J., all 33° Masons are known as "Sovereign Grand Inspectors General" and are members of the Supreme Council, but at most 67 are voting members. In the S.J., only active members are known as "Sovereign Grand Inspectors General"; all others are called "Inspectors General Honorary."

American Scottish Rite Valleys typically have weekly or biweekly meetings with a dinner, a program, and plenty of time for fellowship. There are social events throughout the year—ladies night, family picnic, holiday party, and so on, but the conferral of degrees on new members remains a central activity. Two or three times a year a Valley will hold a *reunion* when some or occasionally all of the 29 degrees will be staged as theatrical performances. Rehearsals of cast and crew provide another opportunity for fellowship.

Scottish Rite Valleys also support various philanthropies and community organizations like the Boy Scouts. Speech and language clinics for children are the major philanthropy of the Scottish Rite. There are 160+ clinics in the S.J. and 50+ in the N.M.J., all providing critical intervention for children who are having difficulties speaking and reading, all at no or low cost to the families. Support to clinic activities, serving on scholarship committees, and participation in community events are just some of the many ways that Scottish Rite Masons are involved in their fraternity.

The Scottish Rite Degrees

The American Scottish Rite is a collection of degrees—initiatory steps and short allegorical plays—that build upon the legends of the Blue Lodge. The rite offers a total of 30 degrees beyond 3° Master Mason. The names of the degrees vary from jurisdiction to jurisdiction, as sometimes do the dramatic contents. What is constant is the idea of progressive ethical awareness and self-knowledge through self-reflection and dramatic allegories.

Degrees of the Scottish Rite

4° Secret Master

5° Perfect Master

6° Intimate Secretary

7° Provost and Judge

8° Intendant of the Building

9° Elu of the Nine

10° Elu of the Fifteen

11° Elu of the Twelve

12° Grand Master Architect

13° Royal Arch of Solomon

14° Perfect Elu

15° Knight of the East

16° Prince of Jerusalem

17° Knight of the East and West

18° Knight of the Rose Croix

19° Grand Pontiff

20° Master of the Symbolic Lodge

21° Noachite, or Prussian Knight

22° Knight of the Royal Axe

23° Chief of the Tabernacle

24° Prince of the Tabernacle

25° Knight of the Brazen Serpent

26° Prince of Mercy

27° Knight Commander of the Temple

28° Knight of the Sun

29° Scottish Knight of Saint Andrew

30° Knight Kadosh

31° Inspector Inquisitor

32° Master of the Royal Secret

33° Inspector General

Not only do the names of the degrees vary by jurisdiction, the administration of the degrees can be different. In the N.M.J. and S.J., the Lodge of Perfection governs the 4–14°. In the Southern Jurisdiction, the Chapter of Rose Croix controls the 15–18°, the Council of Kadosh the 19–30°, and the Consistory the 31° and 32°. Thus a Valley with all four bodies, 4–32°, would have four sets of officers, one for each body. A typical arrangement for a very active valley would be for the Lodge of Perfection to meet during the first week of the month, the Chapter of Rose Croix during the second, and so on. Smaller Valleys might only have the first two bodies, 4–14° and 15–18°, and its members might travel to a larger Valley to receive the rest of the degrees.

In the N.M.J., four bodies administer the 4–32°, but the arrangement is slightly different: Lodge of Perfection, 4–14°; Council of Princes of Jerusalem, 15° and 16°; Chapter of Rose Croix, 17° and 18°; Consistory, 19–32°. And in non-American Supreme Councils the arrangement is sometimes different still.

The Scottish Rite Degrees give insight to the expansion of Masonic legends. The Lodge of Perfection, 4–14°, is concerned with events following the murder of Hiram Abiff: burying him; capturing and punishing his murderers; finding a new master builder; and discovering treasures buried under King Solomon's Temple. The 15° and 16° explain the return of Zerubbabel from Babylon to rebuild the Temple at Jerusalem. The 17° and 18° center around re-instituting the word under the Law of Love as taught by Jesus and other religious reformers. The 19–30° culminate with the Degree of Knight Kadosh, a spiritual knighthood similar to the Knight Templar, and develop the Scottish Rite's myth of Masonic succession from crusading knights. In the 32°, Master of the Royal Secret, the candidate is taught equilibrium in the S.J. and fidelity in the N.M.J.

The Thirty-Third Degree and Other Honors

A few seconds searching on the Internet or on the conspiracy shelf at a bookstore will reveal the most outlandish ideas about Thirty-Third Degree Masons. You can read how we supposedly control all of Freemasonry, the U.S. Congress, the Federal Reserve, the Vatican, all major industries, and most foreign governments. (If this is true, I'm hoping to be given a small mountain resort to control!) The true powers and goals of this inner circle have been kept carefully hidden from the millions of ordinary Masons, but a few brave non-Masons have discovered the secret and are out to warn the world!

The truth is much less breathtaking, but interesting nonetheless. In the S.J. and N.M.J., 32° Masons are nominated to receive the 33° on the basis of service to the fraternity or to humanity. A total of about 1.5 percent of all Scottish Rite Masons have received the 33°, and in America this represents about 0.5 percent or one out of every 200 Masons. The nominations are made in secret before each meeting of the Supreme Council where they are reviewed and approved. A formula based on current membership and recent initiates determines how many Thirty-Third Degrees can be awarded in each Orient. It takes about 8–12 years of active involvement in the Scottish Rite before a 32° Mason is considered for nomination for the 33°.

The Knight Commander of the Court of Honour (KCCH) is an award in the Southern Jurisdiction in recognition of outstanding service by those who have been 32° Masons for at least four years. Exactly twice as many KCCHs are awarded as Thirty-Thirds, and about 2.5 percent of the S.J. membership holds the KCCH. In the S.J., one must be a KCCH for at least four years before being eligible for nomination to the 33°.

The Meritorious Service Award is a Northern Masonic Jurisdiction recognition of outstanding Masonic service, limited to one award per year per Valley. There are bout 1,600 living MSA recipients or about 0.6 percent of the N.M.J. membership.

The Gourgas Medal is given by the Northern Masonic Jurisdiction to 33° Masons in recognition of notably distinguished service in the cause of Freemasonry, humanity, or country. Only twenty-five awards have been made since the decoration was established in 1938.

The Grand Cross of the Court of Honour is the highest honor given by the Southern Jurisdiction to 33° Masons in recognition of exceptional service to Freemasonry or to society at large. It is usually awarded to about three to five recipients a year, and there are rarely more than 50 living Grand Crosses.

The Least You Need to Know

- "Scottish Masonry" meant "High Degree Masonry" in France.
- The immediate "ancestors" of the Scottish Rite came from France via the Caribbean.
- The first Supreme Council was formed in Charleston in 1801; all Supreme Councils today are descended from the "Mother" Supreme Council in Charleston.

◆ The Scottish Rite has large bodies located in regional centers.

◆ Scottish Rite degrees are staged like plays with elaborate scenery, costumes, props, lighting, and make up.

◆ The Thirty-Third Degree has been awarded to 1.5 percent of Scottish Rite Masons for service to the fraternity or humanity.

Part 3

Building Higher, Having Fun, and Doing More

Just when you think you understand the structure of Freemasonry, we're going to throw in a few dozen more groups. It's like first understanding the organization of American colleges, then finding out about sororities and fraternities, and then realizing there are dozens and dozens of other groups on campus. There are several organizations for past presiding York Rite officers, others limited to active Masons by invitation only, and others for historians, magicians, and even Sherlock Holmes fans. There are fun groups like the Shriners, Grotto, and Tall Cedars, and youth groups like DeMolay, Job's Daughters, and Rainbow Girls. Of course we can't tell the story of Freemasonry without talking about the philanthropies they support, from the "Connecticut Cow" 200 years ago to speech and language services and children's orthopedic and burn care today.

Even More Masonic Organizations

In This Chapter

- ◆ The York Rite creates honorary groups
- ◆ Masonic students formed research lodges
- ◆ There's much in addition to the York and Scottish Rites
- ◆ Masonic Week is when it all comes together

Freemasonry is unique for many reasons, not the least of which is the way it attracts so many organizations around it. Other civic groups like the Odd Fellows or Kiwanis or Knights of Columbus never developed this tradition of dozens and dozens of satellite organizations. In Freemasonry, these are known as *appendant* bodies. When these new Masonic bodies are started, no one knows if they'll succeed (like the Shriners, started in 1872) or fizzle (like the Independent International Order of Owls, started in 1890).

All appendant Masonic bodies must be obedient to the policies of the grand lodge of each state in which they operate. Some grand lodges have a laissez faire attitude and let any such group organize in their jurisdiction;

others require a formal vote of approval before a new Masonic organization can start forming bodies in their territory.

Just as you need to understand the York and Scottish Rites, the Eastern Star, and the Shriners to understand the broad organization of Freemasonry, understanding the appendant bodies gives you more insight into the fine structure of the fraternity. We will discuss these appendant bodies in this chapter.

If nothing else, you'll never have the naïve idea that there are only 33 degrees in Masonry—there are scores more than that! Usually only the most active or curious Masons are involved in these groups, and that alone makes them interesting to study.

York Rite Invitational Organizations

The York Rite was created gradually by the addition of sequels, prequels, and spin-offs to the basic Masonic legend about the building of King Solomon's temple. Perhaps because of its method of birth, the York Rite has always been open to new organizations building upon its foundations. The Scottish Rite, presenting itself as a complete self-contained system, has not attracted "add-ons" like the York Rite. The result is a far larger number of organizations built upon Royal Arch or Knights Templar membership.

def•i•ni•tion

A Masonic **invitational** body is one with membership by invitation only. Potential members cannot simply apply; they must be invited. A potential new member is proposed to the group and a ballot taken. If it is favorable, an invitation is extended; if not, nothing is said to the proposed member. An invitational body is sometimes called an honorary body.

Most of the Masonic groups that require their members to be Royal Arch Masons are *invitational* or honorary bodies. Potential members are invited on the basis of their service to Freemasonry and the community. Sometimes other specific requirements exist, such as having presided over certain Masonic bodies. Because membership in these honorary bodies is drawn from the most active Masons, those who have calendars filled with other meetings, the groups meet less frequently—usually quarterly or semi-annually.

Knights of the Red Cross of Constantine

The Knights of the Red Cross of Constantine were organized in England about 1865 and imported to America in 1870, at the beginning of the Golden Age of Fraternalism. A member must be a Christian Royal Arch Mason and "have demonstrated a high level of dedication and performance in his Masonic activities." The legendary history is that Emperor Constantine formed the order in 312 after the Battle of Saxa Rubra to reward those of his soldiers who showed special bravery.

The Imperial Council of the Red Cross of Constantine has restricted the number of bodies in each state and the number of members each body can admit. This limitation on membership usually results in careful selection of new members so that Red Cross members represent some of the most active York Rite Masons in a state. Active Scottish Rite Masons are also members.

Knights of the York Cross of Honor

The year 1930 saw the beginning of the Great Depression and of a new York Rite invitational body, the Knights of the York Cross of Honor (KYCH). This organization was started in Monroe, North Carolina, by a group of young Masons headed by J. Raymond Shute II. To be proposed for membership, one must first preside as Worshipful Master of a Blue Lodge, High Priest of a Royal Arch Mason Chapter, Illustrious Master of a Royal and Select Master Council, and Commander of a Knights Templar Commandery. KYCH bodies have no set size, but the requirement of presiding over each of the four York Rite bodies keeps the numbers down.

The Square Deal

J. Raymond Shute II was one of the great American Masonic innovators. Born in Monroe, North Carolina, in 1904, Ray became a Mason at age 21 and served his lodge as Worshipful Master three years later. His enthusiasm seemed unbounded, as he was responsible for the formation of at least eight Masonic organizations, seven of which are still thriving and successful today. One of Ray's passions was Masonic history, and to encourage this he formed the North Carolina Lodge of Research (1931), the first American lodge devoted to Masonic history (closed in 1953), the Grand College of Rites (1932), and the Society of Blue Friars (1932). He also had a zeal for exclusive organizations whose members were invited to join in recognition of their Masonic accomplishments. Ray created the Knights of the York Cross of Honor (1930), the Holy Royal Arch Knight Templar Priests (1931), the Allied Masonic Degrees (1932), the Knights Beneficent of the Holy City (1934), and the Knight Masons (1936). There is some evidence from his correspondence that his great passion had faded by the late 1930s, and in 1950 he resigned from Masonry. Then after a 36-year absence, he re-affiliated with his lodge in 1986 and died two years later, a Master Mason in good standing. It is testimony to his organizational skills that all but one of these groups formed during the Great Depression have survived. All of his creations are discussed in this chapter.

Holy Royal Arch Knight Templar Priests

J. Raymond Shute II brought the Holy Royal Arch Knight Templar Priests to America from Britain via New Zealand in 1931. The Knight Templar Priests date back to the late 1700s or early 1800s in Britain. In America, members must be Past Commanders of a Knights Templar Commandery. The national body limits the number of members in each state based on the number of active Knights Templar Commanderies.

Allied Masonic Degrees

The process of bringing degrees together into a rite was gradual, and not all degrees were treated the same. For example, the Mark Master Mason Degree became the first degree in the American Royal Arch Chapter; in England it's administered by the Grand Lodge of Mark Master Masons, and in Scotland Blue Lodges can confer the degree.

As the rites coalesced in the eighteenth and nineteenth centuries, some degrees were "orphaned"—never adopted as part of a larger Masonic body. Some of the degrees that fell by the wayside appear to have been of little merit, and their passing was not mourned. Others, however, taught their lessons well and had impressive ritual ceremonies. The solution was the organization of the Grand Council of Allied Masonic Degrees (AMD) in the late 1870s, and it took over administration of several of the orphaned degrees.

In 1892, the AMD was brought to Richmond, Virginia, but it soon went into hibernation. It was not until 1932 when J. Raymond Shute II brought the AMD again to America that it flourished. Membership is by invitation only to Royal Arch Masons; local bodies are limited to 27 members, but there is no limit on the number of local bodies. In America, the AMD is the largest of the York Rite invitational organizations, and it confers the following eleven principal degrees:

Royal Ark Mariner

Secret Monitor

Knight of Constantinople

Saint Lawrence the Martyr

Architect

Superintendent

Grand Tilers of Solomon

Master of Tyre

Excellent Master

Red Branch of Eri

Ye Ancient Order of Corks

Knight Masons

In Ireland, Royal Arch Masons and then Knights Templar conferred the three degrees of the Knight Masons: Knight of the Sword, Knight of the East, and Knight of the East and West. The dramatic legend of the degrees is similar to that of the Order of the Red Cross of American Knights Templar and the 15° and 16° of the Scottish Rite. In 1923, a Grand Council of Knight Masons was formed in Ireland to govern the degrees, and in 1936 J. Raymond Shute II brought yet another Masonic body to our shores and established the Knight Masons in America. Membership is by invitation to Royal Arch Masons. In 2005, there were about 70 local councils and about 7,000 knights.

York Rite Sovereign College

In 1957 in Detroit, Michigan, a group of active York Rite Masons created the York Rite Sovereign College. Potential members must belong to all four bodies of the Rite and have shown strong support for the York Rite before they can be invited. The mission of the York Rite College is "to foster a spirit of service and to promote and support the York Rite in every way possible." The college has grown to 185 local groups, and its Order of the Purple Cross of York is given to members who "have distinguished themselves by their service to humanity or to the Rite." It is from the recipients of the Purple Cross that the governing board of the York Rite Sovereign College is selected.

Research Lodges and History Societies

Much Masonic history has been written by Masons who were more enthusiastic than they were competent. Rumor, speculation, theory, and fact were all given equal credence by some writers. Years ago, a general (and false) assumption that Freemasonry never changed caused some to conclude that the customs and practices common in the early 1800s in America must have been followed by King Solomon!

To counteract the foolishness that sometimes passed for Masonic history, lodges and societies were established devoted to studying the accurate history of Freemasonry. Essays and research papers were written, critiqued, and published that examined everything Masonic from personalities to local lodge histories to origins of degrees and rites. Resulting from more than a century of serious Masonic historical research, a large body of papers now attempts to present accurate and documented histories of Masonic topics. The publications of these research organizations are where one should first turn for any study of the fraternity.

Far from being a "secret society," Freemasonry has scores of publications that regularly explore its history and origins. We give a quick list of some of the more important Masonic research organizations and their papers. Their publications should be the starting point for anyone doing serious research on Freemasonry.

Quatuor Coronati Lodge

In 1884, a group of serious students of Freemasonry came together to form the first lodge devoted to properly documented Masonic history, Quatuor Coronati Lodge No. 2076 of London. The founders called their style of history the "authentic school," and that of their predecessors the "romantic school." Lodge membership is limited to 40, and has rarely approached that number. History papers offered to the lodge are carefully documented and subjected to detailed commentaries by lodge members. Every year since 1885, the lodge has published *Ars Quatuor Coronatorum*, an annual volume of papers presented in the lodge during the previous year. Quatuor Coronati Lodge is indeed the premier lodge of Masonic research.

The Square Deal

"Quatuor Coronati" is Latin for "the four crowned ones" and refers to a legend mentioned only in the Regius Manuscript and none of the other Gothic Constitutions. The Roman Emperor Diocletian ordered four Christian stonemasons to carve a statue of a pagan god. They refused, were put to death, and thrown into the Tiber River. Immediately four crowns appeared above the water where they were thrown. *Ars Quatuor Coronatorum* means "the art of the four crowned ones" and refers to the story of their martyrdom.

National Masonic Research Society

The first major American Masonic research organization was the National Masonic Research Society, formed in 1915 in Iowa. It published an excellent magazine, *The Builder* (back issues of which are still a good source of accurate Masonic history). The Great Depression dealt the society and its magazine a deathblow, and they disappeared in 1930.

Philalethes Society

The Philalethes Society takes its name from two Greek words, *philos* and *alethes*, and means "lover of truth." Students of Freemasonry formed the society in 1928, and it probably weathered the Depression because it didn't have the expense of publishing a magazine. In 1946, the society started publishing its bimonthly magazine, *The Philalethes*. Forty of its members at any time are designated fellows for their exceptional research and publications on Freemasonry. Members and fellows of the Philalethes Society often append the letters "MPS" or "FPS" after their names, especially when signing research papers.

North Carolina Lodge of Research

The first American research lodge, North Carolina Lodge of Research, was formed in North Carolina in 1931 by J. Ray Shute II. Its publication, *Nocalore*, covered a wide range of Masonic topics with high research standards. The Lodge closed in 1954, perhaps because its driving force, J. Ray Shute II, had resigned in 1950.

American Lodge of Research

The American Lodge of Research was formed in 1931 at the beginning of the Depression just after its sister research lodge was formed in North Carolina. The American Lodge of Research has flourished despite its difficult birth year. Its papers are published annually in the *Transactions of the American Lodge of Research*, and cover all aspects of Freemasonry but focus on America and New York. This is a particularly good source for information on American Freemasonry.

Grand College of Rites, U.S.A.

Ritual is the key feature that separates Freemasonry from other civic societies. Its forms and ceremonies have been evolving for centuries and are fascinating to study.

The Grand College of Rites was formed to publish the rituals of extinct organizations in its annual volume, *Collectanea*. There's no need to speculate about what an old Masonic group might or might not have done when you can read the actual ceremonies yourself.

Phylaxis Society

Prince Hall Masonry has a proud and fascinating history, and the Phylaxis Society was formed to publish research papers about African American Freemasonry. Joseph A. Walkes Jr., a Prince Hall Mason, formed the society in 1973 when he was not allowed to be a member of the Philalethes Society because Prince Hall Masonry was not recognized as *regular* (see Chapter 6 for more on Masonic regularity). Since then, the Phylaxis Society has gone on to gain wide recognition for its publications, Joseph A. Walkes Jr. has been elected an Honorary Fellow of the Philalethes Society, and the Phylaxis Society in turn has named several Philalethes Society members as honorary Fellows of the Phylaxis Society. A regrettable beginning has led to cooperation and friendships—the Masonic ideal.

> **The Square Deal**
>
> Heredom is the name of a mythical mountain in Scotland, the supposed site of an early high degree Masonic body. It may have come from *hieros-domos*, Greek for holy house, referring to Solomon's Temple, or from *harodim*, Hebrew for overseers. The mysterious name has been associated with High Degree or Scottish Rite Freemasonry since the 1700s.

Scottish Rite Research Society

One of the newest Masonic research organizations is the Scottish Rite Research Society. Formed in 1991 to promote research on Freemasonry in general and the Scottish Rite in particular, the Society's annual volume of papers, *Heredom*, has established very high academic standards. Its topics are not limited to Scottish Rite, but range over all areas of Freemasonry. This is but one of the most recent efforts to study seriously the history and traditions of the Masonic fraternity.

Other Masonic Groups

The broad structure of American Freemasonry is Blue Lodge for basics, Scottish Rite and York Rite for the enthusiast, Shriners for sociability, Eastern Star for the ladies, DeMolay for boys, and Rainbows and Job's Daughters for girls. As we've seen, Freemasonry is much more complex than this, as illustrated by the York Rite invitational bodies and research organizations. In fact, it's even more complicated. Lots of Masonic groups don't fall into any of the categories just listed, but they still play a part in the broader "Family of Freemasonry." We'll discuss some of the larger ones in this miscellaneous category, skipping over Masonic magicians (the Invisible Lodge), Masonic ham operators (the Masonic Gathering), Masonic Sherlock Holmes fans (the Master's Masons), and many, many more.

Royal Order of Scotland

The Royal Order of Scotland is an invitational Masonic group for Masons who have been members for at least five years, are Trinitarian Christians, and 32° Masons. The last requirement can be waived if the Mason is a Knight Templar. Members also "must be entitled to honor in Freemasonry because of services performed for the Craft, the Church, or the Public." The Provincial Grand Lodge of the U.S.A. was formed in 1877 and usually meets four to six times a year in various locations around the country.

The Royal Order dates back to the 1740s, but by legend, Robert the Bruce established the order after the Battle of Bannockburn to reward the knights who helped him win victory over the English. The hereditary Grand Master of the order is the King of Scots, and the acting head is the Deputy Grand Master. An empty chair for the King of Scots is always placed next to the Deputy Grand Master or his proxy at every meeting of the order.

Masonic Societas Rosicruciana in Civitatibus Foederatis

Plenty of organizations exist for Masons interested in the general history of the fraternity. For those interested in Christian Mysticism, there is the Masonic Societas Rosicruciana in Civitatibus Foederatis (Masonic Rosicrucian Society in the United States). It is not affiliated with any other Rosicrucian organization, nor are its members allowed to belong to other such groups.

The Masonic Rosicrucians formed in 1865 in England and came to America in 1880. Local bodies, called "colleges," are limited to 72 members. About 30 Rosicrucian Colleges are in America, one per state, with around 1700 members. A Chief Adept appointed for life governs each college, which usually meets once or twice a year to hear research papers. There are nine grades of membership, I°–IX°, with the VIII° and IX° conferred only for exceptional service to the society.

Ancient Egyptian Order of Sciots

Following the formation of the Shriners in 1872 and the Grotto in 1889, a group of California Masons met in San Francisco in 1905 to form a new social club for Master Masons complete with fezzes and an Egyptian theme. Originally called Boosters, they changed their name to the Ancient Egyptian Order of Sciots because their ritual legend concerns the interactions between the island of Scio and Egypt. Local groups are called pyramids, and the national organization is the supreme pyramid presided over by the Pharaoh. There are fewer than 20 pyramids, primarily in California, with a few in New Jersey and Illinois. Sciots must promise to attend their Blue Lodge at least once a month.

National Sojourners

Traveling military lodges attached to British regiments helped to spread Freemasonry around the world. As the fraternity grew in organizational and ritual complexity and as the demands of military service changed, traveling military lodges became impractical. But a club for military Masons satisfied the need for fraternal fellowship without much administrative overhead.

A group of Masonic military officers in the Philippines formed an informal club 1899–1907, calling themselves the "Sojourners Club." In 1917 in Chicago, the group revived itself and formed the National Sojourners. Membership is open to Master Masons who are or have been commissioned officers, warrant officers, or senior non-commissioned offices in the U.S. Armed Forces. Local chapters provide assistance and fellowship to sojourning military personnel and support Americanism activities.

High Twelve International

With the formation of Rotary in 1905, Kiwanis in 1915, and Lions Clubs in 1917, businessmen's luncheon clubs became a part of American culture. In 1921, a group of Iowa Masons formed a luncheon club that would meet at "high twelve" for fellowship. High Twelvians, as they call themselves, support local Blue Lodges and college scholarships through their Wolcott Foundation, named after E.C. Wolcott, their founder. There are over 300 High Twelve Clubs.

Society of Blue Friars

Another brainchild of J. Raymond Shute II is the Society of Blue Friars, formed in 1932. It is composed of Masonic authors and meets once a year. Members, known as friars, nominate new members, and the Grand Abbot, who serves at his will, selects one new friar each year. If the total membership drops below 20, two new friars may be selected in one year. Each new friar must present a paper at the annual gathering as evidence of his scholarship. Ninety-four Blue Friars have been selected through 2005, each recognized as a serious student of Freemasonry, making the society an elite recognition of Masonic scholarship.

Knights Beneficent of the Holy City

When J. Raymond Shute II traveled to Switzerland in the 1930s, he joined the Rectified Scottish Rite, a completely different rite from the American Ancient and Accepted Scottish Rite of 33 Degrees. The Rectified Rite is a chivalric order that culminates in the degree of Knight Beneficent of the Holy City (Chevaliers Bienfaisants de la Cité Sainte or C.B.C.S.). Shute established the rite in America in 1934, but limited its membership to 81. This small group could be viewed by conspiracists as the ultimate inner circle of Freemasonry. But holding only one meeting a year doesn't give them much opportunity to plan world domination!

Order of Knights Preceptors

The Sovereign Order of Knights Preceptors was created in 1977 as a way to recognize the service of Past Commanders of a Commandery of Knights Templar. Membership is open to current or Past Commanders and a unanimous ballot is required for election. The order has grown with deliberation and now has nine chapters.

Other Masonic Rites Around the World

It's easy for an American to think that Freemasonry is divided into the York and Scottish Rites, with the Shrine for social activities, and the Eastern Star for the ladies. This chapter has shown the wide diversity of Masonic organizations just within America and that the number of Masonic degrees is far more than just 33. Even more rites exist elsewhere, especially in Europe. There's the Swedish Rite with eleven degrees, found in Iceland, Norway, Sweden, Denmark and Germany; the Rectified Scottish Rite with eight degrees, found in America, Canada, England, France, Switzerland, Belgium, Portugal, and Togo; the Rite of Memphis-Misraim with 90+ degrees, though this rite isn't recognized by any American or British grand lodges; and the French Modern Rite with seven degrees. And this list just scratches the surface.

"Masonic Week" in Washington, D.C.

Masonic Week has been a fixture in Washington, D.C., for about the last 70 years. Many of the organizations described in this chapter hold their annual sessions during this week because they are too small to effectively hold a convention on their own. The meetings, usually held every two hours or so, start on Wednesday afternoon and continue through Saturday evening. The resulting mix of official gatherings and informal fellowship makes for a unique assembly of American Masons.

Probably more Masonic organizations are officially represented at Masonic Week than at any other place. One thing that makes the week fun is membership in a number of unusual Masonic degrees, sometimes created just for Masonic Week. For example, attendees have had the opportunity to join the Wyoming Anti-Horse Thief Association, with all initiation fees going to charity.

The Least You Need to Know

- ◆ The York Rite recognizes high achievers by inviting them to join special organizations.

- ◆ Many groups are devoted to researching accurate Masonic history.

- ◆ Many Masonic organizations exist in addition to the York and Scottish Rites.

- ◆ "Masonic Week" in Washington, D.C., is a gathering of several smaller national Masonic bodies.

Masonic "Fun" and Youth Groups

In This Chapter

◆ Masonic lodges had become formal and stodgy by the late 1800s

◆ Masons formed organizations for fun and fellowship

◆ Masonic organizations for boys and girls

When Freemasonry emerged from the Anti-Masonic Period (1826–1840), it changed the way it did business. Shaken and nearly destroyed, the fraternity sought to avoid activities that could bring public disapproval. It emphasized its tenets of brotherly love, relief, and truth, and its four cardinal virtues of fortitude, temperance, prudence, and justice—especially temperance. The American Temperance Society was formed in 1826, and by the end of the nineteenth century, Masonic grand lodges had almost universally prohibited alcohol at all lodge functions.

After the Civil War (1861–1865), when the Golden Age of Fraternalism started, some Masons became restless with the formal stiffness of Free-masonry. They solved the problem by forming "fun" groups for Masons like the Shriners, the Grotto, and the Tall Cedars of Lebanon, all devoted to socializing and having fun. They eventually picked up impressive charitable activities like the Shriners Hospitals for Children.

As the twentieth century began, Americans started creating organizations for youth. Among those that survived the century are 4-H (formed in 1902), Boy Scouts (1909), Camp Fire USA (1910), and Girl Scouts (1912). Freemasons soon followed the trend with youth groups that reflected their principles: DeMolay for boys (1919), Job's Daughter's International (1920), and the International Order of Rainbow for Girls (1922).

This chapter will discuss fun Masonic groups and organizations for boys and girls.

Setting the Stage for Masonic "Fun" Groups

Alvin J. Schmidt, author of *Fraternal Organizations* (1980), estimates that a little over 40 fraternal organizations were formed in America in the 133 years between 1730–1863. In just the next nine years, 1864–1872, 26 new fraternal groups were formed! These formations represented the beginning of the Golden Age of Fraternalism, when Americans (and also British and Canadians) became interested in all things fraternal.

These new groups patterned themselves after Freemasonry, almost surely relying on printed exposés from the Anti-Masonic Period to create their rituals. They enjoyed the social pleasures of fraternalism and often added insurance as a benefit of membership. A common feature of these fraternal groups was rather pompous names: Benevolent and Protective Order of Elks (formed in 1867); Order of Patrons of Husbandry (1867); Ancient Order of United Workmen (1868); The Ancient and Illustrious Order of Knights of Malta (1870); The Royal Templars of Temperance (1870); Ancient Order of Knights of the Mystic Chain (1871); and International Order of Twelve of Knights and Daughters of Tabor (1872).

In addition to the pretentious names, many groups adopted elaborate uniforms to wear in parades and at other public events. The Knights of Pythias (1864) made up for their simple name with a fancy uniform with braid, epaulets, a sword, and plumed hat. Regalia manufacturers competed with each other to outfit the groups in ever more ornamental garb.

By 1872, Masonic lodge meetings had become formal and serious, with great emphasis put on precise performance of ritual and ceremony. Most grand lodges had adopted policies of abstinence from alcohol, and the "feast and assembly"—the reason for the formation of the Premier Grand Lodge in 1717—was a forgotten custom in

America. Rob Morris, Past Grand Master of Kentucky and founder of the Eastern Star, commented in 1895 on the Masonic emphasis on moral teachings to the exclusion of sociability: "The Order with us has too much of the pulpit, and too little of the table. A due intermixture of both was what the Craft in the olden time regarded."

The Square Deal

The largest regalia supplier of the nineteenth century was M.C. Lilley & Co. of Columbus, Ohio. They begin business printing books and magazines, primarily for the Odd Fellows. As fraternalism boomed in the late 1800s, Lilley began manufacturing banners, costumes, and props for all fraternal groups. When military orders became popular, Lilley employees who were members served on the uniform committees of the different fraternal orders to help them design their uniforms (which Lilley, of course, could manufacture). The company continued until 1953 when it closed its doors.

Shriners

This milieu of fanciful fraternal names and finery coupled with austere Masonic decorum was ripe for something new and different—and a little outlandish. A group of New York City Masons who regularly lunched together often talked about yet another group for Masons to join, but it needed to be devoted to fun and fellowship, with much less emphasis on ceremony. Among the lunch regulars were Walter M. Fleming, M.D., a surgeon, and William J. "Billy" Florence, an actor.

Florence was prominent on the New York stage and performed around the world, always playing to large audiences. According to the Shriners' history, "While on tour in Marseilles, France, Florence was invited to a party given by an Arabian diplomat. The entertainment was something in the nature of an elaborately staged musical comedy. At its conclusion, the guests became members of a secret society."

On returning to New York, Florence shared his notes from several viewings of the entertainment with Fleming, and they agreed this could be the nucleus of their new organization. With the help of others they wrote the ritual, designed the costumes, invented officers' titles, and created an Arabic pedigree for their invention.

The 1904 Officers of the "Divan" of Boumi Shriners, Baltimore, Maryland. From The Book of Boumi (1934).

The Square Deal

Shriner officers' titles reflect their exuberance and tongue-in-cheek attitude: Potentate, Chief Rabban, Assistant Rabban, High Priest and Prophet, Oriental Guide, First and Second Ceremonial Masters, Marshal, Assistant Marshal, Captain of the Guard, and the important—if plainly titled—administrators, Recorder and Treasurer.

The Square Deal

The Shriners' website explains their name. "While there is some question about the origin of the Fraternity's name, it is probably more than coincidence that its initials [Ancient Arabic Order Nobles of the Mystic Shrine], rearranged, spell out the words A MASON."

In 1872, they launched the most flamboyant and exclusive fraternal group yet: the Ancient Arabic Order Nobles of the Mystic Shrine. Shriners, as they came to be called, first had to be a Master Mason, the oldest and most exclusive fraternal order, and then either a Knight Templar or a 32° Mason, the pinnacles of the York and Scottish Rites. Only after this were they eligible to petition the Shrine for membership.

There were thirteen in the initial group of initiates in New York City. By 1876, there were only 43 Shriners, with a second group in Rochester. To spur things on, the Imperial Grand Council was created in 1876 with Fleming as the first Imperial Grand Potentate. The initiation ceremonies were expanded and new members were actively recruited. The strategy worked, because just two years later 425 Shriners existed in thirteen cities, mostly in the northeast.

The growth of the Shrine was exceptional and matched the general growth of American and Canadian fraternal organizations. From 1872 to 1888, the Shrine initiated 7,210 Shriners into 48 centers, including one in Canada. Schmidt counts

106 American and Canadian groups formed during the same period, 1872–1888. The Shriners' growth continued, and in 1898 there were 50,000 Shriners in 79 cities in America and Canada.

Shriners quickly established themselves as the "Playground of Masonry"—a place to have fun "with the boys" (see figure that follows). In an era when parades were major civic events, Shriner units were preeminent. They had drum and bugle units, bands, choirs, and precision drill teams, all with elaborate "oriental" costumes, and every Shriner, whether in a special parade unit or not, wore the Shriners' distinctive red fez. Shriners today have units on horseback, motorcycles, miniature cars, and miniature 18-wheelers.

THE SHRINERS' CREED

This cartoon captures the Shriners' ethos of fun. From The Book of Boumi *(1934).*

The Square Deal

The fez derives its name from Fez, Morocco, where it was first manufactured centuries ago. The "Arabian Nights" has one of the earliest references to the hat, and its distinctive red color comes from Turkish redwood berries. Turkey's Sultan Mahmud Khan II (1808–1839) issued a decree that the fez would replace the turban and become the headdress for all citizens of the Ottoman Empire. Thus by 1872 when the Shrine was formed, the fez was firmly associated with the "exotic" Middle East. Ironically, Mustafa Kemal Ataturk, founder of the modern Republic of Turkey and successor in some sense to Mahmud Khan, outlawed wearing the fez, because it had become a symbol of old-fashioned ways.

The Shrine continued to expand, adding cities even outside the continental United States including Honolulu; Mexico City; Balboa, Panama; and more in Canada. Shriners are organized similarly to the Scottish Rite in that Shrine Centers are large, regional organizations. In the early 1900s, Shriners started sponsoring circuses as fundraisers, and today Shrine Circuses held around the country entertain Shriners and their neighbors.

At the 1920 session of the Imperial Council, the representatives of over 360,000 Shriners made the critical decision to establish a network of hospitals for the care of crippled children. (See Chapter 13 for more details on Shriners Hospitals for Children.) This has grown today to a network of 22 hospitals treating children with orthopedic, burn, and spinal cord injury care, all at no cost to the patients. (Care specialties vary by hospital.) The Shriners in 2005 have 500,000 members in 191 cities and a hospital budget of $625 million! The Shriners' philosophy has evolved to one of elegant simplicity: "Having fun and helping children."

How the Shrine Operates

An interesting "symbiotic" relationship developed between the Shrine and the York and Scottish Rites in some locations. Because many new Master Masons wanted to join the Shrine for its outstanding social and philanthropic activities, the local Shrine coordinated its calendar with the York and Scottish Rites. Typically the Shrine would hold two or three initiations, called "Ceremonials," a year, and the Scottish Rite would nearly always hold their initiations, called "Reunions," a few weeks before. This way Master Masons would receive the 32° and become eligible to join the Shrine shortly before the Ceremonial. The York Rite typically initiates members throughout the year, but they often coordinated their initiations so new Knights Templar were created just before a Ceremonial.

> **The Square Deal**
>
> When a Mason joins the Shrine, he takes a symbolic journey across the desert to the mythical Mystic Shrine. If the ceremony includes the Shriners' famous slapstick initiation stunts and pranks, the new member is said to have crossed the "hot sands." If the initiation is purely ceremonial, then the initiate is said to have crossed the "cold sands."

Each Shrine Temple has within it several special interest groups or "units." A unit is a "club within the club" and brings together Shriners that have special interests. Representative units include clowns, fishermen, sailors, bowlers, hunters, bagpipers, mini-car drivers, and on and on. The interests and imaginations of Shriners are the only limitations on what sort of unit can be formed by a Shrine center.

In 2000, the Shrine dropped its requirement that members be a 32° Mason or a Knight Templar. Membership is now open to all Master Masons, rather than the approximately 40 percent in the York and Scottish Rites. This has had a negative effect on the initiation rates in the Scottish and York Rites as Masons interested primarily in the Shrine now bypass the rites and directly join the Shrine.

Royal Order of Jesters

If there's one thing that Masons like to do, it's form new organizations to join with new offices to serve in and new opportunities for involvement. The Shriners are such a group founded on Masonic membership, and the Royal Order of Jesters is in turn founded on Shrine membership. Formed in 1911, the Jesters are an invitational body of Shriners, and their local branches are called "Courts." Membership requires a unanimous ballot and is limited to no more than 13 new members per court per year. The motto of the Jesters is "Mirth is King," and they let nothing get in their way of having fun.

> **The Square Deal**
>
> John Philip Sousa, known as "the March King," led the U.S. Marine band 1880–1892. In 1896 he composed the official march of the United States of America, "Stars and Stripes Forever." He was also a Mason and a Shriner and composed several marches for the Shrine, including "Nobles of the Mystic Shrine," "The Thunderer," and "The Crusader."

Order of Quetzalcoatl

In 1945, a new opportunity for Shriners was created with the formation of the Order of Quetzalcoatl. Formed in Mexico City, and basing its initiation rituals on Mexican mythology, the order is another invitational body for Shriners. Like the Jesters, the Quetzalcoatl provides an additional outlet for fun and fellowship. Members are known as Coates, local chapters are called Teocallis, and the supreme presiding officer is the Tlaloc. About 100 Teocallis existed in 2005 (compared to 191 Shrine Centers). The order has taken on as a special philanthropy the support of transportation for children traveling to Shriners Hospitals.

The Cabiri

The York Rite is notorious for creating organizations for its past presiding officers. (See Chapter 8 for details.) Why should the Shrine be any different? The Cabiri was organized in 1949 as a Past Potentates association. When elected to office, a

Potentate automatically becomes a probationary member of the Cabiri and can become a full member when he completes his term. In keeping with the tongue-in-cheek attitude of the Shriners, the officers of a Cabiri chapter are known as the Grand Cabar, the Royal Poohba, the High Cockolorum, the Custodian of the Lucre, and the Protector of the Chapter.

Hillbilly Degree

Just as there is a general interest in collecting Olympic pins, Masons have an interest in collecting degrees. Shriners are well known for creating degrees with pompous names and humorous initiations. After going through the ceremony, a Shriner has another dues card to carry and a pin to wear. The Grand and Glorious Order of the Hillbilly was created in 1970 to satisfy the desires of Shriners to have yet a little more fun. However, the Hillbillies have a serious side: all initiation fees must go to the Shriners Hospitals for Children. Thus becoming a Hillbilly is a way to show support for the Shrine's magnificent philanthropy. There were 160 Hillbilly "Clans" in 1999.

The Grotto

By 1889, the Shriners had spread out to over 48 mostly large cities, but it wasn't just big-city Masons who were looking for livelier fun and fellowship than found in the somewhat stuffy Masonic lodges. A group of Masons in Hamilton Lodge No. 120 in Hamilton, New York, about 230 miles north northwest of New York City, had been meeting together for informal merriment. They decided to formalize their organization and created the Mystic Order of Veiled Prophets of the Enchanted Realm in 1889. Local groups of Prophets are called Grottos, and their presiding officer is the Monarch.

The Grotto originally differed from the Shrine in that any Master Mason could join. There was no limitation to 32° Masons or Knights Templars, and thus there was a smaller financial obligation required before joining. The Grotto adopted a black fez as their distinctive "uniform" in 1903. Their rituals are based on the Persian story of Al Mokanna, the Veiled Prophet. In 2005, about 200 Grottos existed in America and Canada. The Grottos have a Humanitarian Foundation that supports cerebral palsy research and dental care for children with special needs. The latter philanthropy reaches out to "forgotten" children who because of severe handicapping cannot have routine dental care except with dentists with special training and sometimes only with anesthesia. (See Chapter 13 for more details.)

The Square Deal

It appears the Shriners established the fez as the unsurpassed fraternal fashion statement. Not only did the Grotto adopt a version of the headgear, but so did many other fraternal orders including the Odd Fellows' Ancient Mystical Order of Samaritans, the Knights of Columbus's Order of Alhambra, the Knights of Pythias's Dramatic Order Knights of Khorassan, the Improved Benevolent and Protective Order of Elks, the Moose Legion, and many others. The rationale for a distinctive headdress—as good as any I've ever heard—was given by Grandpa Barney in the movie *Peggy Sue Got Married:* "It wouldn't be a lodge without hats."

Tall Cedars of Lebanon

The Tall Cedars of Lebanon is another group of Master Masons devoted to "fun, frolic, and fellowship." Their early history is hazy (like that of so many other Masonic bodies), but it appears that from the mid-1800s Masons in the Pennsylvania–New Jersey area created a humorous ceremony they performed after grand lodge or lodge meetings. The ceremony became the initiation of the Tall Cedars of Lebanon. Those who had been initiated recruited new candidates for the fun of seeing them go through the ceremonies.

Eventually in 1902 in Trenton, New Jersey, the activities were formalized with the creation of the Supreme Forest of Tall Cedars of Lebanon. Tall Cedars' Forests are concentrated on the East Coast, though Forests meet as far west as Missouri and Oklahoma. Tall Cedars wear "pyramids" as their distinctive headgear. (See Chapter 19 for a picture.) Their philanthropy is Muscular Dystrophy research, to which they have contributed $17 million since 1951.

Masonic-Sponsored Youth Groups

The twentieth century brought increased leisure time to Americans and a desire for organized, character-building activities for children and youths. This urge to have formal youth groups led to the creation of several youth organizations. Masons were not far behind in forming their own organizations for youth.

DeMolay for Boys

In 1919, an active, young Kansas City, Missouri, Freemason, Frank S. Land, was serving as Director of the Masonic Relief and Employment Bureau of the Scottish Rite of Freemasonry. Land received a call asking if he could find a job for Louis Lower, the son of a recently deceased Mason. Land did more than this; he formed the Order of DeMolay, a group where boys and young men could learn leadership skills, serve their communities, and have fun in a wholesome environment. The nucleus of members for the new organization came from Louis Lower's friends.

Membership in DeMolay requires no kinship with a Mason, but DeMolay Chapters must be sponsored by Masons, and chapters usually meet in a Masonic building. Land patterned the new organization after Masonic bodies with which he was familiar. The Order has two levels of membership: the Initiatory Degree and the DeMolay Degree. The former introduces new members to the Order and presents them with a symbolic Crown of Youth decorated with seven jewels representing the Seven Cardinal Virtues of DeMolay: Love of Parents, Reverence for Sacred Things, Courtesy, Comradeship, Fidelity, Cleanness, and Patriotism. Parents and guardians can attend all meetings, including initiations.

The DeMolay Degree is a dramatic reenactment of the final trial of Jacques De Molay, the last Grand Master of the Knights Templar. Philip the Fair, king of France, had grown jealous of the wealth of the Templars and arrested them in 1307 on trumped up charges of heresy and disloyalty. Though confessing to the charges under torture, De Molay recanted his confession in 1314 and was burned at the stake. He remains a heroic figure of steadfast integrity.

There were 18,000 American DeMolays in 2005 in chapters in every state. Chapters sponsor activities for their members like sports events, dances, parties, and service projects. One of the important benefits of membership is the opportunity for a young man to learn leadership skills by serving as an officer in his chapter.

Job's Daughters International

Mrs. Ethel T. Wead Mick formed Job's Daughters International in Omaha, Nebraska, in 1920, the year after DeMolay was founded in Kansas City. Membership is open to girls and young women related to a Freemason. The group takes its name from the Bible, Job 42:15, "In all the land were no women found so fair as the daughters of Job; and their father gave them inheritance among their brethren."

Like any well-organized youth group, Job's Daughters provide a good mix of fun, leadership training, and service. The girls have their own special charity, the HIKE Fund, Inc. (the Hearing Impaired Kids Endowment Fund). The purpose of HIKE is to provide hearing devices for children with hearing impairments between the ages of newborn and twenty years whose parents are unable to meet this special need financially.

International Order of Rainbow for Girls

The Midwest seemed to be conducive to the formation of Masonic youth groups: DeMolay in Kansas City, Missouri; Job's Daughters in Omaha, Nebraska; and the International Order of Rainbow for Girls in McAlester, Oklahoma. The Reverend William Mark Sexson, pastor of the First Christian Church of McAlester, formed the Rainbow Girls in 1922. Originally limited to girls with a Masonic relative, like the Job's Daughters, Rainbow Girls today are open to interested girls and young women.

The Rainbow initiation ceremony has important teachings for the girls, with a different lesson assigned to each color of the rainbow: Red, Love; Orange, Religion; Yellow, Nature; Green, Immortality; Blue, Fidelity; Indigo, Patriotism; Violet, Service. The girls meet in local Assemblies and learn leadership and planning through organizing and running their activities.

Other Youth Groups

While DeMolay, Job's Daughters, and Rainbow Girls are the "big three" Masonic youth groups, other groups have been formed, some of which are still active today or have changed their membership requirements. The following list is representative of the organizations Masons have formed to support youth activities:

- Acacia Fraternity was formed in 1904 by fourteen Master Masons at the University of Michigan. Membership was originally limited to Master Masons, but this requirement changed as younger men started attending college.

- Sigma Mu Sigma fraternity was formed in 1919 at Tri-State University, Angola, Indiana, by Master Mason students. Like Acacia, they have dropped the requirement that members be Master Masons.

- The Order of the Builders for boys was formed in 1921 in Chicago, and had grown to 4,500 members in 45 chapters within a year. It appears to be out of business.

- The Organization of Triangles was formed in 1925 as Daughters of the Eastern Star, but changed its name in 1961. The Triangles operate only New York State and limit their membership to girls related to Master Masons, Eastern Stars, or Amaranth members.

- The Constellation of Junior Stars, another group limited to New York State, was formed in 1949. Membership is open to all girls and young women.

The Least You Need to Know

- The Shriners started in 1872 to be the "playground of Masonry"; they became the most exclusive and flamboyant group in the Golden Age of Fraternalism.

- Shriners started their Hospitals for Children in 1920 and in 2005 had a budget of over $625 million!

- The Grotto and Tall Cedars of Lebanon are other Masonic groups devoted to fun and fellowship.

- The Order of DeMolay for boys was formed in 1919, and local chapters are sponsored by Masons

- Job's Daughters International was formed in 1920 for girls related to a Mason.

- The International Order of Rainbow for girls was formed in 1922 and is now open to all girls.

Masonic Philanthropies

In This Chapter

- ◆ Masons have a reputation for helping each other
- ◆ Early Masonic relief was local
- ◆ State Masonic charities were built next
- ◆ National philanthropies, such as Shriners hospitals

Freemasons are known for many things: they deal fairly in business; their word is their bond; and they take care of each other. Their reputation—especially for mutual support—is not recent but can be documented going back for centuries. It appears to be an outgrowth of the trade union origins of the fraternity. Once you finished your apprenticeship and had become a Master Mason, the gothic constitutions required you to pay your workers fairly, to not take work away from another Master Mason, and to help traveling unemployed Master Masons.

As the fraternity evolved, so did its philanthropy. From offering work to the unemployed to passing a charity box at lodge meetings to building retirement homes and orphanages, Masonic philanthropy changed to meet the changing needs of its members. The focus of Masonic philanthropy has also broadened until today North American Masonic philanthropies contribute over $750 million a year, or over $2 million a day, of which

70 percent goes to the general public. National networks of childhood speech and language clinics, hospitals for children, scholarship endowments, and funding for medical research typify the breadth of Masonic philanthropy. Charity is a fundamental lesson taught to all Masons, and it sees its fruition in the many, many different Masonic philanthropies.

This chapter will discuss the historical development of Masonic charity and a summary of current major American Masonic philanthropies.

Local Support

Professor Wallace McLeod, an expert on the Gothic Constitutions, has shown that around 1520 the "Standard Original of the Old Charges" was written. In that mother document is found the following regulation for taking care of unemployed Masons:

> "And also that every Mason shall receive and cherish strange Fellows when they come over the country, and set them to work, as the manner is: that is to say, if they have mould stones in place, he shall set him a fortnight at the least on work, and give him his pay, and if he have no stones for him, he shall refresh him with money to the next lodge."

This is simple, practical assistance. If an unemployed member of the trade organization shows up at the lodge at your job site, you either put him to work or give him enough money to travel to the next lodge. This regulation also shows the value of knowing the modes of recognition, including the Mason Word, and keeping them secret. These secrets became a private form of unemployment insurance that allowed you to travel from site to site until you found work. If these secrets were exposed, then anyone could claim support from a lodge without having undergone an apprenticeship or without having assumed the mutual obligation of helping Masons in distress.

There is evidence that some of the first speculative lodges kept charity boxes into which members paid an assessment each meeting and from which they could make withdrawals in times of need. This idea was formalized in the 1733 bylaws of First Lodge of Boston, just 16 years after the formation of the Premier Grand Lodge. "Ninthly—Every Member shall pay at Least two shillings more per Quarter to be applied as Charity Towards the Relief of poor Brethren."

We don't know who was first to use this lodge's charity fund, but the earliest specific case of American Masonic charity that I have found occurred in Fredericksburg,

Virginia, some 20 years after First Lodge of Boston established their charity fund. On November 4, 1754, an indigent brother, John Spottswood, wrote the lodge for assistance, and they gave him one pound, twelve shillings, and sixpence "to relieve his necessity."

While early Masons did provide assistance to each other, they also took a broader view of who were their brothers and sisters. In 1791, the Grand Lodge of Rhode Island was formed, and the Proceedings of the Most Worshipful Grand Lodge of Rhode Island show the first two official actions of the new grand lodge were worship and charity. "The Brethren walked in Regular Procession to Trinity Church where an Excellent discourse was delivered by the reverend William Smith, Rector thereof, & a collection made of £11.9.4 … Money, to be invested into Wood & distributed to the Poor of this Town the ensuing winter."

Dorothy Ann Lipson shows in her book, *Freemasonry in Federalist Connecticut*, how American Masons approached charity differently from others:

> "Masonic charity differed in its underlying assumptions and in its style from civic charity. In Connecticut charity was available to the settled members of a town, regulated by law, and invoked in times of extreme need and as a last resort." (p. 213)

> "Masonic charity was secret unlike civic charity whose administration made the entire town privy to the needs of each recipient. The derogation of character implicit in acknowledging poverty must have compounded suffering. In contract the Masons asked, 'What has the world to do with private transactions whether a widow, an orphan, or a pilgrim has obtained relief?'" (p. 207)

My favorite example of early American Masonic charity is the Connecticut Masonic cow. It's a story of quiet, behind-the-scenes assistance. On April 11, 1821, Federal Lodge No. 17 of Watertown "voted this Lodge furnish a cow for our deceased Bro. D. Thompson's widow and the three young children … This cow is to belong to the lodge." Federal Lodge carried the cow as an asset on its books, presumably to spare the family the embarrassment of publicly accepting charity. The Widow only cared for the lodge's cow (and benefited from the milk and a calf each spring).

The Square Deal

Freemasonry had the radical idea (for its time) that men of different religious backgrounds could agree that God exists, that He is important in their lives, and that the religious discussion should stop there. What they also discovered was that they all felt a duty to God to be charitable. This is perhaps the biggest Masonic "secret" of all. Someone trying to understand how Masons make their connections needs look no further than William Preston's 1771 *Illustrations of Masonry*:

"To relieve the distressed is a duty incumbent on all men, but particularly on Freemasons, who are linked together by an indissoluble chain of sincere affection. To soothe the unhappy, to sympathize with their misfortunes, to compassionate their miseries, and to restore peace to their troubled minds is the great aim we have in view. On the basis we form our friendships and establish our connections."

Statewide Charities

As the country grew, American society changed from small villages to towns and cities with populations spread over larger areas. Where once it was easy for Federal Lodge in Watertown, Connecticut, to know about the needs of Mrs. Thompson and her children or for the Rhode Island Masons to know to whom they should give firewood, it now became increasingly difficult. Further, a cow in the mid-1800s in a city might not be as helpful as it was for Mrs. Thompson and her children.

Orphanages and Retirement Homes

The Grand Lodge of Kentucky took the first step in creating a statewide Masonic charity. In 1867, Kentucky Masons established the Masonic Widows and Orphans Home and Infirmary (now the Masonic Homes of Kentucky). In 1872, North Carolina Masons founded Oxford Orphanage (now the Masonic Home for Children at Oxford), and many other state grand lodges followed suit. The idea of caring for aged Masons, widows, and orphans is an extension of the Gothic Constitutions' requirement that unemployed Masons be given assistance. This was yet another practical value of "knowing the Mason Word," that is, proving you are a Master Mason.

American Masonic institutions not only were meeting the changing needs of their members but also following the lead of the United Grand Lodge of England. The Royal Masonic Institution for Girls was started in 1788. The Royal Masonic Institution for Boys opened in 1798. Several other English Masonic charities, including the Royal Masonic Benevolent Institute for Aged and Decayed Freemasons and their Widows, were established in 1850.

> ### The Square Deal
>
> By 1901, the idea of a Masonic care for orphans was so well established that Rudyard Kipling immortalized it in his novel *Kim*. This is the story of Kimball O'Hara, the orphaned son of a soldier in the Irish regiment who was also a Mason. At one point, when the soldiers are trying to decide what to do with Kim, they say, "the sooner he goes to the Masonic Orphanage the better."

Masonic orphanages and retirement homes continue today, but they are evolving to meet many changes, including higher operating costs from increasing government regulation. Families are smaller, so in case of the death of one or both parents, there are fewer children who need care. There is now an "elder care industry" providing all sorts of housing services and living options. Pensions, Social Security, and investments provide financial support that didn't exist a century ago. I wouldn't be surprised in the future to see "brick and mortar" Masonic homes replaced by foundations that assist children and senior citizens with their needs. The Masonic principle of relief remains constant; it is the delivery system that changes with time.

Masonic Colleges

A little-appreciated aspect of American Masonic philanthropy was the establishment of colleges by grand lodges. The Grand Lodge of Missouri started this ambitious movement in 1841 when it was but 21 years old and had only 1,139 members. By 1847, it laid the cornerstone for the Masonic College of Missouri in Lexington, Missouri. Missouri lodges were allowed to send a certain number of students to the college free of tuition for six months, provided room and board were paid. There were 95 students in 1849 and 175 students by 1857; the endowment was $53,000 in 1853. Sadly, the grand lodge had overreached in its efforts and had to close the college in 1859. The grand lodge eventually gave the college property to Marvin Female Institute, which is today the Central Methodist University in Fayette, Missouri.

Several other grand lodges from the South and Midwest tried their hands at postsecondary education, all with the same unfortunate results as Missouri. Even though none of these schools survived as Masonic institutions, it is a wonderful testimony to the altruism and enthusiasm of the Masons that they would even attempt such an enormous venture.

A partial list of Masonic colleges gives a flavor of the scope of this effort.

◆ Alabama had the Auburn Female Masonic College from the 1840s to the 1850s.

◆ Arkansas established St. John's Masonic College in 1850 and ran the Pea Ridge Masonic College from 1874 to 1930.

◆ Georgia Masons supported the Georgia Masonic Female College and Southern Masonic College, both in Covington.

◆ Kentucky operated the Masonic University from about 1845 to 1857.

◆ North Carolina ran St. John's College from 1858 to 1872.

◆ Ohio had the Dayton Masonic College, 1885, and the Masonic University of Cincinnati.

◆ South Carolina maintained the Masonic Female College in Cokesbury from 1853 to 1874.

◆ Tennessee began the Masonic University of Tennessee in 1848, which has become today's Rhodes College of Memphis.

Regional and National Philanthropies

Because state grand lodges dominate the organizational structure of American Freemasonry, institutional Masonic philanthropies were generally focused within a state. The Scottish and York Rites encouraged their members to be active in their state grand lodges, and did not operate significant philanthropies themselves. All of this changed in 1920 when the Shriners adopted a proposal to establish a hospital for children, and started an era of national Masonic philanthropies.

Scottish Rite Hospitals for Children

Atlanta, Georgia, was the site of the first major Masonic hospital for children. It started simply enough in 1915 as the Scottish Rite Convalescent Home for Crippled Children in Decatur, Georgia, about five miles from downtown Atlanta, offering needy children a place to recover after surgery elsewhere. By 1919, Georgia Scottish Rite Masons opened a 50-bed facility and gave it a new name: the Scottish Rite Hospital for Crippled Children. The hospital grew with the regional population, moved to North Atlanta in the 1970s, expanded its medical services, and changed its name to Scottish Rite Children's Medical Center. In 1998, it merged with the Egleston Children's Health Care System to become Children's Healthcare of Atlanta.

In 1921, Texas Scottish Rite Hospital for Children opened in Dallas, Texas, with a mission to treat young victims of polio. When the Salk and Sabine vaccines stopped the polio epidemic, the hospital shifted its focus to other children's orthopedic problems. Today, the hospital provides extensive treatment and therapy for more than 13,000 children challenged by conditions such as arthritis, cerebral palsy, clubfoot, limb-length differences, scoliosis, and spina bifida.

The hospital also has an extensive research program and is a leading center for professional training in pediatric orthopedics. The Texas Scottish Rite Hospital for Children developed the spinal implant system used in approximately half of the world's surgeries to correct scoliosis, and it has developed a series of videotaped dyslexia and literacy training programs, helping thousands of students learn to read and write. A sense of the hospital's impact is given by a few numbers for 2002: 40,000 outpatient visits, 1,786 surgeries, and more than 100,000 volunteer hours donated in support of the hospital. For contact information on the hospitals, see Appendix B.

> **The Square Deal**
>
> The Texas Scottish Hospital for Children does not charge for its services now, nor has it since its inception. To be admitted, a child's condition should offer hope of improvement; the child must be younger than 18 years of age, and be a resident of the state of Texas. The Hospital operates solely on voluntary gifts from generous individuals, Masons, corporations, and foundations.

Shriners Hospitals for Children

The Shriners formed in 1872 at the start of the Golden Age of Fraternalism. They served as the "playground of Masonry" by offering dances, parties, parades, and other social activities absent from unadventurous lodges' social calendars. At the 1920 Imperial Shrine Session (the Shriners' way of saying "National Convention") it was decided to create a Shriners Hospital for Crippled Children, to be funded by a $2 assessment on each of the 364,000 Shriners—almost $750,000 a year. The inspiration for the hospitals came from a visit by the Imperial Potentate to the Atlanta Scottish Rite Hospital for Crippled children.

A year later the Shriners decided that a single hospital wasn't enough, so they approved a whole network, and in 1922 the cornerstone was laid for the first Shriners hospital in Shreveport, Louisiana. Today there is a network of 22 Shriners hospitals in America, Canada, and Mexico: 14 providing orthopedic care, 3 providing burn care, 2 providing orthopedic and spinal injury care, and the newest hospital in Sacramento providing orthopedic, burn, and spinal cord injury care.

The Square Deal

The Scottish Rite and Shriners Hospitals specializing in orthopedic care for children were built during a period of polio epidemics. The first such epidemic occurred in Vermont in 1894 with a total of 132 cases. By 1916, there were 27,000 instances and 7,000 deaths. The infections continued with 20,000+ cases a year in 1946, increasing to 58,000 in 1952. In 1955, the Salk vaccine proved to be effective protection against the disease, and the number of polio cases was reduced to 5,600 in 1957, and 121 in 1964. Of those who contract polio, about 25 percent endure serious permanent handicaps, about 25 percent have mild handicaps, and 50 percent recover with no permanent symptoms. Thus the Masonic children's orthopedic hospitals filled a pressing national healthcare need.

The prevention of polio and the elimination of the orthopedic problems it caused led the Shriners to branch into other services for children just like the Scottish Rite Hospitals in Dallas and Atlanta. After redirecting their mission to general orthopedic care for children, the Shriners still had room for further expansion. There was only one question: What unmet need could they fill?

The Square Deal

Shriners have a simple admissions policy: any child can be admitted if the child's condition can be cured or substantially helped, if the child is 18 or younger, and if treatment at another facility would place a financial burden on the family. The Shriners' billing policy is even simpler: there's never a charge at a Shriners Hospital—they don't even have a patient-billing department!

The Shriners discovered the only American burn treatment center was part of a military complex, and so in 1962 they undertook to build specialized hospitals for severely burned children. The Shriners opened three such hospitals: Galveston, Texas, 1966, affiliated with the University of Texas Medical Branch; Cincinnati, Ohio, 1968, affiliated with the University of Cincinnati; and Boston, Massachusetts, 1968, affiliated with Harvard Medical School. New facilities were opened at Galveston and Cincinnati in 1992 and at Boston in 1999. Their fourth burn hospital opened at Sacramento, California, in 1997, to spare burned children from western states the necessity of traveling to other Shriners burn hospitals. Since the Shriners opened their burn hospitals, a burned child's chance of survival has more than doubled.

From 1922, when the first Shriners Hospital opened in Shreveport, until 2005, there have been approximately 9,419,130 X-rays taken, 7,112,840 outpatient and outreach clinic visits, 1,254,854 braces and prostheses applied, 740,945 operations performed, and 16,410,800 physical therapy treatments. The entire philosophy of the Shriners Hospitals was captured in a single impromptu photograph taken in 1970 at a local Shrine Temple's annual outing for handicapped children in Indiana. It has become the Shriners' "Editorial without words." For contact information on the Shriners' Hospitals for Children, see Appendix B.

The Shriners' "Editorial without words" personifies Masonic philanthropies.

(Photograph by Randy Dieter. © Shriners Hospitals for Children. All rights reserved.)

Masonic Service Association

The Masonic Service Association of North America was formed in 1919 to give American Grand Lodges a unified method for serving Masons in the Armed Forces and for relief of the distressed. During World War II, MSA operated Masonic Service Centers near major military facilities with voluntary funds from Masonic bodies. As the war wound down, it was a natural transition for the fraternity to continue its concern for the wounded and ill veterans in the military, naval, and veterans hospitals.

At the urging of Past Grand Master Harry S Truman, MSA became one of the original participants in the Veterans Administration Voluntary Services. With a corps of Hospital Representatives and other volunteers, the program has expanded into 157 of the 172 V.A. Medical Centers, several military and naval hospitals, and 25 of the 44 state Veterans Homes. The MSA has set for itself a goal to visit at least once every patient in every hospital it serves.

MSA also serves as the focal point for Masonic disaster relief, coordinating collections from individual Masons and grand lodges and directing the money to affected areas. Another current project is Operation Phone Home, a campaign to provide prepaid international phone calling cards to military personnel serving overseas. For contact information on the Masonic Service Organization of North America, see Appendix B.

Scottish Rite Speech and Language Disorders Clinics

In 1953 in Colorado, Scottish Rite Masons initiated a program to help children with speech and language disorders. The success of the Colorado program led to the establishment of over 210 centers by 2005, in both the Southern Jurisdiction and the Northern Masonic Jurisdiction. Staffed by speech-language pathologists and other trained personnel, RiteCare Childhood Language Programs (Southern Jurisdiction) and 32° Masonic Learning Centers for Children (Northern Masonic Jurisdiction) provide essential services to children with speech, language, and learning disabilities.

Most of these programs are housed in Scottish Rite Temples around the country, so the services are near the children who need them. For those rural areas with thin populations, the Scottish Rite provides mobile clinics that travel to the patients. Regardless of the services provided (which can vary from clinic to clinic), the goal always is to provide timely intervention so the children can read and communicate normally at the earliest age possible. For contact information on these programs, see Appendix B.

Knights Templar Eye Foundation

The Masonic Knights Templar are Christian York Rite Masons. Just as Jesus gave sight to the blind during his ministry, Knights Templar seek to save the sight of others through the work of their Eye Foundation. The foundation, established in 1956, provides assistance to those who face loss of sight due to the need for surgical treatment, if they are unable to pay for it themselves or to receive adequate assistance from government agencies or similar sources. Since 1956, the foundation has handled over 76,000 applications representing more than $91 million. For contact information on the Knights Templar Eye Foundation, see Appendix B.

Dental Care for Children with Special Needs

The image of a child afflicted with physical disabilities evokes immediate sympathy. Some of the needs of these special children are clearly obvious and easily met: wheelchairs, prostheses, and crutches. Other needs are not as obvious but are just as important. Dental care is one of those essential but often overlooked necessities that can be difficult for some patients. Masons in the Grottos of North America, the Mystic Order Veiled Prophets of the Enchanted Realm, saw a need in 1970 and leaped at the opportunity to meet it. Their motto is "Bringing special smiles to special kids." Dentists with specialized training are needed to care for some children with cerebral palsy, muscular dystrophy, and profoundly mentally challenges. In some cases, general anesthesia is required to just do routine teeth cleaning. For contact information on this foundation, see Appendix B.

Camp Chicota

Opposite Chicot State Park in Evangeline Parish, Louisiana, in the center of the state, sits Camp Chicota. It is a testimony to the vision of Prince Hall Masons and an investment in America's children. Owned by the Prince Hall Grand Lodge of Louisiana and Esther Grand Chapter of the Eastern Star, Camp Chicota provides a safe, fun summer experience, a respite from worry and want, for underprivileged children. Each week during the summer 125 boys and girls are guests of the Prince Hall Masonic family of Louisiana. (That's 1,500 children a year!) They get a chance to swim, to explore Chicota's lovely grounds, to play, and to have fun in a safe, secure setting. For one week, they get a real vacation, perhaps their only vacation, and a chance to enjoy being young. For contact information on Chicota Youth Camp, see Appendix B.

The Least You Need to Know

- Since 1520, the Gothic Constitutions have required Masons to help each other.

- Masonic bylaws as early as 1733 established charity funds to relieve members.

- Early Masonic relief was local, practical, and direct, like cash or firewood for a needy family.

- American state grand lodges started forming retirement homes, orphanages, and colleges in the mid-1800s.

- Starting around 1920, Masonic bodies formed national philanthropy programs like the Shriners hospitals.

Part 4

Masonic Myths and Misunderstandings

An organization as old and as widespread as Freemasonry with so many prominent members can't be up to any good, is it? Well, it depends on whom you ask. There are lots of myths and misinformation about Freemasonry, some are malicious lies, but most are urban legends. The focus of much of the malice is Albert Pike, a Confederate general, who led the Scottish Rite for almost 40 years. You'll learn here about Pike and some of the lies told about him. You'll also learn about some of the religious concerns about Freemasonry, including the long-standing objections of the Roman Catholic Church. Then you'll hear the stories of Freemasons inserting their "secret symbols" into the street plans of Washington, D.C., the back of the dollar bill, and even on beer bottles!

Chapter 3

Albert Pike: Sovereign Pontiff of Masonic Mythology

In This Chapter

- Albert Pike was Grand Commander of the Scottish Rite 1859–1891
- The Pike-Lucifer hoax originated in 1894
- The Pike-Ku Klux Klan smear originated in 1905
- The Pike-Mazzini letters are forgeries from after World War II

It doesn't take much searching about Freemasonry on the Internet to find the name Albert Pike popping up time and again. He was a legal scholar and Confederate General who went on to serve as Grand Commander of the Supreme Council, 33°, S.J., for 32 years, from 1859 to 1891. He rewrote the rituals, reorganized the administration of the Scottish Rite, and transformed the organization into what it is today. His book *Morals and Dogma of the Ancient and Accepted Scottish Rite* was given to every new Scottish Rite Mason in the Southern Jurisdiction for almost a century—over 500,000 copies.

Pike has become the favorite target for those who want to "prove" that Freemasonry is evil or plotting world revolution or secretly worshipping Lucifer (to date no one has accused us of being behind global warming, but that may be next). They usually begin by praising Pike before trotting out their laundry list of accusations. A favorite starting point for such attacks is, "Pike was a genius, able to read and write in 16 different languages." Over 150 Internet sites have reprinted this sentence and the attack that follows without attribution. (None of the sites seem to care enough either to do their own thinking or to acknowledge someone else's work.) Once it's proved that Pike was "bad," it's only a small step to argue that the Scottish Rite shares in that "badness," either because Pike was its leader or because they haven't renounced him.

This chapter will discuss the life of Albert Pike and the infamous slanders spread about him.

A Brief Biography

Albert Pike was born on December 29, 1809, in Boston, Massachusetts, a world removed from Arkansas where he later settled. At age 15 he started at Harvard and completed two years of study in one year, making him eligible to become a junior. Harvard demanded tuition for the year skipped, which Pike could not afford, and so he left Massachusetts to find his fortune elsewhere. He journeyed west to Santa Fe, New Mexico, by way of Cincinnati, Ohio; Cairo, Illinois; and St. Louis, Missouri.

This is how Albert Pike looked in 1880 at 71 years of age.

(Courtesy of the Archives of the Supreme Council, 33°, S.J., Washington, D.C.)

After a little less than a year in New Mexico, Pike joined some others and headed out for New Orleans. He soon lost his horse, then lost his way, and eventually wound up in Ft. Smith, Arkansas, over 700 miles east of Santa Fe and still some 650 miles north of New Orleans. He decided to settle in Arkansas as a teacher and began writing for the *Little Rock Advocate*, which he eventually bought and ran himself.

Pike then read *Blackstone's Commentaries on the Laws of England*, was admitted to the bar of Arkansas, and began his legal career. He practiced law in Little Rock, edited eight volumes of the *Arkansas Supreme Court Reports*, and annotated the Arkansas statutes for 1837. During the 1840s, he joined the *Independent Order of Odd Fellows* and went on to serve as Grand Master of their Arkansas grand lodge, 1852–1853.

During the Mexican-American War (1846–1848), Pike recruited a cavalry regiment and served with distinction under General Zachary Taylor at the Battle of Buena Vista. In 1849, he was admitted to the bar of the Supreme Court of the United States, the same year as Abraham Lincoln. Pike soon began representing Native Americans because he could so readily learn their languages. He established his reputation as a trusted friend and advocate in 1859 when he recovered nearly $3 million from the federal government for the Choctaw Nation.

His Masonic activities began in 1850 when he joined Western Star Lodge No. 1 at Little Rock. He first joined the York Rite: Royal Arch Mason, 1851; Cryptic Mason, 1852; Knight Templar, 1853. Then in New Orleans, he met Dr. Albert G. Mackey, Secretary General of the Supreme Council, S.J. Mackey *communicated* the Scottish Rite Degrees to Pike over a period of three days in March 1853. Two years later Pike was appointed a member of the committee revising the rituals, and he found his Masonic calling.

def•i•ni•tion

The **Independent Order of Odd Fellows** is an English fraternity imported into America in the early 1800s. Its members, primarily working class, were considered "odd" because of the mutual support they gave each other. There is a branch for ladies and a system of several degrees similar to the York Rite. The Odd Fellows were larger than the Freemasons in 1900, though they are much smaller today.

def•i•ni•tion

A Masonic degree is **communicated** to a candidate if it is either read or summarized. The Scottish Rite, with 29 degrees, regularly uses this shortcut to reduce 30–60 hours of ritual ceremony. In other Masonic organizations, communication of degrees is reserved for extraordinary circumstances.

Pike was fascinated by the symbolism and allegories of the Scottish Rite Degrees and was convinced there were deeper concepts waiting to be uncovered. It was his theory that the original Scottish Rite ritual writers had hidden deep meaning under obscure symbols, and that a careful study could reveal the hidden treasures. He single-handedly revised the degrees and added rich layers of drama and metaphor to many bare ceremonies. His abilities were recognized, and he quickly advanced to the position of Grand Commander in 1859, on the eve of the Civil War.

In 1856, he spoke at the Southern Convention against resuming the slave trade and was booed off the floor. Pike believed that slavery degraded both slaves and slave owners, and he wanted to eliminate slavery, but by making it economically unnecessary. Despite his abolitionist sentiments, he chose to fight with the Confederacy because of his strong belief in states' rights.

Hits and Myths

A common myth is that Albert Pike was an ardent racist. Albert Pike was a complex man subject to the prejudices of his own time and cannot be described by one simple adjective. He spoke and wrote eloquently against slavery, and yet he owned house slaves. He firmly supported the legitimacy of Prince Hall Masonry: "Prince Hall Lodge was as regular a Lodge as any Lodge created by competent authority." But he also said, "When I have to accept Negroes as brothers or leave Masonry, I shall leave it." But Pike developed a friendship with Thornton Jackson, the Grand Commander of the Prince Hall Scottish Rite, and gave Jackson a copy of his rituals.

The Confederate government appointed Pike to negotiate treaties with the Indian nations, and he was very successful. The Confederacy then commissioned Pike as a Brigadier General in charge of Native American troops defending their own territories. Soon after this, over Pike's great objections, his troops were assigned to fight elsewhere. He and his troops were assigned to Major General Earl Van Dorn, who led the disastrous Battle of Pea Ridge in March 1862. During this battle, some of Pike's Native Americans scalped fallen Union soldiers.

When Pike learned of this, he denounced the mutilations, but the charge of leading "savages" was to follow him the rest of his life. He defended the bravery of his troops, but expressed outrage at their deviation from the accepted codes of warfare. Of course, his soldiers, who had been told they would only be defending their own land, had fought under their code of warfare. When he received no support from Van Dorn, who was maneuvering to disassociate himself from the atrocities, Pike resigned his commission in July 1862.

Following General Robert E. Lee's surrender at Appomattox in April 1865, Pike applied to President Lincoln for amnesty, but charges had been brought against him for inciting Native Americans to war against the government. He moved to Canada to avoid arrest, even though President Johnson granted him an amnesty in August 1865. Pike returned, took an oath of allegiance to the United States in December 1865, but declined a full pardon in April 1866.

Hits and Myths

A common myth is that Andrew Johnson, a Master Mason, granted Albert Pike a pardon in return for Masonic "favors." It's easy to find conspiracists writing that in 1867 "the awed and grateful Johnson was granted advanced degrees 4 through 32 by the Scottish Rite," or that Johnson was Pike's "subordinate" and that Masonic obligations required the president to do the Grand Commander's bidding, or that Pike wasn't pardoned until Johnson received the 33°. The truth is simpler and much less exciting.

Andrew Johnson became a Master Mason in 1851 in Greenville Lodge No. 119 in Greenville, Tennessee. He was a York Rite Mason, joining Nashville Commandery No. 1, Knights Templar, in 1859, but he had no affiliation with the Scottish Rite when he granted Pike's pardon in 1866. Johnson's relationship with Pike was like that of a university president to the president of Phi Beta Kappa (or any other academic honor society): certainly respect, perhaps admiration, but absolutely no subordination.

Johnson issued an order on August 30, 1865, guaranteeing Pike's personal liberty if he took an oath of allegiance. This, however, was not deemed a full pardon, and confiscation proceedings began against his estate in Arkansas. His property, worth $20,000–$25,000, was sold for $2,250. A full pardon came through on April 23, 1866, but Pike refused it because he would have had to pay over $300 in court costs for the sale of his property!

Fourteen months later on June 20, 1867, the Scottish Rite Degrees 4°–32° were communicated to Johnson. Benjamin B. French, 33°, summarized the event: "We met the president in the room known as the Library, where he invited us to partake of a lunch. We then accompanied him to his sleeping room, where we conferred the Degrees. Illustrious Brother Johnson expressed himself much gratified and said that the doctrines inculcated were such as he had been preaching and practicing all his life." Johnson never received the 33°.

The commonsense question is this: "If Pike had so much influence over Johnson, why didn't Johnson immediately grant a full pardon or act to save Pike's property or grant additional and more substantial preference to Pike and the Scottish Rite?" It's silly to think that Masons could influence the president of the United States to obey their orders—unless you prefer conspiracy to history.

After returning to the states Pike worked briefly in Memphis, Tennessee, as a lawyer and as editor of the *Memphis Appeal.* He then moved to Washington, D.C., in 1868, the same year he completed revising the Scottish Rite rituals, began practicing law, and devoted the rest of his life to the Scottish Rite. In 1871, he wrote *Morals and Dogma of the Ancient and Accepted Scottish Rite*, intended to supplement his revised rituals.

Pike had the annoying habit (at least to me) of using words according to their precise and usually original dictionary definition, not how they were generally understood. Thus the title *Morals and Dogma* gets my award for "Most Misleading or Confusing Masonic Book Title," as there's nothing dogmatic about the book. In his introduction, Pike says, "The Ancient and Accepted Scottish Rite uses the word 'Dogma' in its true sense, or doctrine, or teaching; and is not dogmatic in the odious sense of the term. Every one is entirely free to reject and dissent from whatsoever herein may seem to him to be untrue or unsound." This is not the way to introduce the "universally approved doctrinal book" on any subject!

The book is an early study in comparative religion, though it's poorly organized, Victorian in its prose, and unclear about what material is being quoted. Allowing for advances in our knowledge about ancient religions, *Morals and Dogma* is a pretty good book. Pike's motivation for including so much about earlier beliefs is also explained in his introduction. "Of course, the ancient theosophic and philosophic speculations are not embodied as part of the doctrines of the Rite; but because it is of interest and profit to know what the Ancient Intellect thought upon these subjects, and because nothing so conclusively proved the radical difference between our human and the animal sense, as the capacity of the human mind to entertain such speculations in regard to itself and the Deity."

In addition to rewriting the rituals of the Scottish Rite for the Southern Jurisdiction, Pike also reorganized the administration of his Supreme Council. He became recognized as one of the great thinkers on Masonic symbolism and ritual. His international status was established when he railed against a proposal made at the 1875 Lausanne, Switzerland, "Congress of Supreme Councils" to allow Freemasons to believe in a "creative principle" rather than a personal God. Pike continued writing on Freemasonry and administering the Southern Jurisdiction until his death in 1891 in Washington, D.C., at his residence in the Scottish Rite's headquarters.

> ### Hits and Myths
>
> A common myth is that only Scottish Rite Masons are supposed to have a copy of *Morals and Dogma,* a very influential Masonic book. The first printings (1871–1881) had this announcement: "Esoteric Book, for Scottish Rite use only; to be returned upon withdrawal or death of recipient." Hundreds of thousands of copies have been printed since then with no restriction on ownership or use of the books. Anti-Masons also claim that it's only available from a "secret publishing house," or it's "the Bible of the Masons," or it's "the most readily available and universally approved doctrinal book of Freemasonry." All of these statements are false. It was a supplement to the Scottish Rite Degrees in the Southern Jurisdiction and is virtually unknown in Blue Lodges or in the Northern Masonic Jurisdiction.

Taxil's Invention of the "Sovereign Pontiff of Lucifer"

Pike certainly led an adventure-filled life and achieved lasting prominence in the Southern Jurisdiction of the Scottish Rite (though he didn't have much standing with grand lodges, the York Rite, or the Northern Masonic Jurisdiction). How, then, did his reputation become intertwined with the worship of Lucifer? To answer that question we turn to an interesting Frenchman.

Gabriel Antoine Jogand-Pages (1854–1907) is better known by his pen name of "Léo Taxil." He was a French freethinker notorious for his irreligious and pornographic writings. In 1881, he published *The Secret Loves of Pius IX* and received the First Degree in Masonry. By 1882, he had worn out his welcome in his lodge and was expelled without advancing beyond 1° Entered Apprentice. Sometime after this, he concocted his grand scheme to embarrass the Roman Catholic Church and wreak a twisted vengeance on his former Masonic brothers.

Much to the shock of his freethinking friends and to the surprise of French Catholics, Taxil "converted" to Catholicism in 1885. He convinced a priest he was a murderer and did penance in a monastery. He then dropped the bombshell: shortly before joining the church, he had been a Freemason and could reveal their inner workings.

Taxil knew his admission would get special attention, because Freemasonry was a particular concern of Pope Leo XIII; an obsession some have said. Fifteen years before, Giuseppe Garibaldi had liberated the Papal States of Italy from Pope Pius IX. Garibaldi was a Freemason, and it was clear to many that he was acting as part of a Masonic plot to destroy the Roman Catholic Church. The year before Taxil converted, Pope Leo XIII had issued his encyclical on Freemasonry, "Humanum Genus." In it, he expressed his concern about the loss of temporal authority by the Pope. "[A]gainst the apostolic see and the Roman Pontiff the contention of [Freemasons] has been for a long time directed. The Pontiff was first, for specious reasons, thrust out from the bulwark of his liberty and of his right, the civil princedom."

A caricature of Léo Taxil from The Men of the Day.

(Courtesy of Arturo de Hoyos, Grand Archivist and Grand Historian of the Supreme Council, 33°, S.J.)

Like any good con artist, Taxil found the special weakness of his "mark" and focused on it. He soon started writing books about what "really" went on in Masonic lodges, and his output was prodigious. Taxil said of his writing, "My first books on Freemasonry consisted in a mixture of rituals, with short innocent parts inserted, apparently harmlessly interpreted. Each time an obscure passage occurred, I explained it in a way agreeable to Catholics who see Master Lucifer as the supreme grand master of Freemasons."

After writing on Freemasonry for two years, he obtained an audience with Pope Leo XIII in 1887. Following this he revealed (actually invented) the innermost secret of Freemasonry: The New and Reformed Palladian Rite, a Lucifer-worshipping inner circle of men and women that ran Masonry. Palladism is a monstrous deception that never existed except in Taxil's mind. Credulous anti-Masons started writing their own books, interpreting Masonic symbols in the light of the newly revealed Palladism. Taxil incorporated and cross-referenced these books in the growing web of his hoax.

The Square Deal

Pope Leo XIII's 1884 encyclical, "Humanum Genus," is perhaps the best-known Catholic pronouncement against Freemasonry. In condemning Freemasonry the encyclical enumerated some of the unacceptable principles supported by the fraternity:

"states ought to be constituted without any regard for the laws and precepts of the [Roman Catholic] Church"

"marriage … can rightly be revoked by the will of those who made [the contract], and that the civil rulers of the State [and not the Church] have power over the matrimonial bond"

"each [youth] must be left at liberty to follow, when he comes of age, whatever [religion] he may prefer"

"power is held by the command or permission of the people, so that, when the popular will changes, rulers may lawfully be deposed"

"in the various forms of religion there is no reason why one should have precedence of another; and that they are all to occupy the same place [in the state]" (Supporting this objection, the encyclical said earlier, "the Catholic religion, which, as it is the only one that is true, cannot, without great injustice, be regarded as merely equal to other religions.")

He created an evil Grand Mistress of Palladism, Sophia Walder, and her virtuous adversary, Diana Vaughan. He had Diana born in France with her family from Kentucky. She escaped from the evils of Palladism, converted to Catholicism, but now had to remain in hiding to avoid assassination by vengeful Masons. These stories captivated the Catholic hierarchy and the French public, much like a contemporary news story of a missing person. Part of the attraction to Taxil's books was his salacious descriptions of the debaucheries involved in the initiation of young women into Palladism. Sex, devil worship, a narrow escape, a damsel in distress—Taxil sure knew how to appeal to the masses!

Three years after Albert Pike's death, Taxil convinced Abel Clarin de la Rive that Pike had been the "Sovereign Pontiff of Universal Freemasonry" (a nonexistent position). De la Rive subsequently published in *Woman and Child in Universal Freemasonry* (1894) Pike's "announcement" to the "Supreme Confederated Councils of the World" (a nonexistent organization) that the inner circle of High Degree Freemasons worshipped Lucifer (see the figure that follows). The fraud started then and there with malice and continues today through gullibility.

The Square Deal

Pike's "announcement" in de la Rive's book would probably have faded into well-deserved obscurity, except for Edith Starr Miller, Lady Queenborough. In her 1933 book *Occult Theocrasy* (which "exposes" evil forces bent on taking over the world), Miller translated the fictitious announcement, and eager conspiracists have repeated it ever since:

"In *La Femme et l'Enfant dans la Franc-Maçonnerie Universelle* page 578, A. C. De La Rive states that on July 14, 1889, Albert Pike, Sovereign Pontiff of Universal Freemasonry, addressed to the 23 Supreme Confederated Councils of the world the following instructions, which we quote herewith in part …

That which we must say to the crowd is:—We worship a God, but is the God that one adores without superstition.

To you, Sovereign Grand Inspectors General, we say this, that you may repeat it to the Brethren of the 32nd, 31st and 30th degrees—The Masonic religion should be, by all of us initiates of the high degrees, maintained in the purity of the Luciferian doctrine …

Yes, Lucifer is God, and unfortunately Adonay is also God …"

Not quoted by Miller is the footnote from de la Rive identifying Diana Vaughan as the courier of Pike's "Luciferian Doctrine." "It was the sister Diana Vaughan that Albert Pike—in order to give her the greatest mark of confidence—charged to carry his Luciferian encyclical to Paris, during the Universal Exposition." Vaughan is the creation of Taxil's perverse mind, and this alone marks the quote as a hoax. Presumably, Diana carried the encyclical before her conversion to Catholicism and escape from the clutches of Palladism.

A quick Internet search with the keywords "Pike, Lucifer" produces over 30,000 hits, most breathlessly warning readers about the evils of Freemasonry. The warnings remind me of the urban legend about the woman who dried her poodle in a microwave.

Cover of Abel Clarin de la Rive's Woman and Child in Universal Freemasonry *(1894), the original source of the false "Luciferian Doctrine" of Albert Pike. Most of the quotes in English, however, have been plagiarized from Edith Starr Miller's* Occult Theocrasy *(1933).*

(Courtesy of the Archives, Museum, and Library of the Supreme Council, 33°, S.J., Washington, D.C.)

The choice of making Pike "Sovereign Pontiff" was very calculated. Taxil admitted this in his public revelation of the hoax:

> "We located the center of Palladism at Charleston in the United States, with the late General Albert Pike, Grand Master of the Scottish Rite in South Carolina, as Founder. This celebrated Freemason, endowed with vast erudition, had been one of the highlights of the order. Through us, he became the first Luciferian Pope, supreme chief of all freemasons of the globe, conferring regularly each Friday, at 3:00 P.M., with Master Lucifer in person."

The Bishop of Charleston, South Carolina, Msgr. Northrop, traveled to Rome to tell the Pope that the various stories about Palladism in Charleston were false. He knew several of the principal Charleston Masons and visited the Charleston Masonic lodge (said to have statues of Baphomet and Eve that were worshipped by the Masons). After his audience in Rome, Northrop was apparently ordered to keep quiet, and he never spoke on the subject again.

Eventually the deception grew too complicated to be sustained. There were fictitious characters in hiding, threats of assassinations, and more and more details that someone could try to confirm (like the particulars about Palladism in Charleston). Taxil finally announced that he would present Diana Vaughan to the public on April 19, 1897, in the Geographic Hall in Paris. The auditorium was packed with reporters, priests, and interested citizens when he mounted the stage and told them that Diana Vaughan was part of a twelve-year swindle. He ended his confession by saying, "I will admit to a further crime. I committed infanticide. Palladism is now dead for good. Its father just murdered it." A complete transcript of Taxil's confession was published in the weekly Parisian newspaper, *Le Frondeur*, on April 25, 1897. It was translated in volume 5 (1996) of *Heredom*, the transactions of the Scottish Rite Research Society.

The headline reads, "Twelve Years Under the Banner of the Church / The Prank of Palladism / Miss Diana Vaughan—The Devil at the Freemasons / A Conference held by M. Léo Taxil / At the Hall of the Geographic Society in Paris."

(Courtesy of Pierre Molliere, Librarian of the Grand Orient de France)

When de la Rive realized that he had been suckered into publishing the "Pike-Lucifer hoax" as truth, he renounced his writings on Diana Vaughan in the April 1897 issue of *Freemasonry Unmasked*. De la Rive still believed that Freemasonry was plotting against the Catholic Church, but he had enough honesty to admit that Taxil had duped him:

"With frightening cynicism the miserable person we shall not name here [Taxil] declared before an assembly especially convened for him that for twelve years he had prepared and carried out to the end the most extraordinary and most sacrilegious of hoaxes. We have always been careful to publish special articles concerning Palladism and Diana Vaughan. We are now giving in this issue a complete list of these articles, which can now be considered as not having existed."

Tarring Pike with the KKK

The second major attack against Pike is to associate him with the Ku Klux Klan, either as author of the Klan rituals, or as its Chief Judicial Officer, or as the Grand Dragon of Arkansas. Then once the association is made, the natural follow-up is something like "Look how awful that Masonic leader was." Or "Masons sure admire the writings of that vile Klansman." Or "How come those Masons don't renounce Albert Pike? He was a Klansman, after all."

These accusations against Pike at least have the ring of truth. He was an officer in the Confederate Army. He was famous for writing fraternal rituals. He was well known as a legal scholar. He was a leader of fraternal organizations. He was bitter that the federal government had confiscated his property. It's only a small step to go from these facts to conclude that Pike was involved with the Ku Klux Klan. The problem is that there's no evidence—plenty of hearsay, but no evidence—that Albert Pike was in the Klan. The Grand Lodge of British Columbia and Yukon's website said it well: "Research into primary source material will reveal that there isn't any primary source material."

The easiest idea to put to rest is that Pike authored the Klan rituals. Pike had a grandiloquent writing style and a vast vocabulary. Klan rituals (available at Internet auction sites and published on some websites) have none of the distinctive characteristics of Pike's verbal mannerisms. The Klan rituals are quite simply immature and childish and in no way similar to Pike's prose.

All other accusations can be traced back to claims made in two books published after Pike's death:

Fleming, Walter L., introduction to J. C. Lester and D. L. Wilson. *Ku Klux Klan: Its Origin, Growth, & Disbandment.* 1905.

Davis, Susan L. *Authentic History, Ku Klux Klan, 1865–1877.* 1924.

Albert Pike was never associated with the Klan during his lifetime when he might have contested the claim. Lester and Wilson's booklet, *Ku Klux Klan,* was published in 1884 and makes no mention of Pike. In Fleming's 1905 reprint, 14 years after Pike's death, Fleming's preface says that Pike was the "Chief Judicial Officer" of the Klan. This is the source and origin of the claim, and Fleming does not give any references or documentation. Susan L. Davis's *Authentic History* repeats the "Chief Judicial Officer" claim and adds to it that Nathan Bedford Forrest, founder of the Klan, appointed Pike Grand Dragon (state leader) of Arkansas. Like Fleming, Davis gives no sources for her claim, though she does cite Henry and Eppie Fielding of Fayetteville as saying Pike had them assist him in organizing the Klan in Arkansas.

That's it for source material. There are no contemporary letters, minute books, newspaper accounts, or diaries—nothing. In 1871, Pennsylvania Senator and Freemason John Scott chaired a U.S. Senate committee to investigate the Klan. Twelve volumes were required to publish the majority report, summarizing testimony from 52 witnesses. Albert Pike's name was never mentioned.

Fleming's introduction was published when the Klan was being romanticized; Davis's book came on the heels of the 1915 revival of the Klan when it was viewed as a force for civic good. At its peak the Klan had four million members, elected governors and a senator, and controlled several states through sympathetic legislatures. Albert Pike had been a prominent and popular Freemason, and associating him with the Klan was a boost to the organization and any members who could claim to have been in his good graces.

The bottom line is this: there are no primary documents, only secondhand and hearsay evidence published after Pike's death. Like Taxil's fraudulent Lucifer worship, the charges of Klan membership only appeared after Pike couldn't defend himself. If Pike is to be convicted as a member of the Ku Klux Klan, it must be on the basis of hearsay and circumstantial evidence, not fact.

The Elusive Mazzini Letter

Anyone who's spent a little time on the Internet has run into urban legends, and after you've seen several, you develop a sense of when something's wrong. Distant witnesses are a good tip-off: "It was my next door neighbor's old roommate's second cousin." Also telling are vague references to locations that can't be checked: "It was a dark summer night on the road leading to the lake." In this category of urban legends, there are alleged letters between Giuseppe Mazzini, an Italian who worked for the unification of Italy as a democracy, to Albert Pike, reprinted in a few books, but widely quoted on Internet conspiracy sites. Unlike Pike's "Luciferian Doctrine" or his position as "Chief Judicial Officer" of the Klan, I haven't been able to nail down the first appearance of the Mazzini-Pike correspondence.

According to the stories, Mazzini was head of the *Illuminati*, wrote to Pike on January 22, 1870, and outlined his plan to take over Freemasonry. "We must create a super rite, which will remain unknown, to which we will call those Masons of high degree whom we shall select … We will govern all Freemasonry which will become the one international center, the more powerful because its direction will be unknown." This letter was reprinted in *Occult Theocrasy* by Edith Starr Miller (who infamously accepted and translated the Taxil Hoax).

Pike allegedly replied to Mazzini on August 15, 1871, in a letter that was claimed to be on display in the British Museum long enough to be copied. The copy was published in the 1925 book of Cardinal Caro y Rodriguez of Santiago, Chili, *The Mystery of Freemasonry Unveiled*. William Guy Carr published excerpts in his *Pawns in the Game* (4th ed., 1952). Then in his later book, *Satan, Prince of this World*, Carr said, "The Keeper of Manuscripts recently informed the author [Carr] that this letter is NOT catalogued in the British Museum Library. It seems strange that a man of Cardinal Rodriguez's knowledge should have said that it WAS in 1925."

def•i•ni•tion

Adam Weishaupt formed the **Illuminati** (enlightened ones) in Bavaria in 1776. He became a Mason in 1777 and then recruited from lodges. The goal of the Illuminati was to increase morality, oppose evil, and reform the world by creating a secret network of influential people. Bavaria suppressed the order in 1784, though some believe it still exists as a shadowy group controlling world affairs.

Searching for the origins of the Pike letter is like locating "my next door neighbor's old roommate's second cousin." The search is made difficult by Carr's frequent lack of sources and documentation. It is suspicious that the letter is not catalogued in the British Museum. This could be evidence of a forgery—or confirmation of the power of the Freemasons to eliminate anything that exposes their evil plans!

Pike's alleged letter outlines his strategy for three world wars to bring about his evil plan for the world. The third world war, yet to come, will be horrible in its destruction of civilization as we know it. "We shall unleash the Nihilists and the atheists, and we shall provoke a formidable social cataclysm … The multitude, disillusioned with Christianity, … anxious for an ideal, but without knowing where to render its adoration, will receive the true light through the universal manifestation of the pure doctrine of Lucifer, brought finally out in the public view." This fits right in with the fictitious "Luciferian Doctrine" of Pike. Christians concerned about a vast plot working behind the scenes to destroy their religion have anxiously copied and spread the letter so the world knows the true nature of the "evil genius," Albert Pike.

If only those so concerned were equally critical in their reading. The letter has Pike describe the second war in these words, "The Second World War must be fomented by taking advantage of the differences between the Fascists and the political Zionists. This war must be brought about so that Nazism is destroyed and that the political Zionism be strong enough to institute a sovereign state of Israel in Palestine."

Not only was Pike smart enough to plan ahead three world wars for over a century, but he foresaw in 1871 that "Fascists" (a term first used in the 1920s) and "Nazis" (formed in 1919) would be involved in World War II. You have the evidence. Decide for yourself if Albert Pike was a superhuman genius, able to know far in advance about the creation of Fascism and Nazism, or if this is conclusive evidence of a hoax.

The Least You Need to Know

- Albert Pike rewrote the rituals for and reorganized the Scottish Rite, Southern Jurisdiction.

- He was a prominent and respected Masonic leader, but certainly not the head of American Masonry.

- Léo Taxil spent twelve years hoaxing the Catholic Church with his stories of Luciferian Freemasonry.

- Taxil invented the lie that Albert Pike and Masons secretly worship Lucifer.

- There is no evidence, only hearsay, that Albert Pike was an officer in the Ku Klux Klan

- The Pike-Mazzini letters about three world wars are forgeries.

Searching for Hidden Masonic Symbols

In This Chapter

◆ Conspiracists claim Washington, D.C., has hidden Masonic emblems

◆ The House of the Temple

◆ The Great Seal of the United States

◆ The "33" on Rolling Rock beer

There seems to be a natural desire for humans to "leave their marks." This can range from carving initials in a tree, to "Kilroy was here," to spray-painting graffiti on buildings and vehicles. Masons are probably not much different than others in this regard, but their propensity for leaving their marks has become an urban legend of enormous proportions. The purpose is never quite clear (maybe just because they can do it), but there are supposedly secret Masonic symbols just about everywhere—the street plan of Washington, D.C., the Great Seal of the United States, and even beer labels!

Freemasonry has attracted political leaders, scientists, musicians, authors, financiers, revolutionaries, and a surprising array of famous (and occasionally infamous) members. Any group that can connect men this powerful, so the reasoning goes, must be exerting some powerful influence beyond the stated purposes of encouraging brotherly love, relief, and truth. And thus was born the idea of Masonic conspiracies to mark their territory.

This chapter will discuss some of the most popular theories about hidden Masonic symbols: the streets of Washington, D.C., the back of the dollar bill, and Rolling Rock beer.

The Street Plan of Washington, D.C.

When I was younger I enjoyed reading Batman comics. I remember stories where Batman would chase villains who compulsively left "signatures" at crime scenes. Could I figure out the method to the villain's evil madness before Batman? Well, I often feel like I'm reading Batman comics again when I read some of the allegations made by anti-Masons warning an unsuspecting public of the evils perpetrated by the Masons.

Consider just a very few of the many claims put forth about the "giant Satanic talisman" that is the street plan of Washington, D.C. We'll see how well they hold up under rational examination.

◆ The four cornerstones of the District of Columbia were laid with Masonic ceremonies.

◆ Major Pierre L'Enfant, a Freemason, laid out the city.

◆ Freemasons George Washington and Thomas Jefferson added Masonic touches to the plan.

◆ The streets have an inverted pentagram within a pentagon pointing toward the President's House.

◆ The headquarters of the Scottish Rite, the House of the Temple, is on 16th Street, exactly 13 blocks north of the White House and in direct line with the pentagram.

Before looking at the various claims, it might be worthwhile to ask the question, "Why would the Masons do this?" The warnings about the symbols in the street plan all seem to allude to evils that have befallen our country because of the baneful influence of these Masonic talismans. The best conclusion I can reach is that deeply superstitious people concoct and believe these tall tales. In an earlier era, they would have sprinkled holy water everywhere to negate the evil influences; today they post warnings on the Internet.

The Cornerstone of the District of Columbia

On April 15, 1791, Alexandria Lodge No. 22 (later Alexandria-Washington Lodge) laid the southernmost boundary stone of the District of Columbia. The District was originally laid out as a 10-mile-square diamond with its southern tip in Virginia and its northern tip in Maryland. Major Andrew Ellicott and Benjamin Bannecker surveyed the District and placed boundary stones at one-mile intervals around the perimeter. There is no record of a ceremony—much less a Masonic one—associated with any of the other 99 boundary stones.

The Square Deal

Arguing with determined conspiracists can be trying. In their worldview, the absence of evidence is really evidence of how mighty the conspiracy is. According to this line of thinking, Masons are such a powerful secret society that they are able to hold private ceremonies, exclude (or eliminate!) witnesses, and suppress all lodge records, correspondence, and private diaries.

Major Pierre Charles L'Enfant

Major Pierre Charles L'Enfant was commissioned by George Washington to design the city of Washington. L'Enfant served from March 1791 to February 1792, and produced the basic design with two major centers for the city, the Capitol and the President's House, and broad avenues radiating out from each. He had a strong personality and often clashed with his superiors, which led Washington to dismiss him. Eager Freemasons with more enthusiasm than facts have claimed L'Enfant as a brother. It is unfortunate for them that there are no documents, either primary or secondary, showing L'Enfant was a Mason. (Of course the absence of documentation does show the power of the Masonic conspiracy!)

George Washington and Thomas Jefferson

George Washington is perhaps the most famous Freemason who ever lived. Thomas Jefferson, despite claims by enthusiasts and detractors, was not a Mason; there is nothing to connect Jefferson to the fraternity other than wishful thinking. The published papers of Washington, Jefferson, and L'Enfant show that it was Jefferson who corresponded with L'Enfant about the details of the city plan, and it was Jefferson who told him his services must end. Thus the two men with the greatest influence on the design of Washington were not Freemasons.

The Square Deal

Thomas Jefferson is often claimed to be a Mason, with his lodge given variously as Door to Virtue No. 44, Virginia, the Lodge of the Nine Sisters, Paris, or Charlottesville Lodge No. 90, Virginia. There is no mention of Freemasonry among his vast published papers. There is no contemporary evidence that he was a Mason. If a man as famous as Jefferson were a Mason, the smallest Masonic memento of his—even his signature on a lodge register—would be treasured and preserved by any lodge that might own it.

The Inverted Pentagram

In March 1792, an engraving of L'Enfant's city plan, prepared by non-Mason Andrew Ellicott, was published. It shows the major streets, the Capitol, the President's House, the mall, and the major design features familiar to millions of tourists to the city today. It also shows a partial pentagram with its southernmost point on the President's House, and a partial pentagon surrounding it. Anti-Masons have described this as "a giant Satanic talisman, an open door to the demonic world of darkness."

This is the 1792 engraving of the "Plan of the City of Washington." It shows a partial pentagram surrounded by three sides of a pentagon just north of the President's House.

(Geography and Map Division, Library of Congress, from www.freemasonry.bcy.ca.)

The first question to ask is, "Why is an inverted partial pentagram a symbol of evil?" A partial pentagram has no special meaning, but Éliphas Lévi (Alphonse-Louis Constant, 1810–1875) claimed in his 1861 *Doctrine and Ritual of High Magic* that one point up was a symbol of good and light, and one point down was a symbol of evil and darkness. Trevor McKeown, webmaster of the Grand Lodge of British Columbia and the Yukon, said, "No known graphical illustration associating the pentagram with evil appears before this." Years after Lévi's assertion, Anton Levey's Church of Satan adopted it as a symbol of Satan. In other words, an inverted pentagram has been associated with evil for only about 150 years, and certainly had no such connotation in 1792. If the inverted pentagram were such an important "Satanic talisman," wouldn't someone have noticed it earlier in the street plan of Washington?

Overlooking the fact that an inverted pentagram had no particular meaning in 1792, why weren't its lines completed? If it were such a powerful occult symbol, wouldn't its designers have made sure it was complete for full potency? Rhode Island Avenue, which travels southwest to northeast, stops at Connecticut and doesn't make it down to the southwest tip of the star. Wide streets mark only three sides of the surrounding pentagon. The northern edge of the pentagon is formed by normal-width P Street, and the northeast edge doesn't exist at all.

If the Masons were smart enough to include their "giant Satanic talisman" in the Washington's street plan, how could they be so dumb as to leave it incomplete? (Of course we did include a piggy, but I can't tell you where it is—it's a Masonic secret!)

The House of the Temple

One of the most impressive Masonic buildings in the world is located in Washington, D.C., at 1733 16th St., North West, at the corner of 16th and S Streets. This is the House of the Temple, the headquarters of the Supreme Council, 33°, for the Southern Jurisdiction, U.S.A. It was designed by noted architect John Russell Pope and patterned after the tomb of King Mausolos at Halikarnassos, one of the Seven Wonders of the Ancient World. Its cornerstone was laid in 1911 and it was completed in 1915.

The House of the Temple is of supreme importance only to non-Masons who do not understand the relationship between the Scottish Rite and grand lodges. The Supreme Council for the Southern Jurisdiction is called the "Mother Supreme Council of the World" because it was the first Supreme Council from which all others descend, not because it controls anyone. Conspiracists prefer to read Edith Starr Miller's *Occult Theocrasy* with its translation of Taxil's bogus Pike quote about Lucifer worship rather than Taxil's confession and de la Rive's recantation. (See Chapters 13 and 16 for details on the Taxil hoax.)

The Square Deal

John Russell Pope's first public commission in Washington, D.C., was the House of the Temple. It was hailed as one of the most beautiful buildings of the twentieth century when it was completed. After his triumph with the Scottish Rite headquarters building, he received commissions in Washington for the DAR Constitution Hall, the National Archives, the National Gallery of Art, the Thomas Jefferson Memorial, and the National City Christian Church.

According to those who worry about partial pentagrams, "The center of the pentagram is 16th St. where, thirteen blocks due north of the very center of the White House, the Masonic House of The Temple sits at the top of this occult iceberg." As you travel south from the House of the Temple, ten blocks takes you to H Street, the northern edge of Lafayette Park, and eleven blocks takes you to the front entrance of the White House grounds. If F Street, twelve blocks from the House of the Temple, were extended through the White House grounds, the White House would be sitting on top of it. Thirteen blocks south of 16th and S Streets is the northern edge of the Ellipse, a block south of the White House. The profoundly superstitious, who see something fundamentally evil in the number thirteen, will have to find some other symbolism for their twelve-block stroll from the Supreme Council to the White House.

One other complication with the significance of the location of the House of the Temple is that the Scottish Rite did not exist in 1792 when the map was published. The first Supreme Council was formed in 1801 in Charleston, South Carolina, and remained there until after 1868. The land for the current House of the Temple was originally purchased on 16th Street between L and M Streets (across from the National Geographic Society). When the lot proved to be too small for Pope's design, the current lot at 16th and S Streets was purchased some 120 years after the "Plan of the City of Washington" was published.

The Great Seal of the United States

In 1884, Harvard Professor Eliot Norton wrote that the reverse of the Great Seal of the United States, with the all-seeing eye of Providence at the top of an uncompleted pyramid, was "practically incapable of effective treatment; it can hardly, (however artistically treated by the designer,) look otherwise than as a dull emblem of a Masonic fraternity." And with that statement another undying urban legend was launched.

The Great Seal of the United States is not a Masonic emblem, nor does it contain hidden Masonic symbols. While the all-seeing eye is a common symbol used by Masons and others to represent God, when combined with a pyramid it has no official Masonic meaning. (Some lodges have subsequently used the eye in the pyramid as a design element, but it has never been adopted by any grand lodge as a symbol.)

The Square Deal

The motto on the Great Seal underneath the eye in the pyramid is *Novus Ordo Seclorum.* It does not mean "A New World Order." It does not mean "A New Secular Order." The Latin word *seclorum* is a contraction of *saeculorum,* the genitive plural of *saeculum,* which means generation, time, or age. *Novus Ordo Seclorum* thus means "New Order of the Ages"—nothing more, nothing less.

It is unfortunate, but Freemasons have contributed to this popular myth as much as anti-Masons. (With both sides supporting the same conclusion, albeit for different reasons, it has to be true, doesn't it?) The well-meaning Masons are usually amateur symbologists and numerologists who see significance in almost anything. They puff up with pride when they point to the great seal on a dollar and say, "My fraternity put that symbol there!" The anti-Masons want to show that the Masons are powerful and arrogant in foisting their symbolism on the unsuspecting American public, or maybe that the Masons control the Federal Reserve, or perhaps that Masons run everything or … Well, at least the anti-Masons know the Masons put their emblems there, especially the all-seeing eye, and they did it for all the wrong reasons.

The Square Deal

According to conspiracists, the date under the pyramid on the reverse of the Great Seal, MDCCLXXVI (1776) doesn't refer to the date of the Declaration of Independence. This actually refers to the date of the founding of the Illuminati of Bavaria, the shadowy group working to take over everything and establish a New World Order. It's only a coincidence that the year is the same as that of the Declaration of Independence.

The all-seeing eye of Providence is a long-established emblem of the omniscience of God, based on passages from the Bible.

> "Behold, the eye of the LORD is upon them that fear him, upon them that hope in his mercy." (Psalms 33:18)

> "The eyes of the LORD are upon the righteous, and his ears are open unto their cry." (Psalms 34:15)

> "The eyes of the LORD are in every place, beholding the evil and the good." (Proverbs 15:3)

> "For the ways of man are before the eyes of the LORD, and he pondereth all his goings." (Proverbs 5:21)

The Great Seal of the United States grew out of three separate Congressional committees. Like the design of the streets of Washington, D.C., there was virtually no Masonic involvement in the design of the Great Seal. It was after the fact that the story of Masonic involvement was added and inflated.

The First Committee

The first committee was created on July 4, 1776, and its members were Benjamin Franklin, Thomas Jefferson, and John Adams, with Pierre Du Simitière as artist and consultant. Of the four men involved, only Benjamin Franklin was a Freemason. Each of the three committee members proposed an allegorical design: that of Franklin, the only known Freemason involved at any stage, was Moses at the Red Sea with Pharaoh being overwhelmed; Jefferson's was Israel being led through the wilderness; and Adams's, the choice of Hercules between the rugged path of Virtue and the flowery meadow of Sloth. Not much Masonic here!

Du Simitière, the committee's consultant and a non-Mason, contributed several major design features that made their way into the final design of the Great Seal: the shield, "E Pluribus Unum," and the eye of providence in a radiant triangle. (See figure that follows.) The eye of providence on the current seal thus can be traced not to the Masons, but to a non-Mason consultant to the committee.

The design of the Great Seal proposed by Pierre du Simitière. This is the source of the eye of providence in a radiant triangle Great Seal.

(From the Library of Congress)

The Second and Third Committees

Congress declined the first committee's suggestions as well as those of its 1780 committee. Francis Hopkinson, consultant to the second committee, had several lasting ideas that eventually made it into the seal: white and red stripes within a blue background for the shield, a radiant constellation of thirteen stars, and an olive branch. Hopkinson's greatest contribution to the current seal came from his layout of a 1778 50-dollar colonial note in which he used an unfinished pyramid in the design. (See figure that follows.)

The third and last seal committee of 1782 produced a design that finally satisfied Congress. Charles Thomson, Secretary of Congress, and William Barton, artist and consultant, borrowed from earlier designs and sketched what at length became the Great Seal of the United States.

The "Remarks and Explanations" of Thomson and Barton are the only explanation of the symbols' meaning. Despite what others may believe, there's no reason to doubt the interpretation accepted by the Congress. "The Pyramid signified Strength and Duration: The Eye over it and the Motto [Annuit Coeptis, He (God) has favored our undertakings] allude to the many signal interpositions of providence in favor of the American cause."

The $50 colonial note de-signed by Francis Hopkinson. This is the source of the un-finished pyramid in the Great Seal of the United States.

(From Charles A. L. Totten, The Seal of History [1897])

Freemasons probably all along used the all-seeing eye as a symbol in the same way that it was used in the Bible. The first "official" use and definition of the all-seeing eye as a Masonic symbol seems to have come in 1819 with *The True Masonic Chart of Hieroglyphic Monitor* of Jeremy Ladd Cross—37 years after Congress adopted the design of the great seal. Here's how Cross explains the symbol: "And although our thoughts, words and actions, may be hidden from the eyes of man, yet that All-Seeing Eye, whom the Sun, Moon and Stars obey, and under whose watchful care even comets perform their stupendous revolutions, pervades the inmost recesses of the human heart, and will reward us according to our merits."

Rolling Rock Beer

Since I'm not superstitious, the "great Satanic talisman" in the street design of Washington doesn't do anything for me. The idea of Masonic symbols on the back of a dollar bill is nice, but only if I could get some free samples. Another urban legend involving Masons, however, is the motto on the back of Rolling Rock beer bottles, and I know exactly what to do with the beer I had to buy for my research!

The Latrobe Brewing Company started in 1893 in Latrobe, Pennsylvania. It closed during Prohibition, and started up again in 1933. In 1939, they introduced the

Rolling Rock brand of beer, and put the following statement on the back of their bottles:

> *Rolling Rock. From the glass lined tanks of Old Latrobe we tender this premium beer for your enjoyment, as a tribute to your good taste. It comes from the mountain springs to you.* "33"

From almost the first day the beer was introduced, people wanted to know what the mysterious "33" meant on the back of the bottles. The company maintains it stands for the year Prohibition ended, 1933, and the number of words in the statement. Many other reasons have been offered:

- Beer tastes best at 33°.

- Rolling Rock was brewed at 33°.

- The workers at the brewery belonged to union local number 33.

- The number of letters in Rolling Rock's ingredients—water, malt, rice, hops, corn, brewer's yeast—adds up to 33.

- It's somehow related to the 33° of Scottish Rite Freemasonry (my favorite reason).

Journalist Cecil Adams, author of *The Straight Dope*, contacted James Tito, whose family owned the brewery. Tito explained that the "33" got there by accident. As the family argued over the slogan to put on the bottle, a family member wrote "33" in large numbers under one slogan to emphasize how short it was. This was the slogan chosen, and the copy with the "33" was sent to the printer who assumed it was part of the slogan. The rest is history and the source of many a discussion at bars. The number 33 has assumed a certain mystique for Rolling Rock, and they use it in all sorts of advertising promotions. The myth that 33° Masons had something to do with Rolling Rock Beer has been put to rest. It is perhaps the only time I've been saddened to learn the truth about an urban legend.

The Least You Need to Know

- Pierre L'Enfant, the designer of the Washington, D.C., was not a Mason.

- The "great Satanic talisman" in the street plan of Washington, D.C., is nothing when carefully examined.

- The Scottish Rite was created after the city plan of Washington was published.

- The House of the Temple is not 13 blocks north of the White House.

- Masons did not design the Great Seal of the United States and the eye in the pyramid is not a Masonic symbol.

- The mysterious "33" at the end of the slogan on Rolling Rock beer bottles has nothing to do with Freemasonry.

Masonic Mythology: Knights Templar and Egypt

In This Chapter

- ◆ The Knights Templar were created in 1118
- ◆ Philip IV of France and Pope Clement V
- ◆ Templars go "underground"
- ◆ Chevalier Andrew Michael Ramsay's Oration of 1737
- ◆ Other myths that have been grafted onto the Templar legend

Of all the myths and legends swirling around Freemasonry, none has been as enduring or romantic as that of the Knights Templar. The connection of crusading knights with Freemasonry was first published in 1737 with Chevalier Andrew Michael Ramsay's *Oration before the Grand Lodge of France*. Soon thereafter all sorts of knightly orders appeared and attached themselves to Freemasonry. Eventually the Knights Templar came to be the principal crusaders associated with Ramsay's Oration. The Knights Templar of the York Rite and various Templar legends of the Scottish Rite followed.

The legend in its simplest form is that the Templars during their stay in Jerusalem discovered "secrets" buried beneath King Solomon's Temple. They carried these back to Europe with them when the crusaders were forced out of the Holy Land. After being suppressed by the king of France and the pope, the Templars went underground with their secrets and used Freemasonry as a "front organization." Those Masons that proved themselves were then invited to join the inner circle of Knights. Working backwards from the secrets found in Jerusalem, some have speculated they originated with the pharaohs in Egypt. These theories (built with virtually no factual evidence) provide a romantic epic that ends with the modern fraternity of Freemasonry.

This chapter will discuss the origin and destruction of the Knights Templar, Chevalier Ramsay's Oration, and the source of the myth that Freemasonry is descended from the Knights Templar.

The Historical Knights Templar

The Knights Templar were formed in 1118 by Hughes de Payens and eight other knights for the purpose of protecting pilgrims to and from the Holy Lands. They took the name "Poor Fellow Soldiers of Christ," and were unique in that members were soldiers who took monastic vows of the Catholic Church. King Baldwin of Jerusalem gave them quarters near the site of King Solomon's Temple; they became the "Poor Fellow Soldiers of Christ and the Temple of Solomon," and eventually the Knights of the Temple or Templars. As roving monastic soldiers, the Templars reported directly to the Pope, and were free from any control of local priests of bishops.

The Templars recruited from among the nobility, lived under austere conditions, and gained a reputation—especially among their enemies—as fierce warriors. They were not allowed to retreat if only outnumbered three to one, and if ordered by their leaders they would fight to the death or to victory, whichever came first. Templars joined the Order expecting to die in battle.

> **The Square Deal**
>
> The seal of the Knights Templar, adopted about 50 years after their founding, depicts two knights riding a single horse. It was symbolic of the knights' vows of poverty. They were so poor they had to share a horse. In later years, the Order had more than enough wealth for knights to have several horses.

The Square Deal

The Templar's banner was half black, half white, and called the "Beauséant." The black referred to the sins of the world they had left behind, and the white to the purity of the Order of the Temple. Alternatively the black referred to fierceness with which they fought their enemies, and white to the mercy they showed their allies. The banner always flew in battle and served as a rallying point for the knights.

When a knight joined the Templars he turned over his possessions, including land, to the Order. From time to time, the Order would inherit land and other wealth from grateful citizens. Over the centuries, the Templars amassed quite a fortune. Knights Templars met in preceptories spread throughout Europe, and they also became bankers. The Order would accept a deposit at one preceptory and issue a "letter of credit" that could be redeemed at another. The Templars gradually amassed a great fortune. The fact that they answered only to the Pope and were wealthy made them powerful indeed.

Philip the Fair, Clement V, and the Fall of the Templars

Philip IV, king of France, was called "the Fair" because of his good looks. Clement V was the first of the "Avignon Popes," settling in France in 1309. Clement appeared to fear Philip and to accede to his wishes. What Philip wished for was the wealth of the Templars.

On Friday, October 13, 1307, Philip had the Templars arrested and thrown into prison. One of Philip's counselors accused them of heresy and other crimes, and they were tortured until they confessed. On March 18, 1314, Jacques De Molay, the Grand Master of the Templars, was brought before the public to confess his sins and those of his Order. Instead he recanted his confession and was led off and burned at the stake. Thus ended the Poor Fellow Soldiers of Christ and the Temple of Solomon. Templars in some countries were absorbed into other orders, for example the Order of Christ in Portugal and the Teutonic Knights in Germany.

The Square Deal

A great legend has grown up around De Molay's last words. As he was being bound to the pyre, he denounced the treachery of the pope and king and summoned them to join him within a year at a tribunal before God. Philip and Clement both died within a year of De Molay's execution. True or not, there is a satisfying justice to the story.

Escaping Arrest and Going Underground in 1314

The few preceding paragraphs briefly outline the bare details of the Templars. Scores of books expand on the details, if you want to know more. It is everything that came afterward—hints, legends, rumors—that make the story lasting. The wealthiest and most powerful body of fighting men in the world was eliminated almost overnight. Were they really guilty of the horrible crimes to which they confessed under torture? Had greed and idleness supplanted their bravery and monastic simplicity? What happened to their money? What happened to their fleet of ships? What happened to all the rest of the knights that escaped torture?

The papal condemnation arrived in England on December 15, 1307, but no Templars were arrested until January 7, 1308. Strange to tell, few of the knights could be found and arrested, and less than £200 of their treasure remained in their London headquarters when it was raided. King Robert the Bruce of Scotland had already been excommunicated for other reasons, and so had little concern for the papal orders when they arrived in his country. Legend has it that those knights known to the Bruce were welcomed into the Scots army.

Hits and Myths

There are enough Templar legends to fill several books—just check out a bookstore and see for yourself. Some say the Shroud of Turin was a Templar relic that avoided confiscation by the pope. Others speculate about the disappearance of the Templar fleet from La Rochelle, France. There's even a persistent legend that much of the Templar treasure left La Rochelle and was buried on Oak Island in Nova Scotia, Canada. In the movie *National Treasure,* starring Nicholas Cage, it is implied that the Templar's treasure helped underwrite the American Revolution. At the end of the movie, Cage's character finds the buried treasure, which includes the lost Library of Alexandria!

Here's where the romance and legends start in full force. Faced with horrible tortures if captured, the Knights Templar in England went into hiding. Some say they became Freemasons and lost themselves in the artisans' lodges in England and Scotland. The heavy work of a stone masonry was nothing to men who had expected to die in battle. To more fully protect their sheltered existence, they introduced into Freemasonry the severe judicial penalties of the day for violation of the Mason's oath of membership. This explains why such stern penalties are associated with revealing what were just trade secrets.

Further, as they became better established in their new protective identities, they established an inner organization. The most faithful Masons, those who had proven their trustworthiness and loyalty in the lodge, were invited into this hidden "lodge within a lodge" and initiated into the Knights Templar to keep the tradition alive. Some 350 years after the suppression of the Order in 1314, the inner order of Freemasons revealed itself as the Masonic Knights Templar.

That's the story in a nutshell. Many, Masons and non-Masons alike, find it compelling and accept it as the origin of modern Freemasonry. The theory has gaps, but so does the Transition Theory of the transformation of a trade organization into a gentlemen's fraternity. For me, the gaps in the Templar Theory of Freemasonry are too big to handle and the Transition Theory makes the most sense.

The Square Deal

There are several non-Masonic orders of Knights Templar, such as the Sovereign Military Order of the Temple of Jerusalem. These are Christian organizations that encourage their members to charity and service. Most make no claim to descent from the original Poor Fellow Soldiers of Christ, though some hold out that they are the true descendents of the original order through some complicated genealogy. The only way to know if someone who calls himself a "Knight Templar" is a Mason is to ask.

Turning the Tide at Bannockburn

There's even more romance to the underground Templar story. By 1314, the Scots had been trying for years to gain independence from the English. King Edward II of England had brought an army of 40,000 into Scotland to crush the revolt. King Robert the Bruce had just 13,000 to oppose the English. The decisive battle occurred on St. John the Baptist Day, June 24, 1314, at Bannockburn. During part of the battle, several hundred English knights were routed by the sudden appearance of Scots supporters who emerged from the woods. The startled English didn't know who or how many were coming out of the woods and retreated.

The Templar legend is that it wasn't shouting camp followers with pitchforks that emerged from the woods but mounted, armored Knights Templars. The elite fighting men, so the story goes, were so devastating in their attack that the English turned and ran, giving the victory to the Scots. The Templars thus repaid Robert for giving them sanctuary from the papal torturers.

The Square Deal

The Royal Order of Scotland, dating back to the 1740s, is one of the oldest "high degree" groups basing membership on Freemasonry. The Royal Order's legend is that following the Battle of Bannockburn King Robert the Bruce created this special order of knighthood to recognize the knights who helped him win the victory. The hereditary Grand Master of the Royal Order is the King of the Scots, and an empty chair is left for him at gatherings.

The Oration of Chevalier Ramsay

There is one other significant player in Masonic-Templar connection. Chevalier Andrew Michael Ramsay, a Scotsman, was tutor to Charles Edward Stuart, "Bonnie Prince Charlie," and his brother in their French exile. Ramsay joined the Horn Lodge in Westminster in 1730, about the same time the Third Degree was being introduced. In 1737, he was the Grand Orator of some Masonic body in Paris, and gave an oration, apparently as part of the initiation of new members. It is famous because it contains in one place most of the major components of the high degrees.

Here are a few excerpts from Ramsay's oration, which was published in 1741 and later found in a manuscript version:

> "Our ancestors, the Crusaders, gathered together from all parts of Christendom in the Holy Land, desired thus to reunite into one sole Fraternity the individuals of all nations …
>
> Our founders were not simple workers in stone, nor yet curious geniuses; they were not only skilled architects, engaged in the construction of material temples, but also religious and warrior princes who designed to enliven, edify, and protect the living Temples of the Most High.
>
> King Solomon wrote in hieroglyphic characters, our statutes, our maxims and our mysteries, and this ancient book is the original Code of our Order. … After the destruction of the first Temple … the Great Cyrus … appointed Zerubbabel as Grand Master of the Lodge of Jerusalem and instructed him to lay the foundation of the Second Temple, where the mysterious book of Solomon was deposited. … This book … was lost until the time of the Crusades, when a part of it was rediscovered after the relief of Jerusalem.

The Kings, princes, and lords returned from Palestine to their own lands and there established divers Lodges …

By degrees, our Lodges and our Rites were neglected in most places. … Nevertheless, it preserved its splendor among those Scotsmen to whom the Kings of France confided during many centuries the safeguard of their royal persons."

Consider these points that Ramsay makes in his oration:

♦ The ancestors of the Masons were the "Crusaders."

♦ The founders were not just stone workers but skilled architects working to glorify God.

♦ King Solomon prepared the original Code of the Masons.

♦ A "mysterious book" is buried in the foundation of the Temple and later found.

♦ Returning royalty from Palestine established lodges in Europe.

♦ The Scots best preserved the traditions of the Crusading knights.

One of Ramsay's purposes seems to have been to give Freemasonry a more impressive genealogy, satisfactory to the French nobility being attracted to the fraternity. The crusading ancestors did this, as well as the skilled architects and warrior princes. Not in particular that Ramsay elevates Freemasonry above mere stone workers. Further it is "Kings, princes, and lords" returning from Palestine who establish lodges in Europe. There's enough in this pedigree of the fraternity to make anyone proud.

The "Crusaders" of Ramsay morphed into the Knights Templar. This makes sense as after 400 years the Templars had an aura of mystery and intrigue surrounding them. They were considered the bravest of the crusaders at a time of renewed interest in knightly chivalry. The betrayal, martyrdom, and legendary revenge of Jacques De Molay, the last Grand Master of the Knights Templar, is an inspiring tale.

The Square Deal

No one really knows where Ramsay got the idea that Crusaders were the ancestors of Freemasons. It could have been his own invention, or he could have repeated some tradition he heard in lodge. His Oration has had influence far beyond its length. He did not create a Masonic rite of several degrees as is asserted by some.

Finally, Ramsay has his countrymen, the Scots, preserve Freemasonry in its true "splendor." This is consistent with the Scots Masters, the superior Masons whom the Grand Lodge of France needed to regulate in 1743, just six years after Ramsay's Oration. (See Chapter 9 for more details.)

It is after his 1737 Oration that the theory of Masonic descent from the Templar grafts itself onto Masonry. There is, of course, a "chicken or the egg" argument here. Which came first: Ramsay's oration or the theory of Templar descent? In the absence of the slightest hint of any knightly connection with Freemasonry before 1737, I'm inclined to give the nod to Ramsay.

Other Connections to the Templars

The legends surrounding Masonry seem to grow by gradual additions. The Templar story is great, but there's the issue of what they discovered in the foundation of the Temple. Was it indeed a "mysterious book" written by King Solomon or something else? Some have conjectured that while in Egypt Moses learned "initiation" secrets of the Pharaohs, he passed these secrets on to his successors, and this was the knowledge that was hidden in the foundation of King Solomon's Temple.

There have been other speculations about what was buried and discovered in the foundation of King Solomon's Temple. Michael Baigent, Henry Lincoln, and Richard Leigh's *Holy Blood, Holy Grail* speculates that the secret found concerned the secret bloodline of Jesus. They speculate that Jesus and Mary Magdalene married and that she traveled across the Mediterranean Sea to France with their son.

The holy bloodline of Jesus is preserved in that of the kings of France. Supposedly the Roman Catholic Church didn't want this information known and went to great lengths to destroy those in possession of this "dangerous" knowledge. The Albigensian Crusade and the suppression of the Templars are two examples of the alleged Catholic attempts to destroy those who knew the secret of Jesus' bloodline. Dan Brown's *The Da Vinci Code* incorporates this idea of the secret bloodline of Jesus into its plot.

The Least You Need to Know

- The Knights Templar were a fierce order of warrior-monks formed in 1118 to protect pilgrims to the Holy Lands.

- The Templars' wealth led to their betrayal and suppression in 1314 by Philip IV of France and Pope Clement V.

◆ Legend says some of the Templars escaped torture and death by becoming Freemasons.

◆ Legend also says that new Templars first proved themselves as Freemasons before being selected as Knights.

◆ Chevalier Ramsay gave an oration in 1737 that attributed the origins of Freemasonry to crusading knights.

◆ There are many other extensions of the Knights Templar legend, not all connected with Freemasonry.

Chapter 16

Religious Concerns About Freemasonry

In This Chapter

- ◆ The Gothic Constitutions
- ◆ Anderson's 1723 *Constitutions of the Free-Masons*
- ◆ The first *Papal Encyclical* in 1738
- ◆ The 1784 *Papal Encyclical* "Humanum Genus"
- ◆ Other religious objections

Convincing evidence shows that Freemasonry began as a trade organization of members faithful to the Catholic Church. As they evolved into a gentlemen's club, they adopted the then-radical idea of religious toleration—agreeing that God exists, is central to their lives, and compels them to serve humanity, but stopping the discussion there. They've been in trouble ever since.

Freemasons have been attacked on religious grounds since shortly before the formation of the Premier Grand Lodge in 1717. Most notably, the Roman Catholic Church has issued a series of encyclicals against the fraternity accusing it, among many other things, of deposing the Pope from his civil princedom and supporting the liberty of youths to follow whatever religion they prefer when they come of age. (See Chapter 13 for more details.) The Portuguese Inquisition captured and tortured Freemasons to obtain confessions about the "true" inner workings of lodges. Most recently some Protestant Christians have raised objections to the fraternity and have tried to disfellowship them from their churches. There are also concerns from Christians about the ecumenical tendencies of Freemasonry.

One chapter is hardly adequate to consider the issue of Freemasonry and religion. But I'll try to address some of the most important historical objections and those heard frequently today.

The Religious Language of the Gothic Constitutions

Wallace McLeod, retired Professor of Classics, University of Toronto, and expert on the Gothic Constitutions, reconstructed and modernized the spelling of the "Standard Original" of the Gothic Constitutions in his 1986 Prestonian Lecture. All quotes that follow are from Professor McLeod's reconstruction.

The Gothic Constitutions were the governing documents of a group of Christian workers. This is not surprising as England was a Catholic country at the time, and the Freemasons were engaged in a great deal of church construction. The Constitutions all begin with a clearly Christian invocation. "The might of the Father of Heaven, with the wisdom of the glorious Son, through the grace and goodness of the Holy Ghost, that be three persons in one Godhead, be with us at our beginning, and give us grace so to govern us here in our living that we may come to His bliss that never shall have ending. Amen."

After the invocation and traditional history of Freemasonry, the Gothic Constitutions then give "charges" or instructions for the guidance of their members. The first two require that Freemasons are faithful to church and king. "The first charge is that ye shall be true men to God and the Holy Church; and that ye use no error nor heresy, by your understanding or by discreet or wise men's teaching. And also that ye shall be true liege men to the King without treason or falsehood; and that ye know no treason or treachery, but that ye amend it if ye may, or else warn the King or his council thereof."

Reverend James Anderson's 1723 *Constitutions of the Free-Masons* summarized the existing regulations and introduced religious toleration in Charge I. Concerning God and Religion.

A Mason is oblig'd by his Tenure, to obey the moral Law; and if he rightly understands the Art, he will never be a stupid Atheist, nor an irreligious Libertine. But though in ancient Times Masons were charg'd in every Country to be of the Religion of that Country or Nation, whatever it was, yet 'tis now thought more expedient only to oblige them to that Religion in which all Men agree, leaving their particular Opinions to themselves; that is, to be good Men and true, or Men of Honour and Honesty; by whatever Denominations or Persuasions they may [be] distinguish'd; whereby Masonry becomes the Center of Union, and the Means of conciliating true Friendship among Persons that must else have remain'd at a perpetual Distance.

The puzzlement with Anderson's summary charge is what exactly did he mean by "that Religion in which all Men agree." The Premier Grand Lodge had been formed in 1717, just 29 years after the Glorious Revolution of 1688 had deposed the Catholic James II in favor of the Protestant William and Mary. Tensions were still high between Catholics and Protestants, and it was a radical religious and political idea to suggest any friendship could exist between the two sides. While there has never been a formal pronouncement from the Grand Lodge of England, Charge I has generally been interpreted to mean that a beneficent God created the world and that He is the creator-father of all humankind.

The First Religious Attack

John Wycliffe (1330–1384), the reformer and translator of the Bible into English, attacked Freemasons in 1383 on economic—not religious—grounds, for behaving like a trade union. "For they conspire together that no man of their craft shall take less on a day than they set. ... And that none of them shall do ought but only hew stone, though he might profit his master ... by laying on a wall ..." In other words, Freemasons would not work for less than the set wage and they, as hewers of stone, would not take on work of another craft, the layers. Wycliffe, however, had no religious concerns with Freemasonry.

The first published religious attack appeared much later in 1698, nineteen years before the Premier Grand Lodge was formed in London in 1717. (This, by the way, is nice evidence that there was enough Masonic activity in London in 1698 for Mr. Winter to issue his warning.)

The leaflet that follows contains basically two charges against the fraternity. First, the members swear oaths "against all without their following" and presumably to support each other. Second, Freemasons are "meeters in secret," which is the way of "Evil-doers."

TOALLGODLYPEOPLE,

In the Citie of

LONDON.

Having thought it needful to warn you of the Mischiefs and Evils practiced in the Sight of GOD by those called Freed Masons, I say take Care lest their Ceremonies and secret Swearings take hold of you; and be wary that none cause you to err from Godliness. For this devllish Sect of Men are Meeters in secret which swear against all without their Following. They are the Anti Christ which was to come leading Men from Fear of God. For how should Men meet in secret Places and with secret Signs taking Care that none observe them to do the Work of GOD; are not these the Ways of Evil-doers?

Knowing how that God observeth privilly them that sit in Darkness they shall be smitten and the Secrets of their Hearts layed bare. Mingle not among this corrupt People lest you be found so at the World's Conflagration

---

Set forth as a Warning to this Christian Generation by

M. Winter, and Printed by R. Sare at Gray's

Inn-gate, in Holbourn.

1 6 9 8 .

Only one copy of Winter's 1698 anti-Masonic leaflet exists. It was discovered in 1943 in the collection of a Sheffield, England, Mason. It is only 4½" × 7⅞" in size and appears to have been stored between the pages of a book. It is now in the Library of the United Grand Lodge of England in London.

The Square Deal

The only actual penalties enforced by Masons are permanent expulsion from membership, suspension of membership for a fixed period, and reprimand. The symbolic judicial penalties vary from grand lodge to grand lodge, and have been eliminated by many.

The Freemasons' oath or obligation of membership goes back to the time of the Gothic Constitutions. "These charges that we have rehearsed, and all other that belong to Masonry, ye shall keep, so help you God and Halidom [that which you regard as sacred], and by this Book [the Bible] to your power. Amen." Over the years the wording has expanded to include specific injunctions for keeping the secrets and eighteenth-century English criminal penalties (traditional, but severe by modern standards).

Commenting on the penalties, Dr. Jim Tresner, Masonic student and author, said, "they are entirely symbolic and refer exclusively to the shame a good man should feel at the thought he had broken a promise."

It's not clear if the leaflet's objection is to Masons swearing to support each other, or to their swearing anything at all. I and many others would disagree that only "Evil-doers" meet in secret.

Papal Pronouncements Against Freemasonry

Pope Clement XII took notice of Freemasonry and in 1738 issued the first encyclical against the fraternity, "In Eminenti." The encyclical is too long to quote in full, but excerpts give a flavor for the condemnation. (From www.papalencyclicals.net, accessed October 7, 2005.)

> "Men of any Religion or sect, satisfied with the appearance of natural probity, are joined together ... by a strict and unbreakable bond which obliges them, both by an oath upon the Holy Bible and by a host of grievous punishment, to an inviolable silence about all that they do in secret together. ... All prudent and upright men have passed the same judgment on them as being depraved and perverted. For if they were not doing evil they would not have so great a hatred of the light. ... Therefore, bearing in mind the great harm which is often caused by such Societies ... and realizing that they do not hold by either civil or canonical sanctions and for the other just and reasonable motives known to us ... these same societies ... are to be condemned and prohibited ... under pain of excommunication ... from which no one can obtain the benefit of absolution, other than at the hour of death, except through Ourselves or the Roman Pontiff of the time. ... Moreover, We desire and command that ... inquisitors for heresy ... are to pursue and punish them with condign penalties as being the most suspect of heresy."

The Square Deal

There are many different kinds of papal pronouncements: constitutions, encyclicals, decrees, decretals, rescripts, and others. These popularly and often incorrectly are referred to as "bulls." A "bull" refers to the lead seal used to authenticate papal documents. According to the *Catholic Encyclopedia*, "For practical purposes a bull may be conveniently defined to be 'an Apostolic letter with a leaden seal.'" Generally a papal bull is used for more solemn pronouncements. None of those issued against Freemasonry have been bulls.

It appears Clement XII followed the same logic of the 1698 London leaflet: Freemasons bind themselves together by a solemn obligation and they meet in private. (Lodge meetings were hardly secret since Masons met in public taverns, wore distinctive regalia, and were well known for drinking and singing after their meetings.) Some have suggested that Clement was trying to influence the Hanoverian-Jacobite struggle in England and the restoration of the exiled Catholic James II. There has also been much fruitless speculation over what "the other just and reasonable motives known to" Clement were. A more practical motive for the condemnation could be the concern that the Masonic obligation might prevent a penitent from making a full confession.

About 20 papal pronouncements, some dealing very indirectly with Freemasonry, have been issued since "In Eminenti" in 1738. In 1864, Pius IX acknowledged in "Quanta Cura" that the Vatican's effects on Freemasonry were limited by civil authorities. "For they are not ashamed of affirming … that the Apostolic Constitutions, whereby secret societies are condemned (whether an oath of secrecy be or be not required in such societies), and whereby their frequenters and favorers are smitten with anathema—have no force in those regions of the world wherein associations of the kind are tolerated by the civil government." (From www.papalencyclicals.net, accessed October 7, 2005.)

The most sweeping condemnation was in Leo XIII's 1884 "Humanum Genus." He says mankind is "separated into two diverse and opposite parts, of which the one steadfastly contends for truth and virtue, the other of those things which are contrary to virtue and to truth. The one is the kingdom of God on earth, namely, the true Church of Jesus Christ … The other is the kingdom of Satan …" Leo said that Freemasonry belongs to the kingdom of Satan. He went on and condemned Freemasonry for supporting various unacceptable principles including that "power is held by the command or permission of the people, so that, when the popular will changes, rulers may lawfully be deposed" and that "each [youth] must be left at liberty to follow, when he comes of age, whatever [religion] he may prefer." Leo XIII also seemed to blame the demise of Papal civil authority on a Masonic conspiracy led by Freemason Giuseppe Garibaldi, the liberator and unifier of Italy. (From www.papalencyclicals.net, accessed October 7, 2005.)

Soon after he issued "Humanum Genus" in 1884, Leo XIII fell hook, line, and sinker for the hoax perpetrated by Léo Taxil. (See Chapter 13 for more details.) Taxil published a series of increasingly lurid books giving the "true inner secrets" of Masonic Lodges and what "really went on" in the fictitious coed "Palladium Lodges." Taxil's books are rife with tales of satanic worship and the conjuration of demons. All of

Taxil's "revelations" confirmed Leo XIII's conspiratorial ideas about Freemasonry. Taxil finally made a full and public confession of his hoax in 1897.

Canon Laws Against Freemasonry

The Roman Catholic *Code of Canon Law* further condemns Freemasonry. *Canon* 2335 of the *Code of Canon Law* (1918) says, "Those who join a Masonic sect or other societies of the same sort, which plot against the Church or against legitimate civil authority, incur ipso facto an excommunication simply reserved to the Holy See."

This canon puzzled British-American Freemasons, who never discuss either topic. (It's awfully hard to plot against the Church or civil authority if you can't talk about politics and religion!) It's as if the Vatican authorities confused British-American Freemasonry, staunchly apolitical and areligious, with French-style Grand Orient Masonry, which endorses candidates and has made strong anti-religious pronouncements. The fact that the Grand Orient is in the Vatican's next-door neighbor may explain their confusion.

def•i•ni•tion

A **canon** generally means a law or rule. "Canon Law" refers to the laws of the Roman Catholic and some other churches. It derives from the Greek word *kanon*, meaning a "measuring rod" or "rule."

During the pontificate of Paul VI (1963–1978), local church authorities were allowed to decide if Freemasonry in their areas violated Canon 2335. Freemasonry never formally prohibited Catholics from joining, but centuries of name calling left bitter feelings on both sides. Nonetheless, with case-by-case approval by local Church authorities, many Catholics became Freemasons.

In 1983, Canon 1374 of the new *Code of Canon Law* replaced Canon 2335. "One who joins an association which plots against the Church is to be punished with a just penalty; one who promotes or moderates such an association, however, is to be punished with an interdict." This new Canon seemed to remove the condemnation from British-American Freemasonry.

But just before the *Code of Canon Law* went into effect in 1983, Joseph Cardinal Ratzinger, then Prefect of the Office of the Sacred Congregation for the Doctrine of the Faith, and now Pope Benedict XVI, issued a clarification:

> "Therefore, the Church's negative judgment in regard to Masonic associations remains unchanged since their principles have always been considered

irreconcilable with the doctrine of the Church and, therefore, membership in them remains forbidden. The faithful who enroll in Masonic associations are in a state of grave sin and may not receive Holy Communion.

It is not within the competence of local ecclesiastical authorities to give a judgment on the nature of Masonic associations which would imply a derogation from what has been decided above ...."

The situation in 2005 thus seems to be where it was in 1738, though there are now many Catholics in Masonic lodges. Freemasons still hold private meetings and take a solemn obligation upon joining, and the Roman Catholic Church apparently still doesn't like this. The old condemnation of plotting against Church and civil authority seems to have fallen away, but "the other just and reasonable motives" known now to the Sacred Congregation appear to carry the day.

Who Speaks for Freemasonry?

Freemasonry is so decentralized that it's a wonder the organization holds together at all. Many men have had strong opinions about Freemasonry and what it means and what it should do. On occasion they have published books that have gained popularity, but this doesn't make them official spokesmen for Freemasonry. More importantly, it in no way makes their ideas about the fraternity binding on any other Mason.

Since the organization is hundreds of years old and has millions of members, it's easy to find Masons who have published just about any idea about the fraternity. And it's also easy to confuse the relationship between a Sovereign Grand Commander, an Imperial Potentate, a General Grand High Priest, and a Grand Master.

Thus it's not uncommon for a "researcher" to discover something written by "Illustrious Albert Pike, 33°, Sovereign Grand Commander of the Mother Supreme Council of the World," and to think it is a universal pronouncement, binding on all the fraternity. The reaction from most Masons is likely to be, "Albert who?" The reaction from knowledgeable Masons is likely to be, "I read it over and can't agree with all Pike said. He had a few good ideas, but his facts were a little off." This, by the way, was how Pike wanted it.

It's also not uncommon to find all sorts of people claiming to be Freemasons. For example, Helena Petrovna Blavatsky, founder in 1875 of the Theosophical Society (created "to investigate the hidden mysteries of Nature under every aspect possible, and the psychic and spiritual powers latent in man especially"), is claimed by Anti-Masons to have been a Freemason as a prelude to attacking the fraternity because of her writings. Blavatsky in fact attacked regular Freemasonry in her book *Isis Unveiled.* Aleister Crowley, notorious occultist, belonged to several irregular and unrecognized Masonic bodies, all beyond the reach of any regular grand lodge. Annie Besant, president of the Theosophical Society in 1907, was a Co-Mason, but this is no more a reflection on regular Freemasonry than a mail order "university" is a reflection on the academic policies of Harvard.

Who speaks for Freemasonry? The grand lodges alone have that authority, and then only within their jurisdiction. Anyone else is free to expound on the purposes or principles of the fraternity, but their opinions remain their own and are not binding on any Mason or any lodge.

General Religious Concerns

Much of the religious concern about Freemasonry comes from critics taking a few passages of Masonic ritual out of context, applying their interpretation to the words, and then condemning Freemasonry. There's also a tendency to criticize the activity if the Masons do it, but to turn a blind eye if someone else does it.

The "Worshipful" Master

The 1993 *SBC Report on Freemasonry*, issued by the Southern Baptist Convention, identified eight "tenets and teachings" of Freemasonry that it found incompatible with Christianity. The first incompatibility included, "The prevalent use of offensive concepts, titles, and terms such as 'Worshipful Master' for the leaders of the lodge."

First the title "Master" caused concern. Jesus said, "Neither be ye called masters: for one is your Master, even Christ." (Matthew 23:10) If this admonition were followed consistently, then we wouldn't have scoutmasters, concert masters, masters of ships, or master plumbers. The word means "A worker qualified to teach apprentices and carry on the craft independently," and this is exactly how Freemasonry uses the term.

Then there is the adjective "worshipful." Freemasonry is an old institution that proudly (and perhaps stubbornly) insists on preserving traditions. The Regius Manuscript of about 1390, the oldest document dealing with Freemasonry, ends with the words, "Amen! Amen! So mote it be! So say we all for charity." When prayers are offered in a lodge today, the Masons present will all say, "So mote it be" after the "Amen," thus continuing a 600-year-old tradition.

Similarly, the presiding officer of a Masonic lodge, the Master, is given the old British honorific title of "worshipful." He is thus known as the "Worshipful Master." The definition of "worshipful" in modern American English is moving toward "Given to or expressive of worship; reverent or adoring," and away from its original meaning of "honorable."

The Square Deal

Freemasons have developed an adjectival hierarchy for describing their officers. As generally used by most grand lodges, "Most Worshipful" is reserved for the Grand Master and Past Grand Masters. "Right Worshipful" and sometimes "Very Worshipful" are used for most other grand officers. (The Grand Master and Past Grand Masters of Pennsylvania are "Right Worshipful.") The naming convention is idiosyncratic enough that you must consult each grand lodge's constitution to know what adjectives apply to a specific officer.

John Wycliffe's 1384 English translation of the Bible shows early usage of the word "worship" which Freemasons continue to employ. Wycliffe translates Matthew 19:10 as "Worschipe thi fadir and thi modir" while the King James Version (1611) renders this as "honor thy father and thy mother." English mayors and judicial officers are still addressed as "Your Worship" or "Worshipful," but this doesn't bother Masonic critics. It's only when Masons use old language that there's a problem.

The Secret Worship of Lucifer

One of the most repeated urban legends about Freemasonry is that the "secret" of High Degree Freemasonry is the worship of Lucifer carried on in secret coed "Palladian Lodges." The infamous lie was concocted by Léo Taxil, published by A. C. de la Rive, and translated by Edith Starr Miller, Lady Queenborough. "To you, Sovereign Grand Inspectors General, we say this, that you may repeat it to the Brethren of the 32nd, 31st and 30th degrees—The Masonic religion should be, by all of us initiates of the high degrees, maintained in the purity of the Luciferian doctrine … Yes, Lucifer is God, and unfortunately Adonay is also God …"

The quote and the "doctrine" are lies, part of a hoax perpetrated on the credulous by Taxil. After stringing along his "marks" for twelve years and making his living from publishing his "revelations," Taxil's hoax began to crumble under the weight of too many contradictions. In 1897, Taxil mounted the stage of the Geographic Hall in

Paris and confessed everything before slipping out of the auditorium. (See Chapter 13 for more details.) Taxil had the smug satisfaction of pulling off a masterful hoax, and the gullible, willing to believe the worst about their neighbors, continue to discover the "secret religion" of the Freemasons.

The Square Deal

A. C. de la Rive was an ardent anti-Mason and editor of the magazine *Freemasonry Unmasked*. After Taxil exposed his hoax, de la Rive wrote, "We have always been careful to publish special articles [in *Freemasonry Unmasked*] concerning Palladism … We are now giving in this issue a complete list of these articles which can now be considered as not having existed." It is a shame that Edith Starr Miller didn't do enough research to discover de la Rive's recantation.

Salvation by Works

In America, most lodges explain the presentation of the white lambskin apron to new members with these words, "The Lamb in all ages has been deemed an emblem of innocence. He therefore, who wears the Lambskin as the 'Badge of a Mason' is continually reminded of that purity of life and conduct, which is so essentially necessary to his gaining admission into the Celestial Lodge above, where the Supreme Architect of the Universe presides."

Critics of Freemasonry latch onto the phrase, "that purity of life and conduct, which is so essentially necessary to his gaining admission into the Celestial Lodge above," as evidence that Freemasonry is teaching works salvation. That is, it is through your own works that you gain salvation and not through faith in Jesus Christ. A Christian Mason understands that good works are necessary, not essential, to salvation, but that faith is essential, and through it one is necessarily moved to a purity of life and conduct.

Freemasonry is not a religion and does not teach salvation or any religious doctrine. Masons are expected to be mature in their faith when they join, and to seek greater knowledge in their own houses of worship. Freemasonry only provides fellowship for men who agree that God is central in their lives and compels them to greater service.

The Prevention of Evangelizing

Freemasonry has a long tradition of not discussing religion or politics in the lodge. This was codified in 1723 with the publication of Reverend James Anderson's *Constitutions of the Free-Masons*. "Charge VI. Of Behavior: No private piques or quarrels must be brought within the door of the lodge, far less any quarrels about religion, or Nations, or State policy ..."

Christians have an even longer tradition of evangelizing. Jesus instructed his followers, "Go ye therefore, and teach all nations, baptizing them in the name of the Father, and of the Son, and of the Holy Ghost." (Matthew 28:19)

Some critics conclude—incorrectly—that Freemasonry is designed to prevent Christians from performing the command from Jesus to tell the "good news" and evangelize, since religion is not discussed at lodge meetings. This flies in the face of common sense (not to mention good marketing). It would be just as inappropriate (and ineffective!) to stand up and evangelize during PTA, Scouting, or Little League meetings. There is nothing to prevent a Christian Mason (or PTA member) from contacting another member after a meeting and inviting them to church. In fact, I found out about my current church from a Brother Mason—after a lodge meeting.

Praying to the Great Architect of the Universe

God is infinite, and no finite expression can adequately describe more than a small aspect of Him. Prayers of the faithful may address Him by a characteristic appropriate to the need: Comforter, Guardian, or Father. Boy Scouts address God as the Great Scoutmaster, some physicians call Him the Divine Healer, and Freemasons often call him the Great Architect Of The Universe (abbreviated G.A.O.T.U.).

As explained in Chapter 2, this phrase was introduced in Reverend James Anderson's 1723 *Constitutions of the Free-Masons*, and he no doubt picked it up from John Calvin's *Institutes of Christian Religion*. God is referred to as "the Architect of the Universe" and his creation as "Architecture of the Universe" no less than ten times. In Calvin's Commentary on Psalm 19, God is called the "Great Architect" or "Architect of the Universe."

The first lesson taught in nearly every American Lodge is that no man should enter into any great or important undertaking without first invoking the blessing of Deity. Masons therefore pray frequently at their meetings to seek God's blessing on their efforts, to bless their food, and to seek health and recovery for sick members. A typical prayer given at the opening of a lodge is, "Supreme Grand Master of the

Universe: We would reverently invoke Thy blessing at this time: Wilt Thou be pleased to grant that this meeting, thus begun in order, may be conducted in peace, and closed in harmony. Amen."

The prayers at a lodge meeting are ecumenical, like those at a Lions Club or similar civic club. The prayers are not addressed to some "composite deity" or to some "Masonic God," but to the one living God who created the world, the Great Architect Of The Universe. A Masonic lodge knows nothing more about its members' beliefs than that they each believe in the God who created the universe. People not comfortable praying with others without knowing more about the specific religious beliefs would not be comfortable being Masons.

The Square Deal

I had a somewhat unpleasant discussion with a man at a public forum on Freemasonry. He started by asking in an accusatory tone, "To whom do Masons pray at lodge meetings?" I replied, "To God." "Well, to which god do you pray?" "To the God who created the universe." He pressed on, "Can you be more specific?" "I'm not sure I have the vocabulary to satisfy you. How many gods do you think created the universe?" He retorted, "That's not what I meant. I want to know to whom do Masons pray at Lodge meetings." Very little was resolved with that discussion.

Freemasonry Is a Religion

If a researcher manages to avoid the obvious pitfall of Taxil's "secret Luciferian worship," it's still possible to fall for the subtler trap that Freemasonry is a "religion." The members don't know it, the Worshipful Master has never been told, and the grand lodge is clueless. Nonetheless, erstwhile people have discovered this important secret that no Mason knows, and they want to save Freemasons from the errors of their ways.

The best response is from the "Statement on Freemasonry and Religion" prepared by the Masonic Information Center of the Masonic Service Association of North America in December 1993, and revised September 1998. As follows:

> **Basic Principles.** Freemasonry is not a religion, nor is it a substitute for religion. It requires of its members a belief in God as part of the obligation of every responsible adult, but advocates no sectarian faith or practice. Masonic ceremonies include prayers, both traditional and extempore, to reaffirm each individual's dependence on God and to seek divine guidance. Freemasonry is open to men of any faith, but religion may not be discussed at Masonic meetings.

The Supreme Being. Masons believe that there is one God and that people employ many different ways to seek, and to express what they know of God. Masonry primarily uses the appellation, "Grand Architect Of The Universe," and other nonsectarian titles, to address the Deity. In this way, persons of different faiths may join together in prayer, concentrating on God, rather than differences among themselves. Masonry believes in religious freedom and that the relationship between the individual and God is personal, private, and sacred.

Volume of the Sacred Law. An open Volume of the Sacred Law, "the rule and guide of life," is an essential part of every Masonic meeting. The Volume of the Sacred Law in the Judeo/Christian tradition is the Bible; to Freemasons of other faiths, it is the book held holy by them.

Freemasonry Compared with Religion. Freemasonry lacks the basic elements of religion: (a) It has no dogma or theology, no wish or means to enforce religious orthodoxy. (b) It offers no sacraments. (c) It does not claim to lead to salvation by works, by secret knowledge, or by any other means. The secrets of Freemasonry are concerned with modes of recognition, not with the means of salvation.

Freemasonry Supports Religion. Freemasonry is far from indifferent toward religion. Without interfering in religious practice, it expects each member to follow his own faith and to place his Duty to God above all other duties. Its moral teachings are acceptable to all religions.

The Least You Need To Know

- The Gothic Constitutions required Masons to be faithful Christians.

- The first religious attack on Freemasons in 1698 accused them of swearing oaths and meeting in secret.

- Anderson's 1723 *Constitutions of the Free-Masons* obliged Masons "to that Religion in which all Men agree."

- The first Papal Encyclical in 1738 against Masons accused them of swearing oaths, meeting in secret, and other unnamed charges.

- Leo XIII's 1884 encyclical accused the Masons of supporting the rights of citizens to change their government and youths to choose their own religion when they came of age.

- The Masonic worship of Lucifer is a lie, part of a hoax started in 1885.

Part 5

A Field Guide to Masonic Symbols and Jewelry

It wouldn't be surprising if you've run across Masonic jewelry before—maybe among your family heirlooms or in a flea market. This part gives you an overview of the many symbols used by the Masons and their meanings. Once you have a handle on the symbols, we'll show you how they're used in dozens of examples of pins, watches, medals, and costumes used by Masons. You should be much better prepared to identify things the next time you're in an antique shop.

Chapter 17

Masonic Symbols

In This Chapter

♦ Symbolism is a "private language" for Masons

♦ Working tools teach moral lessons

♦ King Solomon's Temple provides symbols

♦ Other borrowed symbols

A symbol is "something that represents something else by association, resemblance, or convention, especially a material object used to represent something invisible." An image of a mortarboard can convey the complex idea of graduation from high school or college. A picture of a jagged lightning bolt next to a wire fence immediately warns of electricity. The American flag—"Old Glory"—the "Stars and Stripes"—carries such powerful symbolism that people can be reduced to tears on seeing it.

Masonic symbols work much the same way. They usually represent abstract ideas that focus the thinking of those to whom they have been explained. But it's not enough that you know the symbolism of the stars and stripes or the battles it's been through for you to feel anything about it. Nor is it enough that you know that the square reminds Masons of the "square of virtue" for the symbol to mean something to you. It requires a deeper appreciation of the symbol for the significance to come out.

Symbols have served as a "private language" of Masons for centuries. Architectural tools and other symbols are presented and explained to new members. These symbols decorate lodges, aprons, and jewelry, and constantly remind Masons of the moral lessons they teach. This chapter takes a representative but not exhaustive look at Masonic symbols. You should get an appreciation of the private language of Masonic symbols, and you should be able to identify some attic and flea market treasures.

Working Tools

Every Mason belongs to a Blue Lodge that confers the first three degrees. It is here where you find the largest number of symbolic working tools. Of course not every grand lodge uses the same tools and symbols, especially when American and non-American lodge symbols are compared, and the symbols do not necessarily have the same precise meaning. What is the same, however, is that Masonic lodges use symbols to teach moral lessons and ethical behavior. We'll give the meanings of tools found in most American lodges that are derived from the books of William Preston of England and Thomas Smith Webb of Massachusetts. Some of the tools here are associated with the York Rite.

Unless noted otherwise, quotations that follow are from Jeremy Ladd Cross's *The True Masonic Chart or Hieroglyphic Monitor* (1860).

The square.

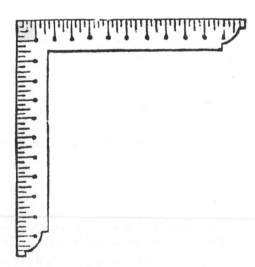

The *square* is one of the universal symbols of Freemasonry. It is the emblem of the Worshipful Master, worn on a ribbon or collar around his neck, and it is one of the working tools given to a Fellowcraft Mason. It teaches Masons to square their actions by "the square of virtue."

The Square Deal

Some have speculated that the square is an emblem of the Master because it represents the innermost secret of operative Masons: how to make and test a right angle (nothing here about Knights Templar bringing back secrets from the Holy Lands!). Without a local hardware store nearby, it's hard to make a square unless you know the "secrets" (or theorems) of geometry. This is also a possible explanation of why geometry and the 47th Problem of Euclid are so prominent in Masonic symbolism.

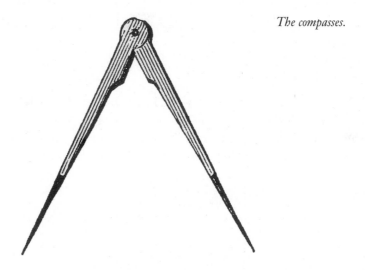

The compasses.

The *compasses* (or compass) are another universal Masonic symbol. As they draw a circle around a center point, the Mason is reminded to circumscribe his desires and keep his passions within due bounds. It is a constant reminder to a Mason to exercise self-restraint and self-control. Compasses, however, are never symbolically presented to a candidate as a working tool of a degree.

The Square Deal

The 1730 exposé *The Mystery of Free-Masonry* gives the following question and answer: "Q. How was the Master cloathed? A. In a yellow jacket and Blue Pair of Breeches." The explanation is a subtle allusion to the compasses: "The Master is not otherwise cloathed than common; the Question and Answer are only emblematical, the Yellow Jacket, the [brass] Compasses, and the Blue Breeches, the Steel Points."

The level.

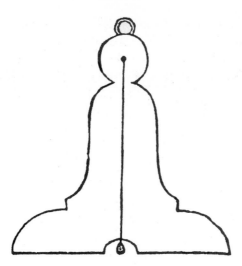

This tool usually appears with a plumb line suspended from the top. A line is drawn or engraved on the tool perpendicular to the base, and when the plumb line aligns with the drawn line, the base is level. The *level* reminds Masons they are "traveling upon the level of time to 'that undiscovered country from whose bourne no man ever returns.'" The Senior Warden of a lodge wears a level around his neck as the emblem of his office, and it is another one of the working tools presented to a Fellowcraft Mason. In many lodges as part of the final closing ceremony, all members and officers step down to the lodge floor so the meeting ends with everyone on a symbolic common level.

The plumb.

This tool works on a similar principle to a level. A plumb line is suspended from the top of the tool, and a line is drawn or etched parallel to the two edges. When the plumb line aligns with the drawn line, the sides are upright or plumb. The *plumb* is the emblem of the Junior Warden of a lodge, and admonishes Masons to walk uprightly in their several stations before God and men. It is the third of the working tools presented to a Fellowcraft Mason.

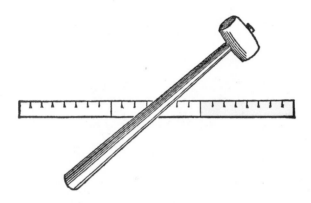

Twenty-four-inch gauge and common gavel.

These are the working tools presented to an Entered Apprentice Mason. The *twenty-four inch gauge* teaches a Mason to divide his day into three equal parts with "eight hours for the service of God, and a distressed worthy brother; eight for our usual vocations; and eight for refreshment and sleep." The *common gavel* is for a Mason to divest his heart and conscience of all the vices and superfluities of life, thereby fitting his mind as a living stone for that spiritual building, that house not made with hand, eternal in the heavens.

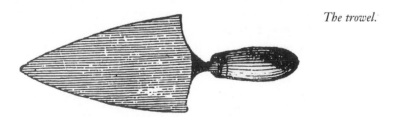

The trowel.

"The working tools of a Master Mason are all the implements of Masonry indiscriminately, but more especially the trowel. The *trowel* is an instrument made use of by operative masons, to spread the cement which unites a building into one common mass; but we, as free and accepted masons, are taught to make use of it for the more noble and glorious purpose of spreading the cement of Brotherly Love and affection;

that cement which unites us into one sacred band, or society of friends and brothers, among whom no contention should ever exist, but that noble contention, or rather emulation, of who can best work and best agree."

The chisel and mallet.

"The *chisel* morally demonstrates the advantages of discipline and education. The mind, like the diamond in its original state, is rude and unpolished. But as the effect of the chisel on the external coat soon presents to view the latent beauties of the diamond; so education discovers the latent virtues of the mind, and draws them forth to range the large field of matter and space to display the summit of human knowledge, our duty to God and to man. The *mallet* morally teaches to correct irregularities, and reduce man to a proper level; so that, by quiet deportment, he may, in the school of discipline learn to be content. What the mallet is to the workman, enlightened reason is to the passions; it curbs ambition, it depresses envy, it moderates anger, and it encourages good dispositions; whence arises among good masons that comely order, 'Which nothing earthly gives, or can destroy, the soul's calm sunshine, and the heart-felt joy.'" These are the working tools of a Mark Master Mason (the first degree in a Royal Arch Mason Chapter in the York Rite).

The crow, pickaxe, and spade.

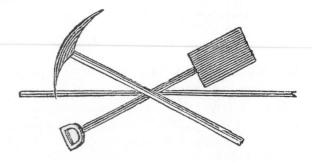

"The working tools of a Royal Arch Mason are the *crow, pickaxe,* and *spade.* The crow is used by operative masons to raise things of great weight and bulk, the pickaxe to loosen the soil and prepare it for digging, and the spade to remove rubbish. But the Royal Arch Mason is emblematically taught to use them for more noble purposes. By them, he is reminded that it is his sacred duty to lift from his mind the heavy weight of passions and prejudices which encumber his progress towards virtue, loosening the hold which long habits of sin and folly have had upon his disposition, and removing the rubbish of vice and ignorance, which prevents him from beholding that eternal foundation of truth and wisdom upon which he is to erect the spiritual and moral temple of his second life." Albert G. Mackey, *The Book of the Chapter,* 4th ed. (New York: Maynard, Merrill, & Co., 1858).

Past Master emblems: two variations seen in most American grand lodges and that of Pennsylvania and England.

(Latter courtesy of www.freemasonry.bcy.ca)

In the United States, the two most common forms of the *Past Master's emblem* are 1) compasses on a protractor with a sun in the middle, or 2) compasses, protractor, sun, and a square. A Worshipful Master should rule and govern his lodge with the same regularity as the sun. Some grand lodges, Pennsylvania and England, for example, use 3) the 47th Problem of Euclid (the Pythagorean Theorem) within a square.

Architectural Features of King Solomon's Temple

Masonic traditions about King Solomon's Temple are elaborations based on the Bible, and are not intended to be historically accurate. These allegories lead Masons to contemplate God's wondrous creation and their relationship with their Creator. They fit in the same class of literature as *The Littlest Angel*, a touching story based on the birth of Jesus, designed to inspire and move the reader. (I still have the copy read to me as a child, and I get a little misty when I read it even now.)

A Good Rule

Many American lodge rooms today have floors that are either tiled with black and white squares or carpeted with a black and white pattern. Some lodges have a small rectangular rug with a black and white pattern that's placed near the center of the lodge room. All of these are reminders of the legendary design of the floor of King Solomon's Temple.

According to Masonic tradition, the ground floor of King Solomon's Temple was paved with black and white stones. "The *Mosaic pavement* is emblematical of human life, checkered with good and evil; the *beautiful border* which surrounds it, those manifold blessings and comforts which surround us, and which we hope to enjoy by a faithful reliance on Divine Providence, which is hieroglyphically represented by the *blazing star* in the center."

The Mosaic pavement, border, and blazing star.

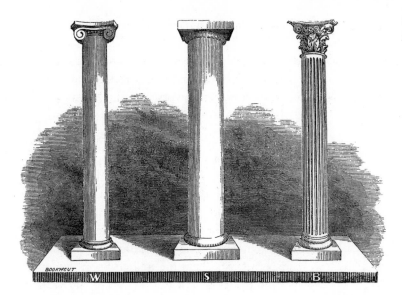

Representatives of wisdom, strength, and beauty.

Freemasonry "is said to be supported by *Wisdom*, *Strength*, and *Beauty*; because it is necessary that there should be wisdom to contrive, strength to support, and beauty to adorn, all great and important undertakings." These virtues are represented by three columns: wisdom by an Ionic column, strength by a Doric column, and beauty by a Corinthian column. The three legendary Grand Masters at the building of the Temple also represent these virtues. King Solomon symbolizes wisdom; Hiram King of Tyre, strength, since he supported Solomon in this massive building project; and Hiram Abiff, beauty, since he adorned the Temple with his castings.

A Good Rule

Often the Worshipful Master's podium is fashioned from an Ionic column, the Senior Warden's podium from a Doric column, and the Junior Warden's podium from a Corinthian column. Thus Masons seeing the podiums are reminded of the three principal supports of the lodge, the three legendary grand masters, and the roles they had in building the Temple at Jerusalem.

Perfect and rough ashlars.

"The *rough ashlar* is a stone as taken from the quarry in its rude and natural state. The *perfect ashlar* is a stone made ready by the hands of the workmen to be adjusted by the working tools of the Fellowcraft … by the rough ashlar, we are reminded of our rude and imperfect state by nature; by the perfect ashlar that state of perfection at which we hope to arrive by a virtuous education, our own endeavors, and the blessing of God …"

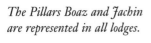

A Good Rule

Most American lodges will have rough and perfect ashlars, stones usually about 1'×1'×2', sitting on the dais in the east of the lodge room. These are constant reminders to Masons to strive for self-improvement.

The construction, placement, and naming of the *two pillars* outside King Solomon's temple are detailed in the Bible. "And king Solomon sent and fetched Hiram out of Tyre. He was a widow's son of the tribe of Naphtali, and his father was a man of Tyre, a worker in brass: and he was filled with wisdom, and understanding, and cunning to work all works in brass. And he came to king Solomon, and wrought all his work. For he cast two pillars of brass, of eighteen cubits high apiece: and a line of twelve cubits did compass either of them about … And he set up the pillars in the porch of the temple: and he set up the right pillar, and called the name thereof *Jachin:* and he set up the left pillar, and called the name thereof *Boaz.*" (1 Kings 7:13-15, 21 [KJV])

The Pillars Boaz and Jachin are represented in all lodges.

The name Boaz means "in strength" and Jachin means "Jah [Jehovah] will establish." Taken together they mean, "In strength Jehovah will establish," alluding to God's promise to King David to establish his kingdom in strength. Masonic tradition has the two pillars topped by globes, celestial and terrestrial, which are emblematic of the extent of God's creation. "Contemplating these bodies, we are inspired with a due reverence for the Deity and His works …"

A Good Rule

All of the early exposés of Masonic ritual give the passwords as **Boaz** and **Jachin**. Virtually all lodge rooms have two pillars in the west near the Senior Warden's station, and the exteriors of lodge halls are sometimes decorated with two pillars, in remembrance of those outside the porch of King Solomon's temple.

Winding stairs.

A short passage in the Bible describes the *winding stairs* leading to the middle chamber of King Solomon's temple. "And against the wall of the house he built chambers round about, against the walls of the house round about, both of the temple and of the oracle: and he made chambers round about … The door for the middle chamber

A Good Rule

Many American Masonic halls have a flight of three, five, and seven steps, either leading to the front door of the building, or somewhere within. A Mason walking up such a flight of stairs is presented with a wealth of imagery as he symbolically advances up and into King Solomon's Temple.

was in the right side of the house: and they went up with winding stairs into the middle chamber, and out of the middle into the third." (1 Kings 6:5, 8 [KJV])

Masonic tradition has the stairs consisting of three, five, and seven steps, each with a symbolic representation. The first three steps represent the principal officers of a lodge: Worshipful Master, Senior Warden, and Junior Warden. The middle five represent the five orders of architecture: Tuscan, Doric, Ionic, Corinthian, and Composite. The last seven remind the Mason of the seven liberal arts and sciences: grammar, rhetoric, logic, arithmetic, geometry, music, and astronomy.

Masonic legend has the *middle chamber of King Solomon's Temple* used as a meeting place of the craftsmen during the construction of the Temple. It is depicted with a blazing letter "G" suspended over the Worshipful Master, symbolizing geometry and God.

Symbolic middle chamber of King Solomon's Temple.

A Good Rule

All American lodge rooms have a large "G" over the Master's station in the east of the lodge. It is illuminated only when the Worshipful Master declares the lodge opened, and it is turned off as soon as he declares it closed.

Punched tin lantern with a "G."

(Courtesy of the Archives, Museum, and Library of the Supreme Council, 33°, S.J., Washington, D.C. Photo by Lee B. Ewing.)

An early American lodge used this *tin lantern with a "G"* either suspended over the Worshipful Master's station as the illuminated "G" or hung outside of the lodge hall to indicate a meeting was being held that evening.

Other Symbols

Freemasonry is omnivorous in its use of symbols. The most common are working tools and features of King Solomon's Temple. Masons, however, use a wealth of symbols, some borrowed, some invented, to teach and to inspire.

The tenets of a Mason's profession are Brotherly Love, Relief, and Truth. Masons are taught to practice the four cardinal virtues of *Fortitude, Prudence, Temperance,* and *Justice.*

A Good Rule

American lodges are often decorated with murals or sometimes statues of the female figures depicting the four cardinal virtues.

The Four Cardinal Virtues:
Fortitude, Prudence,
Temperance, and Justice.

"The *pot of incense* is an emblem of a pure heart, which is always an acceptable sacrifice to the Deity, and, as this glows with fervent heat, so should our hearts continually glow with gratitude to the great beneficent Author of our existence, for the manifold blessings and comforts we enjoy." The pot of incense is one of the symbols of the Master Mason Degree.

Pot of incense.

The beehive.

"The *beehive* is an emblem of industry, and recommends the practice of that virtue to all created beings, from the highest seraph in heaven, to the lowest reptile of the dust. It teaches us, that as we came into the world rational and intelligent beings, so we should ever be industrious ones, never sitting down contented while our fellow-creatures around us are in want, when it is in our power to relieve them, without inconvenience to ourselves." The beehive is one of the symbols of the Master Mason Degree.

The all-seeing eye.

The *all-seeing eye* is one of the emblems most commonly associated in the public mind with Freemasonry. It's widely believed (but hardly possible) that Masons put their eye on the Great Seal of the United States and thereby on the dollar bill. Hollywood loves to use the emblem as visual shorthand that a character is a Mason.

"Although our thoughts, words and actions, may be hidden from the eyes of men, yet that all-seeing eye, whom the Sun, Moon, and Stars obey, and under whose watchful care even Comets perform their stupendous revolutions, pervades the inmost recesses of the human Heart, and will reward us according to our merits." The imagery of God watching the actions of people probably came from the Bible, Psalms 33:13, "Behold, the eye of the LORD is upon them that fear him, upon them that hope in his mercy …" The all-seeing eye is one of the symbols of the Master Mason Degree.

Hits and Myths

Many say Freemasons inserted some of their emblems (chief among them the all-seeing eye) into the reverse of the Great Seal of the United States. But Benjamin Franklin was the only Mason to serve on any of the design committees (Thomas Jefferson served on the first committee, but there are no records that he was a Mason), and Franklin's suggested design had Moses parting the Red Sea. Pierre Du Simitiere, a non-Mason on the first committee, suggested the eye. Francis Hopkinson, a non-Mason on the second committee, had used an uncompleted pyramid (without an eye) on a 1778 50-dollar colonial note. The third committee took elements from the previous committees and produced our current seal—with no apparent Masonic input.

The anchor and the ark.

"The *anchor* and *ark* are emblems of a well-grounded hope, and a well-spent life. They are emblematical of that divine Ark, which safely wafts us over this tempestuous sea of troubles, and that Anchor which shall safely moor us in a peaceful harbor, where the wicked cease from troubling, and the weary shall find rest." The anchor and ark are symbols of the Master Mason Degree.

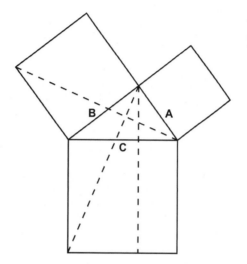

Forty-seventh Problem of Euclid or Pythagorean Theorem.

The *Forty-seventh Problem of Euclid* or Pythagorean Theorem is the famous theorem about right triangles: the sum of the squares of the legs is equal to the square of the hypotenuse: $A^2 + B^2 = C^2$.

"[The Forty-Seventh Problem of Euclid] was an invention of our ancient friend and brother, the great Pythagoras ... This wise philosopher enriched his mind abundantly in a general knowledge of things, and more especially in geometry, or masonry. On this subject, he drew out many problems and theorems; and among the most distinguished, he erected this, which, in the joy of his heart, he called Eureka, in the Grecian language signifying, 'I have found it' ... It teaches masons to be general lovers of the arts and sciences." The Forty-seventh Problem of Euclid is one of the symbols of the Master Mason Degree.

"The *hourglass* is an emblem of human life. Behold! How swiftly the sands run, and how rapidly our lives are drawing to a close! We cannot without astonishment behold the little particles which are contained in the machine—how they pass away almost imperceptibly! And yet, to our surprise, in the short space of an hour, they are all exhausted. Thus wastes man! Today, he puts forth the tender leaves of hope; tomorrow, blossoms, and bears his blushing honors thick upon him; the next day comes a frost, which nips the shoot; and when he thinks his greatness is still aspiring, he falls, like autumn leaves to enrich our mother earth." The hourglass is one of the symbols of the Master Mason Degree.

The hourglass.

The scythe.

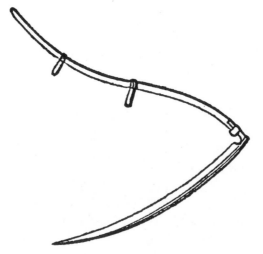

"The *scythe* is an emblem of time, which cuts the brittle thread of life, and launches us into eternity. Behold! What havoc the scythe of time makes among the human race! If by change we should escape the numerous evils incident to childhood and youth, and with health and vigor arrive to the years of manhood; yet, withal, we must soon be cut down by that all-devouring scythe of time, and be gathered into the land where our fathers have gone before us." The scythe is one of the symbols of the Master Mason Degree.

The Triple Tau of Royal Arch Masonry.

The *triple tau* within a triangle is the emblem of Royal Arch Masonry. Its origin is unknown, but it is thought to be a stylized "T" over an "H" standing for, perhaps, Hiram of Tyre or Holy Temple or Templum Hierosslyma (the Temple at Jerusalem).

Past High Priest emblem.

The *Past High Priest emblem* of a Royal Arch Chapter is three triangles with the four-lettered name of God (Jehovah or Yahweh in Hebrew) on each triangle. Resting on the triangles is a representation of the breastplate of the High Priest with twelve stones, one for each of the twelve tribes of Israel. (Ex. 28:15-21)

Fourteenth Degree Ring.

All Scottish Rite initiates are formally presented with a *Fourteenth Degree Ring* as part of the ritual of that degree. The ring ceremony is often a public event for family and friends where the new member's wife or special friend presents his ring to him. It is a plain gold band on which is a triangle with the Hebrew letter *yod*, the first letter of the unpronounceable name of God—Jehovah—Yahweh. The ring serves as a constant reminder to the wearer of his duty "in never mentioning His name, but with that reverential awe which is due from a creature to his Creator." Inside the ring is engraved the motto, "Virtus junxit, mors non separabit" (What virtue has joined, death cannot separate).

Thirty-Third Degree Ring.

Part of the ceremony of the Thirty-Third Degree in the Scottish Rite involves the presentation of a *Thirty-Third Degree Ring* to the candidate. The ring is composed of three gold bands, each about ⅛" wide, usually with a triangle containing the number "33." Some jewelers offer the ring with a row of small diamonds around the triangle. Inside the ring is engraved the motto *Deus meumque jus* ("God and my right"). This is the Latin version of the motto of Richard the Lion-Hearted (*Dieu et mon droit*).

Scottish Rite 33° double-headed eagle.

The *double-headed eagle* is the most widely used emblem of the Scottish Rite. If it is crowned (like the one here), it is the emblem of the Thirty-Third Degree. The triangle with "33" in it is optional as is the banner with the motto *Deus meumque jus*. Without the crown it is the emblem of the Thirty-Second Degree, and the motto is now *Spes mea in deo est* ("My hope is in God"). In the Northern Masonic Jurisdiction, USA, the eagle with wings up is reserved for active (voting) members of the Supreme Council. (The eagle shown here has its wings down.) The Southern Jurisdiction, USA, attaches no significance to the position of the wings.

> **A Good Rule**
>
> Like so many Masonic emblems, the origins of the double-headed eagle are confused. One of the ancestors of the Scottish Rite was a French high-degree system called the "Emperors of the East and West," and this group's emblem was the double-headed eagle, looking both east and west. But the family of Frederick the Great of Prussia, the legendary founder of the Scottish Rite, had a coat of arms that showed a double-headed eagle. Whatever the source, the eagle is now firmly associated with the Scottish Rite.

Knights Templar cross and crown.

The Knights Templar are the fourth Masonic body in the York Rite, and their membership is limited to Christian Masons. Their emblem is the *cross and crown*, taken from the promise in Revelation 2:10 (KJV), "Fear none of those things which thou shalt suffer: behold, the devil shall cast some of you into prison, that ye may be tried; and ye shall have tribulation ten days: be thou faithful unto death, and I will give thee a crown of life."

A Good Rule

The Knights Templar also use the motto from the vision of Constantine the Great, *In hoc signo vinces* ("In this sign [the cross] conquer"). The Roman Emperor Constantine saw these words and a cross in the sky before the battle of Saxa Rubra. He painted crosses on the shields of his soldiers, won the battle, and later made Christianity the official religion of the Roman Empire.

Eastern Star Emblem.

The *Eastern Star emblem* is a five-pointed star with points of red, yellow, blue, green, and white. Each point stands for a woman from the Bible: Adah, the daughter, represented by a sword and veil; Ruth, the widow, represented by a sheaf; Esther, the wife, represented by a crown and scepter; Martha, the sister, represented by a broken column; and Electa, the mother, represented by a cup. The qualities they symbolize are Fidelity, Constancy, Loyalty, Faith, and Love. In the center of the five star points is an altar with an open Bible.

The Least You Need to Know

- Masonic symbols and their meanings can vary from grand lodge to grand lodge.

- All Masons use symbols to teach the moral lessons of their degrees.

- Working tools are the most frequent source of symbols.

- Features of King Solomon's Temple are also a rich source of symbols.

- Many Masonic symbols have been borrowed from general cultural icons.

Chapter 18

Masonic Regalia

In This Chapter

- All branches of Freemasonry have distinctive regalia
- The apron is the unique Masonic badge
- Masons proudly wear jewelry, emblems, and costumes
- Other organizations have emblems that look Masonic

Freemasons are proud of their fraternity and show that pride by wearing Masonic emblems: rings, tie bars, lapel pins, cuff links, and more, though embroidered baseball caps and polo shirts are today as popular as jewelry for displaying emblems. It's no different from someone wearing the emblems of the Boy Scouts, Rotary, Kiwanis, their school, or their branch of the armed services. What does separate Freemasonry from other groups, however, is the sheer number of emblems associated with the fraternity and the centuries they have been used.

I became interested in Masonic and other emblematic jewelry when I worked in downtown Dallas, Texas, in the late 1960s. As I walked to lunch each day, I'd play a game of identifying lapel pins. My game might not interest you, but you might want to identify a piece of jewelry among your family heirlooms, an item at a flea market, a badge on a car, or an emblem on a grave marker or building. In this chapter I'll give you some broad guidelines for distinguishing common Masonic jewelry items—*A Field Guide to Masonic Jewelry*, if you will.

Aprons—Masonry's Unique Badge

Certain craftsmen—carpenters, blacksmiths, and stonemasons, for example—wear aprons to protect their clothes. Freemasons acknowledge their craft heritage by wearing aprons at their meetings. These are not worn for protection, but are now entirely symbolic of their craft heritage. When a Mason puts on his apron he is said to be "properly clothed." We'll give a sample of the sorts of aprons you might find in an attic or flea market.

William Hogarth, the English painter, satirist, and Freemason, depicted early English Masonic aprons in his satirical 1738 painting, *Night*, which was engraved by Charles Spooner and sold on the streets. The figure that follows shows a drunken Sir Thomas de Veil wearing a large apron and a square around his neck, the jewel of a Worshipful Master. The Tyler with a lantern, also in an apron, leads his tipsy brother home. It satirizes the social foibles of the day, and abounds with humorous details.

William Hogarth's Night
(1738) depicts two Masons in aprons walking home from a meeting.

In the following detail from Hogarth's *Night*, you can see that the Worshipful Master, Sir Thomas de Veil, wears his "jewel of office," a carpenter's (or mason's) square, on a ribbon or collar and a large white apron. He also wears a tricorn hat with oak bough (indicating that it's Restoration Day, May 29) and carries a walking stick in his right hand. The faithful Tyler assisting him home also wears a large white apron and carries a lantern. His sword, the emblem of his office, is under his left arm.

This detail from Hogarth's Night *clearly shows the large aprons of the two brothers and the Worshipful Master's square.*

Early Masonic aprons, prior to about 1800, are fine examples of folk art. They could be embroidered by a wife or mother for a Mason and can be wonderful examples of craftsmanship. Some aprons of this period were painted on the fabric.

The apron of Daniel D. Tompkins (1774–1825) is typical of an early home-decorated apron. It has an all-seeing eye on the flap, and on the body the sun, moon, square and compasses, level, trowel, anchor of hope, and beehive of industry. In the middle, steps lead up to the symbolic ground floor of King Solomon's Temple as represented by the checkered pavement. Centered on the pavement are the "three great lights" of the lodge, the Holy Bible, square, and compasses illuminated by three candles representing the sun, moon, and Master of the lodge. Pineapples, traditional symbols of hospitality, rather than the more common celestial and terrestrial globes, top the two pillars that represent Boaz and Jachin, the two pillars in front of King Solomon's Temple. Tompkins joined Hiram Lodge No. 72, Westchester County, N.Y., in 1800. He was governor of New York, 1807–1817, Vice President of the United States, 1817–1825, and Grand Master of New York, 1820–1821.

This is the handmade apron of Daniel D. Tompkins (1774–1825), Vice President of the United States and Grand Master of New York.

(From the collection of the Chancellor Robert R. Livingston Masonic Library of the Grand Lodge of New York.)

As Masonry became more popular and the demand for aprons increased, they began to be produced by local milliners or manufactured by regalia companies, still with unique designs. By the 1850s, most grand lodges had specified the design and color of aprons. Today nearly all aprons are commercially produced to grand lodge specifications, though there's still lots of room for local variations of design.

A typical apron that would have been presented years ago to a new Master Mason is white leather with dark blue ribbon borders and with a square, compasses, and "G" (for God and geometry) on the body and an all-seeing eye on the flap. In America, most lodges provide plain white canvas aprons for attendees, and presentation aprons are kept at home as valued mementos. Most contemporary American presentation aprons are plain white leather with no decorations.

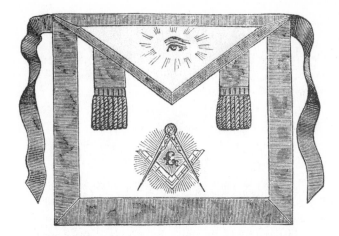

This Master Mason leather presentation apron would have dark blue ribbon borders imprinted with an all-seeing eye, square, compasses, and "G."

Apron designs in Britain and Europe are somewhat different from America. A Master Mason there is presented with a white leather apron with light blue silk borders, tasseled silk ribbons, and three silk rosettes. Upon becoming a Past Master the three rosettes would be replaced with silver "T"s (called "taus" after the Greek letter). There is not as much variation in British and European Past Master aprons as in America.

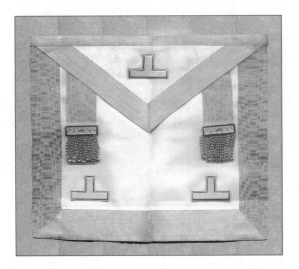

This British and European style Past Master apron has three "taus"; a Master Mason apron would have silk rosettes in place of the "taus."

A Good Rule

English and most European Masons are expected to carry their regalia with them when they attend lodge, though a lodge usually has a few "loaner" aprons if someone forgets. American lodges usually furnish white canvas aprons for all Master Masons and canvas aprons with the Past Master emblem printed on it for Past Masters. Past Masters may bring their own presentation apron to American lodges, especially if it's a special meeting.

American lodges have a set of "officer aprons" with the emblems of each office embroidered on them. They are worn by the officers during the meetings and can be simple or ornate. Upon completing a term as Worshipful Master, most American lodges give the outgoing Master a presentation apron to wear on special occasions. These have dozens of styles, some unique to the lodge. Usually the name of the lodge and year of service are embroidered on the apron.

On the left is an ornate Worshipful Master apron with a square (the emblem of office) and gavel. On the right is my Past Master apron from Patmos Lodge No. 70, Ellicott City, Maryland.

(Courtesy of the Museum of the Supreme Council, 33°, S.J., Washington, D.C.)

Royal Arch Masons, the first York Rite body after the Blue Lodge, wear aprons bordered in red with a triple tau on the flap. The red denotes the fervency and zeal of Royal Arch Masons who have advanced thus far beyond the Master Mason Degree. A Past High Priest apron is decorated with fringe and a Past High Priest emblem.

On the left is the apron worn by Royal Arch Masons at meetings, and on the right is my Past High Priest apron from Zeredathah Chapter No. 35, Laurel, Maryland.

Awards for Past Service

Upon completing a year presiding as Worshipful Master of a lodge, a Mason becomes a Past Master. This is the highest honor that can be bestowed on a member by a Blue Lodge. Many lodges give their Past Masters an ornately embroidered apron and a medal or a jewel. A Past Master jewel nearly always includes the Past Master emblem with bars for engraving the recipient's and lodge's names, and a gavel is often included in the design. The designs are limited only by the imagination of the jeweler and the treasury of the lodge. You can find past officer jewels with coats of arms and monograms as well as tools of every sort.

The Square Deal

A jewel is an emblem worn by a Mason to indicate membership or position. A Masonic officer wears a collar or cord around his neck with the jewel of his office suspended from it. For example, the Worshipful Master wears a carpenter's (or mason's) square, the Senior Warden a level, and the Junior Warden a plumb. After presiding over a Masonic organization, a Mason is usually presented with a past officer's jewel. The jewels of current officers are usually larger, simpler, and less expensive than past officer's jewels.

This plate from Daniel Sickel's General Ahiman Rezon and Freemason's Guide *(1865) shows the jewels worn by lodge officers during a meeting, usually hung from a ribbon or collar*

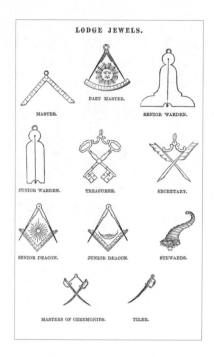

My Past Master jewel falls into the large middle ground of presentation jewels. The bar at the top is engraved with my name and decorated with a small all-seeing eye and a square and compasses. The name of the lodge and date of presentation are engraved on the back. Note that this jewel has the compasses and protractor, but no square. It has a pin back and is worn on the jacket breast pocket.

This is my 1979 Past Master jewel from Patmos Lodge No. 70, Ellicott City, Maryland.

Some lodges produce unique medals for their Past Masters. A fine example of a custom Masonic jewel is from Holland Lodge No. 8, New York City. Tiffany & Co. made this gold and platinum jewel in 1938 for Martin L. Scott. It is worn on a ribbon around the neck.

A custom 1938 Past Master jewel from Holland Lodge No. 8 of New York City.

(Courtesy www. phoenixmasonry.org)

Royal Arch Mason Chapters provide Past High Priest jewels for their outgoing presiding officers, though not as often as decades before. These jewels incorporate three triangular plates with Jehovah engraved in Hebrew and a replica of the High Priest's breastplate. Sometimes the breastplate is enameled, sometimes it is set with stones. A keystone, the emblem of the Mark Master Mason Degree in the Royal Arch Chapter, is frequently incorporated in the design. Presentation information is usually engraved on the back, and nearly all the other features are variable.

A Past Commander of a Knights Templar Commandery does not have a rigidly specified emblem, like a Past High Priest. The jewels usually incorporate a cross in their design and the words, *In hoc signo vinces* ("In this sign [the cross] conquer"). Presentation information is usually engraved on the back, and nearly all the other features are variable.

A 1902 Past High Priest jewel with stones set on the High Priest's breastplate presented to John Cheshire.

(Courtesy of the Museum of the Supreme Council, 33°, S.J., Washington, D.C.)

The 1837 Past Commander's jewel of Lew E. Worth, presented by Aurora Commandery No. 22, Illinois.

(Courtesy of the Museum of the Supreme Council, 33°, S.J., Washington, D.C.)

The two most important elements of an Eastern Star Past Matron's jewel are the star emblem and a gavel. The jewels can look like a Past Master's jewel, or a brooch. They can be enameled or they can have colored stones on each star point.

The 1902 Past Matron's jewel of Sophia Dietz of Golden Rod Chapter No. 205, Chicago. The gavel pin guard indicates she was a Past Matron.

(Courtesy of the Museum of the Supreme Council, 33°, S.J., Washington, D.C.)

Thirty-Third Degree Masons can wear a jewel suspended from a white ribbon, called the "Grand Decorations of the Order." "The Grand Decorations of the Order rest on a Teutonic Cross. It is composed of a nine-pointed star, formed by three triangles of gold, one upon the other, and interlaced. From the lower part of the left side toward the upper part of the right extends a sword, and, in the opposite direction, a hand of Justice. In the middle is the shield of the Order, blue; upon the shield is [a double-headed eagle holding a sword]; on the [right] side of the shield is a golden balance, and on the [left] a golden compass resting on a golden square. Around the whole shield runs a stripe of blue, lettered in gold with the Latin words *Ordo ab Chao* "Order from Chaos"; and this stripe is enclosed by a double circle formed by two serpents of gold, each holding his tail in his mouth. Of the smaller triangles formed by the intersection of the principal ones, those nine that are nearest the blue stripe are colored red, and on each is one of the letters that constitute the word *SAPIENTIA* "wisdom."

A Good Rule

Under normal circumstances it's considered bad form to wear the official regalia of one branch of Masonry at a meeting of another. (Lapel pins, tie bars, cuff links, etc., are not considered official regalia and can be worn anywhere.) Thus a Thirty-Third Degree Mason or Past Commander of a Commandery of Knights Templar would not be recognizable at a Blue Lodge meeting by their regalia. In fact, they would be "outranked" by the Worshipful Master and always by the Grand Master.

A Thirty-Third Degree Mason wears a jewel like this on his jacket pocket.

(Courtesy of the Museum of the Supreme Council, 33°, S.J., Washington, D.C.)

This is a close-up of the "Grand Decorations of the Order."

(Courtesy of the Museum of the Supreme Council, 33°, S.J., Washington, D.C.)

Lapel Pins and Other Personal Jewelry

Styles and tastes in jewelry change, and ornate breast jewels are not worn as often today as in earlier years. (The cost of gold is another factor limiting their popularity!) Watch fobs were common when vests and pocket watches were popular, but are more likely found among the family's heirlooms. Today you're most likely to see fraternal emblems on a lapel pin or on a car badge (a 2–3" circular emblem, usually attached to the rear of a car).

The square and compasses with a "G" is the most common Masonic emblem, either by itself or with other elements. The emblem reminds the wearer to square his actions by the square of virtue, to circumscribe his passions and desires, and to remember that God should be in the center of his life. The emblem can be found incorporated into hundreds of designs.

The square and compasses, usually with a "G" in America, is the most common emblem worn by Masons. It's shown here by itself, and incorporated into state designs for Texas and Maryland.

The trowel is the particular symbolic tool of a Master Mason, for with it he spreads "the cement of Brotherly Love and affection." Its shape lends itself nicely to a tie bar.

The trowel is a popular design for a Masonic tie bar, shown here with a square and compasses.

After-meeting refreshments are humorously referred to as the "Knife and Fork Degree." Any design with a knife, fork, and square and compasses would be a good-natured gift to a brother who either worked in the kitchen or who was known for his enjoyment of food.

A presiding Worshipful Master could wear a square as a lapel pin during his year "in the East." It is a miniature of the jewel he wears around his neck at every meeting. Lodges often have a pin that is passed down from Master to Master.

The "Knife and Fork Degree" tie bar is a humorous recognition of enthusiasm for after-lodge refreshments.

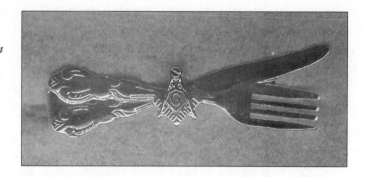

A presiding Worshipful Master could wear this Master's square lapel pin.

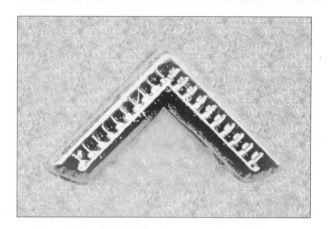

There are three common emblems used by Past Masters: compasses, protractor, and sun; compasses, protractor, square, and sun; and a square over the 47th Problem of Euclid. The first two are almost exclusively American, the latter is seen in Pennsylvania, Europe, and a few other grand lodges.

The keystone is the emblem of the Mark Master Mason Degree, the first degree in American Royal Arch Mason Chapters. It is used to represent Royal Arch Masonry in America. In Scotland, the Mark Master Mason Degree is controlled by Craft Lodges, and in England it is controlled by the Grand Lodge of Mark Master Masons. In neither country is it part of the Royal Arch.

These three pins are the usual designs of an American Past Master emblem. The third is seen almost only in Pennsylvania and Europe.

This Mark Master Mason keystone lapel pin represents the Royal Arch Chapter, the first body in the York Rite.

The past presiding officer of a Royal Arch Mason Chapter could wear a miniature Past High Priest emblem: three triangles with Jehovah or Yahweh engraved on them in Hebrew on which is a miniature of the breastplate of the high priest as described in the Bible (Exodus 28:15–21).

This lapel pin is the emblem of a Past High Priest (presiding officer) of a chapter of Royal Arch Masons.

The presiding officer of a Royal & Select Masters Council, the third body in the York Rite, is the Illustrious (or sometimes Thrice Illustrious) Master. His emblem is a pair of compasses opened on a protractor with a trowel in the center.

This is the emblem of a Past Illustrious Master of a Council of Royal and Select Masters, the third body in the York Rite.

While the York Rite does not have a central governing body, it has very loyal members. They proudly wear emblems of the various York Rite bodies, or a pin representing all four. The "union emblem" has the square and compasses of the Blue Lodge, the triple tau of the Royal Arch Mason Chapter, a sword, trowel, and broken triangle for the Royal and Select Masters Council, and the cross and crown of the Knights Templar Commandery.

This lapel pin is a union of the principal emblems of the four York Rite bodies: Blue Lodge, Royal Arch Mason Chapter, Royal & Select Masters Council, Knights Templar Commandery.

The Knight of the York Cross of Honor (K.Y.C.H.) was created in 1930 to honor exceptional service to the York Rite. The emblem is a crown with the emblems of the four bodies of the York Rite across the front. Membership is by invitation only to those who have presided over all four York Rite bodies. If you're a K.Y.C.H. and have served over a grand York Rite body, you become a Knight Grand Cross of Honor (K.G.C.H.). Depending on how many of the grand York Rite bodies you have served (up to four), you're known as a "one-star" through "four-star general."

The Red Cross of Constantine is a very exclusive invitational body for Christian Royal Arch Masons, generally limited to the most active Masons. Its emblem is an equal-armed cross with the letters "I," "H," "S," and "V" on the arms. They stand for *In hoc signo vinces*, "In this sign conquer."

This Knight of the York Cross of Honor emblem can be worn only by those who served as Past Master, Past High Priest, Past Thrice Illustrious Master, and Past Commander.

Members of the Red Cross of Constantine wear this emblem. The letters on the arms stand for In hoc signo vinces.

The double-headed eagle grasping a sword in its talons is the general emblem of the Scottish Rite. If it has a triangle on its breast with "32," then it's a 32° eagle; if the eagle's heads are crowned and the triangle has "33," then it's a 33° eagle. It makes no difference if the triangle is point up or point down; that's up to the jeweler.

Scottish Rite double-headed eagle pins. The one with the crown and "33" in the triangle is for 33° Masons, the other is for 32° Masons.

Several other emblems are used for the Thirty-Third Degree. The most common one in the Southern Jurisdiction is a patriarchal cross on a slant. It was adopted from the emblems of the leaders of the medieval Knights Templar. Another popular emblem is a crowned triangle with a "33" within it.

Thirty-Third Degree Masons can wear several emblems, including the slanted patriarchal cross and the crowned triangle with "33" in it.

The emblem of a member of the Ancient Arabic Order Nobles of the Mystic Shrine, or a Shriner, is a crescent formed by two tiger claws joined by a sphinx head, encircling a star, resting on or suspended from a scimitar. After the square and compasses, probably more variations exist on the Shriner emblem than any other Masonic emblem.

This pseudo-Arabic emblem with a crescent and scimitar identifies its wearer as a Shriner. Most people know them better for their red fezzes and little cars.

The Tall Cedars of Lebanon are another "fun" group for Master Masons to join, like the Shriners. The Tall Cedars wear distinctive pyramidal, tasseled hats decorated with a cedar, representative of those sent by Hiram, king of Tyre to King Solomon to help build the Temple at Jerusalem.

This pin is a miniature of the pyramid-shaped hats worn by Tall Cedars.

It would be possible to devote an entire book to nothing but personal items decorated with Masonic emblems. We don't have room for that, but there are a few others you should see. The Dudley Masonic pocket watch is a classic of watch-making excellence. Designed by William Wallace Dudley and manufactured by the Dudley Watch Company of Pennsylvania about 1920–1925, only a few thousand were ever made. The unique design feature of the watch is that Masonic working tools were used as the bridgework to support the gears. The watch had a crystal on the back so the beauty of the internal watch works could be enjoyed.

This is a back view of one of the few thousand Dudley Masonic pocket watches manufactured 1920–1925. The back has a crystal to show off the bridgework, made from a trowel, a square and compasses with a "G," and two levels (a plumb level and a modern spirit level).

Any Mason who owned a Dudley Masonic pocket watch surely would have had a fine Masonic fob on his watch chain. The Knights Templar emblem was a popular design for fobs, as was the double-headed Scottish Rite eagle and other emblems. The basic Knights Templar emblem is a circle with the motto *In hoc signo vinces*, "In this sign conquer." On top of the circle is a cross with a crown, reminding Christians that their faithfulness will be rewarded with a crown of life (Rev. 2:10).

The jewelry base of many fraternal fobs was a black enameled Maltese cross with crossed swords surmounted by a helmet with hinged visor. Jewelers used this common base for watch fobs for many different fraternal orders during the "Golden Age of Fraternalism," about 1870–1920.

A Knights Templar watch fob with a jeweled cross.

Car Badges

You don't need to drive very far in traffic before you'll see a car that's "advertising" something: a political candidate, a school, a sports team, or perhaps a Masonic organization. Masonic car badges are enameled metal, about 2½" in diameter, and are usually seen on the backs of cars. We'll show you some of the emblems you're likely to see on the road other than the easily recognized "standards" like the square and compasses and Shriners emblem.

Whether used for a lapel pin or a car badge, the primary emblem of a Thirty-Third Degree Mason is the crowned double-headed eagle.

This is the car badge of a Thirty-Third Degree Mason.

The Royal Order of Jesters is an invitational group limited to active Shriners. The Jesters' emblem is a crowned "Billiken," a mascot of good luck and fun; their motto is "Mirth Is King."

A Royal Order of Jesters car badge features their mascot, a crowned "Billiken."

The Order of the Amaranth is a group for women with a Masonic relative and Master Masons. The Amaranth was originally part of a three-degree system for women and men: Eastern Star, Queen of the South, and Amaranth. The emblem of the Amaranth is a crown surrounded by a wreath sitting on a sword.

This is the crown, sword, and wreath car badge of the Order of the Amaranth.

The Shriners are famous for their fun-loving attitudes, their parades, and their wonderful hospitals. The wives and other female relatives of Shriners have formed several organizations for fun, fellowship, and philanthropy. Everything they do is for fun and a good cause. The Ladies Oriental Shrine of North America's emblem is the Shrine emblem with a lotus blossom replacing the Shriners' star and the letters "L.O.S.N.A." on the scimitar and crescent. The Daughters of the Nile emblem replaces the Shriners' star with a rose and has "Daughters of the Nile" on the scimitar. The Daughters of Isis is affiliated with the Prince Hall Shriners, the Ancient Egyptian Arabic Order Nobles of the Mystic Shrine.

The female relatives of Shriners have formed several groups for fun, fellowship, and philanthropy: The Ladies Oriental Shrine of North America; Daughters of the Nile; and Daughters of Isis.

Prince Hall Royal Arch Masons have an organization for their female relatives: the Heroines of Jericho. The ritual ceremony derives from the biblical story of Rahab and the capture of Jericho by Joshua and the Hebrews (Joshua 2:1–21).

Membership in the International Order of the White Shrine of Jerusalem ("White Shrine" for short) is open to Christian Masons and their female relatives. Their emblem is a cross and shepherd's crook. Their motto is *In hoc signo spes mea*, "In this sign is my hope."

The car badge of Heroines of Jericho features the principal emblem of the group, a spinning wheel.

The car badge of the White Shrine of Jerusalem is a white cross and shepherd's crook.

Headgear: Hats, Fezzes, and Chapeaux

After aprons, unique headgear may be the most distinctive regalia worn by various branches of the Masons. Everyone knows the Shriners as "the guys in the red fezzes" who ride the little cars in the parades. (They're also the guys who spend over $625 million a year to provide free orthopedic care and burn treatment for children!) The Knights Templar wear military uniforms with swords and a plumed "chapeau" (and their foundation pays for sight-saving emergency eye operations).

These elaborate costumes and unusual hats were adopted during the "Golden Age of Fraternalism," approximately 1870–1920. During this fifty-year period, over 300 fraternal organizations were formed, including the Elks, Moose, Daughters of America, B'Nai B'Rith, Knights of Columbus, Degree of Pocahontas, and on and on. One of the appeals of these groups, in addition to mutual support (often in the form of formal insurance policies), philanthropy, and fellowship, was "non-normative" clothing, especially costumes and uniforms worn during parades.

Shriners wear a red fez with a Shrine emblem on the front and a black tassel. It is all part of the exotic pseudo-Arabic theme they adopted for themselves as a way to poke good-natured, tongue-in-cheek fun at the inflated and self-important titles of fraternal groups. The name of the member's local Shrine is on the fez, and the decoration can range from simple embroidery to elaborate beads and sequins.

This is my red fez from the Boumi Shriners of Baltimore, a fun social group for Master Masons.

Scottish Rite Masons wear small caps at their meetings, patterned after the dress regalia of British military orders. The caps are worn more widely in the Southern Jurisdiction than in the Northern Masonic Jurisdiction, with colors and emblems varying somewhat between the jurisdictions. The descriptions that follow are for the Southern Jurisdiction.

- ◆ Thirty-Second Degree Masons wear a black hat with a double-headed eagle embroidered on the front.

- ◆ The Knight Commander of the Court of Honour (KCCH) is a rank only in the Southern Jurisdiction, between the 32° and 33°. About 2.5 percent of S.J. Scottish Rite Masons have been awarded the KCCH, and they wear red caps with their cross emblem embroidered on the front.

- ◆ A white cap embroidered with a patriarchal cross is worn by 33° Inspectors General Honorary. About 1.5 percent of Scottish Rite Masons have received the 33°. (Active members of the Supreme Council, S.J., wear a purple cap.)

These caps are worn by Scottish Rite Masons in the Southern Jurisdiction at their meetings. The colors and emblems indicate the degree of the wearer: black—32°; red—32°, Knight Commander of the Court of Honor; white—33°.

While the Shriners are the largest Masonic fun group, they're certainly not the only one, and Shriners have no monopoly on unusual hats. The Grotto, Mystic Order Veiled Prophets of the Enchanted Realm (MOVPER), has a black fez with red tassel. The face of Mokanna, "the Veiled One," is on the front as is the name of the member's local grotto.

Usually the men wear the fezzes, but ladies in the Prince Hall Order of the Eastern Star, an organization of Prince Hall Masons and their female relatives, often wear white fezzes embroidered with the Eastern Star emblem and their chapter name or "O.E.S." for "Order of the Eastern Star."

The Tall Cedars of Lebanon are another fun group for Master Masons. Their distinctive hat is a green three-sided "pyramid" with a tassel and an image of a cedar on each side.

This image of Mokanna, "the Veiled One," is used by the Grottos as their emblem.

The distinctive headgear of the Tall Cedars of Lebanon is a green "pyramid" with a tassel.

(Courtesy of the Archives, Museum, and Library of the Supreme Council, 33°, S.J., Washington, D.C.)

Knights Templar and Other Uniforms

During 1870–1920, the heyday of American fraternalism—the "Golden Age"—the Knights Templar uniform represented the height of sartorial splendor for fraternal parade drill units. Their black uniforms were patterned after Civil War uniforms and were copied by other fraternal groups such as the Knights of Pythias, Knights of Columbus, Patriarchs Militant, Knights of the Maccabees, and many more.

Embellished with medals, sashes, swords, and gloves, the Templars' uniforms and distinctive plumed bicorn chapeaux attracted members who found parade-ground militarism romantic. The uniform worn by American Knights Templar today is a normal-length black uniform jacket (not a frock coat), with all the Victorian accoutrements except the sash.

The chapeau of a Knight Templar is a plumed hat that looked dashing in parades.

Prince Hall Knights Templar shown in full uniform of the 1800s. Insignia of rank on the jacket cuffs and shoulders distinguish members and officers.

(Courtesy of www. phoenixmasonry.org)

Scottish Rite uniforms were not common, but they followed the general style of the Knights Templar with sash, sword, gloves, medals, and distinctive hat. It's easy to imagine the striking image cut by a marching unit of men in uniforms like this.

A nineteenth-century 33° Mason in his fashionable uniform.

(Courtesy of www. phoenixmasonry.org)

The Shriners enthusiastically adopted exotic costumes for their parades and theatrical initiations. They had oriental bands, military parade units armed with scimitars, and mounted "Arabian" cavalry. Their officers also wore costumes in parades, at initiation ceremonies, and for special Shrine occasions.

James D. Robertson, M.D., the 1915 "Assistant Rabban" of Aleppo Shriners' Temple, Boston, Massachusetts. Other officers had colorful costumes, some simpler and some more(!) exotic.

(Image from History of Aleppo Temple, *2 vols., 1915)*

Similar Emblems of Other Groups

One of the ironies of the anti-Masonic movement of 1826–1840 is that the best attempts to destroy the "secret societies" backfired. The many published exposés of Masonic ritual provided easy templates for others to follow when they created new fraternal orders during the Golden Age of Fraternalism. Thus it's not surprising that the lodge room layout, officers, regalia, government structure, and emblems of many fraternal organizations are very similar to those of Freemasonry.

When trying to identify emblems on jewelry, a grave marker, or regalia, it's very easy to get confused. The various orders of fraternal knighthood had uniforms similar to the Knights Templar, generally varying only by the insignia, buttons, or buckles. One factory might produce swords for Knights Templar, Patriarchs Militant, Knights of Pythias, and many more. The swords would differ only with the engraving on the handles and blades, and the emblems on the scabbards. For example, the all-seeing eye is a common icon used to represent the omnipresent oversight of God (Psalm 33:18), and was used as an emblem by many fraternal groups. Other fraternities have "borrowed" Masonic regalia: Odd Fellows and Elks used to wear aprons, and the Junior Order of United American Mechanics modified the square and compasses as their logo.

It's not possible here to give a complete catalog of fraternal emblems, but we can point out some of the common ones likely to be found at a flea market, on grave markers, or in your family's chest of heirlooms. Associated with these groups are certificates, sashes, past officers' jewels, lapel pins, watch fobs, and such.

The Odd Fellows are known as the "Three Link Fraternity," and the links represent friendship, love, and truth. They started in the United States in 1819 in Baltimore, and by 1900, were the largest American fraternal organization. Odd Fellows were more of a working-class organization than Freemasonry and emphasized "cash and carry benefits" like insurance and help in finding a job if unemployed. After joining an Odd Fellow lodge a member could become a Patriarch and then a Patriarch Militant, the latter with uniforms like the Knights Templar.

The three-link emblem of the Independent Order of Odd Fellows. The three links stand for friendship, love, and truth.

(Image from www.ioof.org)

Not all fraternal aprons are Masonic. Up until about 1870, Odd Fellows wore aprons, usually decorated with their three links, and ornate collars. After that, they discontinued the aprons but retained the collars.

This photo shows an Odd Fellow with an apron and a collar from before 1870, when the Odd Fellows dropped the apron as part of their regalia. The three links on the apron identify the man as an Odd Fellow, and the crossed keys are the usual emblem of the treasurer.

(Courtesy www. phoenixmasonry.org)

The Rebekah is the ladies auxiliary of the Odd Fellows Lodge. Their emblem has many versions, usually involving an "R," three links, and a dove carrying an olive branch.

This is the emblem of the Rebekah, the female auxiliary of the Odd Fellows.

(Image from www.ioof.org)

The Encampment of Patriarchs of the Odd Fellows holds a position similar to the Chapter of Royal Arch Masons in Freemasonry. During the Golden Age of Fraternalism, the Patriarchs started wearing military-style uniforms, but they later spun off their uniformed rank as the Patriarchs Militant.

The Patriarchs of the Odd Fellows have as an emblem a tent with crossed shepherd crooks and three links.

(Image from www.ioof.org)

The Junior Order of United American Mechanics' emblem and lodge halls are often confused with the Masons. This group was started in 1853 as a junior branch of the Order of United American Mechanics. Within 30 years it had become an independent organization with no requirement that its members be "junior" in any way. The JOUAM was pro-native-born Americans and anti-immigrant. It is today a patriotic organization that promotes American principles. It has no connection at all with Freemasonry. I have heard it incorrectly referred to as the "Jr. Masons," probably because their emblem is so similar to the Masons' and their name includes "Junior."

The principal emblem of the Junior Order of United American Mechanics is the square and compasses with an arm and hammer in the center (where Masons would put a "G").

(Emblem from Constitution of the State Council of New Hampshire, JOUAM, 1903)

The Knights of Pythias were formed in 1864 with the idea of creating a fraternal order that could "rekindle the brotherly sentiment" between North and South. Their emblems are usually red, yellow, and blue with the letters "F," "C," and "B" for friendship, charity, and benevolence. Their designs nearly always incorporate a helmet, a shield, crossed battle axes, and a death head (memento mori).

During the heyday of fraternalism, 1870–1920, it would not be uncommon to find men belonging to many fraternal organizations. You can sometimes find custom-made jewelry items that incorporate the emblems of several organizations. The combinations of emblems are limited only by the jeweler's skill and the member's finances! The Masons' square and compass sitting on top of the Odd Fellows' three links was common enough that it was listed in jewelry catalogs.

The Knight of Pythias watch fob shown here has a knight's helmet on top of a shield with the letters "F," "B," and "C," crossed battle axes, crossed swords, and a skull and cross bones, an admonition to remember death (memento mori).

A custom-made fob or charm with the Odd Fellows' three links over the Knights of Pythias triangular emblem with "F, C, B," and a Masonic square and compass in the center of the triangle.

(From the collection of Arturo de Hoyos)

The Least You Need to Know

- All Masons wear aprons with the designs indicating their rank.

- Some Masonic groups give medals and special aprons to their past presiding officers.

- While scores of emblems exist for Masonic organizations, they use a few basic symbols.

◆ Some Masonic groups wear distinctive hats and uniforms.

◆ Other fraternal orders' emblems are similar because they borrowed from Freemasonry.

Appendix A

Glossary

all-seeing eye   A symbol of God watching humanity. "Behold, the eye of the LORD is upon them that fear him, upon them that hope in his mercy ..." (Psalms 33:13).

Ancient Landmarks   The Ancient Landmarks are those fundamental principles of Masonry that cannot be changed. Any deviation from them results in an organization that is not regular Freemasonry. There is no universally agreed-upon list of landmarks; groups of grand lodges that recognize each other rely upon consensus.

apron   Freemasons wear aprons as part of their guild inheritance. These are usually 18–24" square with a triangular flap at the top and are decorated to indicate rank. New Masons are presented with white lambskin aprons, symbolic of innocence and purity. American lodges provide white canvas aprons for meetings. The style of aprons varies widely around the world.

Blue Lodge   See *Symbolic Lodge*.

body   Body is the generic term used to refer to Masonic organizations rather than lodge, chapter, council, commandery, consistory, preceptory, priory, conclave, and so on. Thus Masons would say, "The York Rite is composed of four bodies," rather than, "The York Rite is composed of lodges, chapters, councils, and commanderies."

Capitular Masonry   Royal Arch Masonry is called Capitular Masonry because its bodies are called chapters, and capitulum is Latin for chapter.

chair degree   In many Masonic organizations, the presiding officer goes through a special installation ceremony, another degree in fact, where he receives the chair degree. A chair degree, with passwords, signs, and grips, is called such because it's only given to those who sit in the presiding officer's chair.

chartered lodge   A chartered lodge is a local lodge with a charter or warrant from a state or regional grand lodge. The lodge is obligated to obey the rules and regulations of the grand lodge that granted its charter.

clandestine   A lodge is clandestine if it works without a valid charter from a recognized grand lodge.

communicate   A Masonic degree is communicated to a candidate if it is either read or summarized. The Scottish Rite, with 29 degrees, regularly uses this short cut to reduce 30–60 hours of ritual ceremony. In other Masonic organizations, communication is reserved for extraordinary circumstances.

cowan   The 1647 records of Kilwinning Lodge explain that a cowan is a "Mason without the Word," which is a skilled craftsman who didn't belong to a lodge. In contemporary union terms, this would be a "scab worker." The dictionary definition is "a dry stone dyker," someone who builds without mortar.

Cryptic Masonry   The Degrees of Royal and Select Masters are called Cryptic Masonry because they deal with the legend of a crypt hidden under King Solomon's Temple to preserve Masonic secrets.

degree   A Masonic degree is a level of membership or the ceremony required to attain that level of membership. The first three degrees correspond to membership levels in a trade union: 1° Apprentice; 2° Fellowcraft (or journeyman); 3° Master Mason. Hundreds of degrees have been invented over the years, both serious and humorous.

Freemason   Freemasons are members of the "Ancient, Honorable Fraternity of Free and Accepted Masons." The terms Freemason and Mason are interchangeable as are Freemasonry and Masonry. The word is thought to refer originally to "freestone masons," skilled craftsmen who carved freestone (a soft, easily carved stone). Professor Andrew Prescott, Director of the Center for Research into Freemasonry, University of Sheffield, discovered the earliest known use of the word in the London Coroners' Rolls for 1325–1326.

"G"   The letter "G" stands for both geometry and God. Geometry was central to the work of operative masons, and God is central to the lives of speculative Masons.

G.A.O.T.U.   Great Architect of the Universe. See *Great Architect of the Universe.*

grand lodge   A grand lodge is the state or provincial or national organization that has final authority over all Freemasonry within its borders or jurisdiction. Most American grand lodges meet annually to conduct business.

Grand Orient   Grand Orient is another name for a grand lodge. It means "Grand East," and refers to the location of the seat of the Grand Master in the grand lodge. While the Grand Orient de France will admit atheists, the name "Grand Orient" itself says nothing about an organization. For example, the Grand Orient d'Haiti is a regular grand lodge formed in 1822.

Great Architect of the Universe   The Great Architect of the Universe is a title for God as Creator. Its first Masonic use was in Reverend James Anderson's 1723 *Constitutions of the Free-Masons.* Anderson, a Presbyterian minister, no doubt picked it up from John Calvin's *Institutes of Christian Religion.* Calvin, whose teachings formed the basis of theology for Presbyterian and Reformed Churches, refers to God as "the Architect of the Universe" and refers to His works as the "Architecture of the Universe." Masons sometimes abbreviate the phrase as G.A.O.T.U.

heal   Healing is the process of making an irregular Mason or Masonic lodge regular, usually authorized and under the supervision of a Grand Master. The Mason or lodge to be healed must acknowledge that they have deviated from accepted Masonic norms. The healing process usually involves at least repeating the solemn obligation of membership.

high degree   A high degree is any Masonic degree after 3° Master Mason, for example the Royal Arch Degree of the York Rite or the 32° Master of the Royal Secret of the Scottish Rite. "High Degree Masons" only have authority in the organization that gave them the high degree. The Grand Master is the highest Mason in any grand lodge.

honorary body   See *invitational body.*

Illuminati   Adam Weishaupt formed the Illuminati (enlightened ones) in Bavaria in 1776. He became a Mason in 1777 and then recruited from lodges. The goal of the Illuminati was to increase morality, oppose evil, and reform the world by creating a secret network of influential people. Bavaria suppressed the order in 1784, though some believe it still exists as a shadowy group controlling world affairs.

invitational body A Masonic invitational body is one with membership by invitation only. Potential members cannot simply apply; they must be invited. A potential new member is proposed to the group and a ballot taken. If it is favorable, an invitation is extended; if not, nothing is said to the proposed member. An invitational body is sometimes called an honorary body.

irregular A lodge or grand lodge is irregular if it does not adhere to Masonic standards (for example allowing political discussions or not requiring a Volume of Sacred Law in each lodge).

jewel A jewel is an emblem worn by a Mason to indicate membership or position. A Masonic officer wears a collar or cord around his neck with the jewel of his office suspended from it. For example, the Worshipful Master wears a square. After presiding over a Masonic organization, a Mason is usually presented with a past officer's jewel.

jurisdiction The jurisdiction of a Masonic body is the geographic area over which it has Masonic control.

legitimate origin A grand lodge or lodge (except for the few time-immemorial lodges like Mother Kilwinning No. 0 of Scotland) has legitimate origin if it can trace its origin back to a grand lodge with legitimate origin in an unbroken succession of regular charters. The British grand lodges—England (1717), Ireland (1725), and Scotland (1736)—are "grandfathered" in as being of legitimate origin, since the first grand lodges there were self-created.

lodge A Masonic lodge is a local chapter of the fraternity of Freemasons. Like the word school, the word lodge can refer to both the group of members and to the physical building. Other Masonic-related organizations use the words chapter, council, commandery, consistory, priory, court, and so on to refer to specific local organizations.

military lodge A lodge whose charter is granted to members of a military unit. The lodge is not limited to one city, but moves about with the unit. Freemasonry was spread throughout much of the world by traveling military lodges.

Mother Council of the World Founded in 1801, the Supreme Council for the Southern Jurisdiction was the first supreme council in the world. It is called the Mother Council of the World because all legitimate Supreme Councils can trace their origins back to it.

Odd Fellows   The Independent Order of Odd Fellows is an English fraternity imported into America in the early 1800s. Its members, primarily working-class, were considered "odd" because of the mutual support they gave each other. There is a branch for ladies and a system of several degrees similar to the York Rite. The Odd Fellows were larger than the Freemasons in 1900, though they are much smaller today.

operative Mason   An operative Mason is a worker who constructs a building with stone.

operative Masonry   "By operative masonry, we allude to a proper application of the useful rules of architecture, whence a structure will derive figure, strength and beauty, and whence will result a due proportion and a just correspondence in all its parts ...." (J. L. Cross, 1819)

Orient   The Scottish Rite refers to states as Orients and the cities or regions where Scottish Rite bodies are located as Valleys.

patent   A patent is an official document conferring a right or privilege. In Masonry, it nearly always refers to a Scottish Rite document either certifying membership or granting authority and power. Modern patents only certify membership.

petition   A membership petition is what Masons call an application. The typical petition usually asks for name, age, residence, occupation, references, and the recommendations of two members of the lodge.

Private Lodge   A Private Lodge is a local lodge usually held in a member's home without a charter or regular meetings. Found occasionally in the eighteenth century, such lodges are never seen today.

recognition   A grand lodge or other Masonic body "recognizes" another if it accepts it as a legitimate Masonic organization. Recognition usually allows intervisitation membership by members and transfer of members. It's similar to one college "recognizing" another by allowing the transfer of credits.

reunion   A reunion is a Scottish Rite event when a Valley gathers to confer the degrees on new members. A reunion may be a long weekend or it could be spread out over several weeks. While all 29 degrees are rarely conferred during one reunion, members can usually see all of the degrees over a few years in a region.

Saint John's Days   Saint John's Days are June 24 for St. John the Baptist, and December 27 for St. John the Evangelist. The Saints John are the patron saints of Freemasonry, dating back to at least the formation of the Premier Grand Lodge on June 24, St. John the Baptist's Day, 1717. It is a traditional day for feasting, parading, and attending worship.

side degree   A side degree is a Masonic degree that's not under the control of any central governing organization. Generally anyone who has received the degree can give it to someone else. Some side degrees created their own governing body, but most died out from lack of interest. Modern side degrees tend to be humorous fund-raisers with the fees going to a designated charity.

speculative Mason   A speculative Mason is a member of the modern fraternity and one who "fits himself as a living stone for that house not made with hands, eternal in the heavens."

speculative masonry   "By speculative masonry, we learn to subdue the passions, act upon the square, keep a tongue of good report, maintain secrecy, and practice charity … It leads the contemplative to view, with reverence and admiration, the glorious works of creation, and inspires him with the most exalted ideas of the perfection of his divine Creator …" (J. L. Cross, 1819)

square and compass   Freemasons are members of the "Ancient, Honorable Fraternity of Free and Accepted Masons." The terms Freemason and Mason are interchangeable as are Freemasonry and Masonry. The word is thought to refer originally to freestone masons, skilled craftsmen who carved freestone. It may have referred to the fact that Masons were free to travel.

Symbolic or Blue Lodge   A Symbolic or Blue Lodge confers the first three degrees: 1°, Entered Apprentice; 2°, Fellowcraft; and 3°, Master Mason. All Masons belong to a Blue Lodge. They may be "Blue" because their aprons are usually trimmed with blue, or because their symbolic covering "is no less than the clouded canopy, or starry-decked heavens" which is blue. In England and Europe, these are known as "Craft Lodges."

third degree, giving someone the   The expression, "Giving someone the third degree," often referring to intense questioning, is thought to have originated from the supposed rigors of initiation into the Third or Master Mason Degree.

Time Immemorial Lodge   A Time Immemorial Lodge is a local lodge that meets without a grand lodge charter. Before grand lodges established procedures, several Masons could come together and decide to create a lodge. There were very few such lodges, but two examples are Mother Kilwinning Lodge No. 0 of Scotland and Fredericksburg Lodge of Virginia, George Washington's mother lodge.

Tyler   The Tyler (or Tiler) is the outer guard of a lodge room. The position is first referred to in James Anderson's *The New Book of Constitutions*, 1738. Its origin is unknown, but it likely originated from protecting a building by tiling its roof.

Valley   The Scottish Rite refers to states as Orients and the cities or regions where Scottish Rite bodies are located as Valleys.

Volume of Sacred Law   In a Masonic lodge, the *Volume of Sacred Law* is the book or books held sacred by the members. In British and American lodges, it is nearly always the Holy Bible. The Volume of Sacred Law represents God's revelation to mankind.

Worshipful Master   The presiding officer of a lodge is called the Worshipful Master, not because the members "worship" him, but because it's a traditional English title of respect. (English magistrates today are still addressed as "worshipful.") The Grand Master is Most Worshipful, and other officers may be Right Worshipful or Very Worshipful, depending on their rank. Other Masonic bodies use different superlatives to describe their local presiding officers: Excellent, Illustrious, Eminent, Venerable, and so on. When the word Most is used, that usually indicates the presiding officer of a state or national organization.

Appendix B

Further Reading, Websites, and Contact Information

There is no "official voice" of Freemasonry except for a grand lodge. If you look hard enough, you can find a Freemason who will say anything you want to hear. The books recommended here are generally conservative in their conclusions and demanding of their references. Many other excellent (and not so excellent) volumes on Freemasonry are not listed here.

Most Masonic grand bodies publish annual "Transactions" or "Proceedings." These contain committee reports, floor debates, motions proposed, officer lists, and so on. Earlier years often list the names of all members of lodges. While reading these volumes can be tedious, they give a detailed account of what really goes on in Masonry.

Then there's always the "research lodge," which is a lodge whose members are interested in the history of Freemasonry. They usually publish an annual volume that contains the research papers published during that year. A state research lodge is an excellent source for biographies of Masons or histories of lodges from that state.

The premier research lodge is Quatuor Coronati Lodge No. 2076, London, founded in 1885; they have published their annual transactions, *Ars Quatuor Coronatorum*, since 1886.

The American Lodge of Research of New York is the oldest existing American research lodge; they have published their annual *Transactions* since 1930.

The Philalethes Society, "the international Masonic research society," has published its bimonthly magazine, *The Philalethes*, since 1946.

The Phylaxis Society is devoted to Prince Hall Masonic research and has published their quarterly magazine, *The Phylaxis*, since 1974.

The Scottish Rite Research Society of Washington, D.C., is devoted to the study of Freemasonry in general and the Scottish Rite in particular; they have published their annual transactions, *Heredom*, since 1992.

Books on Freemasonry

American Lodge of Research. *Transactions of the American Lodge of Research*. New York: 1930.

Bérage, M. de Les Plus. *Secrets Mystères des Hauts Grades de la Maçonnerie Dévoilés (The Most Secret Mysteries of the High Degrees of Masonry Unveiled)*. Jerusalem [Geneva]: 1766.

Brockman, C. Lance, ed. *Theatre of the Fraternity: Staging the Ritual Space of the Scottish Rite of Freemasonry, 1896–1929*. Minneapolis, MN: Frederick R. Weisman Art Museum, Univ. of Minnesota, 1996.

Brown, Walter Lee. *A Life of Albert Pike*. Fayetteville, AR: Univ. of Arkansas Press, 1997.

Bullock, Steven C. *Revolutionary Brotherhood: Freemasonry and the Transformation of the American Social Order, 1730–1840*. Chapel Hill, NC: Univ. of North Carolina Press, 1996.

Carnes, Mark. C. *Secret Ritual and Manhood in Victorian America*. New Haven, CT: Yale Univ. Press, 1989.

Clegg, Robert I. *Mackey's History of Freemasonry, 6 vols., rev. ed.* New York, NY: Masonic History Co., 1921.

Coil, Henry W., et al. *Coil's Masonic Encyclopedia, rev. Allen E. Roberts*. Richmond, VA: Macoy Publishing and Masonic Supply Co., 1999.

Coil, Henry W. *Freemasonry Through Six Centuries, 2 vols., ed.* Lewis C. "Wes" Cook. Richmond, VA: Macoy Publishing and Masonic Supply Co., 1967.

de Hoyos, Arturo, and S. Brent Morris. *Is It True What They Say About Freemasonry? 3rd ed.* New York: M. Evans & Co., 2004.

Denslow, William R. *10,000 Famous Freemasons, 4 vols.* Richmond, VA: Macoy Publishing and Masonic Supply Co., 1957.

Fox, William L. *Lodge of the Double-Headed Eagle: Two Centuries of Scottish Rite Freemasonry in America's Southern Jurisdiction.* Little Rock, AR: Univ. of Arkansas Press, 1997.

Franco, Barbara. *Bespangled, Painted, & Embroidered: Decorated Masonic Aprons in America, 1790–1850.* Lexington, MA: Scottish Rite Masonic Museum of Our National Heritage, 1980.

Gould, Robert Freke. *The History of Freemasonry, 4 vols., rev. ed.* Philadelphia: John C. Yorston, Pub. Co., 1898.

Hamill, John. *The Craft: A History of English Freemasonry.* London: Lewis Masonic, 1994.

Hamilton, John D. *Material Culture of the American Freemasons.* Hanover, NH: Univ. Press of New England, 1994.

Heaton, Ronald E. *Masonic Membership of the Founding Fathers.* Silver Spring, MD: Masonic Service Association, 1974.

Horne, Alex. *King Solomon's Temple in the Masonic Tradition.* Wellingborough, Northamptonshire, England: Aquarian Press, 1972.

Jones, Bernard E. *Freemasons' Book of the Royal Arch.* London: Harrap, 1957.

———. *Freemasons' Guide and Compendium, new & rev. ed.* London: Harrap, 1977.

Lipson, Dorothy Ann. *Freemasonry in Federalist Connecticut, 1789–1835.* Princeton, NJ: Princeton Univ. Press, 1977.

Morris, S. Brent. *Cornerstones of Freedom: A Masonic Tradition.* Washington, D.C.: Supreme Council, 33°, S.J., 1993.

———. *Masonic Philanthropies: A Tradition of Caring, 2nd ed.* Lexington, MA and Washington, D.C.: Supreme Councils, 33°, 1997.

Philalethes Society. *The Philalethes* magazine. Toronto, Ontario: 1946—.

Phylaxis Society. *The Phylaxis* magazine. Tacoma, WA: 1974.

Putnam, Robert D. *Bowling Alone: The Collapse and Revival of American Community.* New York: Simon & Schuster, 2000.

Quatuor Coronati Lodge No. 2076. *Ars Quatuor Coronatorum, transactions of Quatuor Coronati Lodge No. 2076.* London: 1886.

Roberts, Allen E. *House Undivided: The Story of Freemasonry and the Civil War.* New York: Macoy Publishing and Masonic Supply Co., 1964.

Schmidt, Alvin J. *Fraternal Organizations.* Westport, CT: Greenwood Press, 1980.

Scottish Rite Research Society. *Heredom, transactions of the S.R.R.S.* Washington, D.C.: 1992.

Stevenson, David. *The Origins of Freemasonry: Scotland's Century.* Cambridge, England: Cambridge Univ. Press, 1988.

Tabbert, Mark A. *American Freemasons: Three Centuries of Building Communities.* Lexington, MA: National Heritage Museum; New York: N.Y. Univ. Press, 2005.

Vaughn, William Preston. *The Antimasonic Party in the United States, 1826–1843.* Lexington, KY: University Press of Kentucky, 1983.

Walkes, Joseph. A., Jr. *Black Square and Compasses: 200 Years of Prince Hall Masonry, rev. ed.* Richmond, VA: Macoy Publishing and Masonic Supply Co., 1979.

Wesley, Charles H. *Prince Hall: Life and Legacy, 2nd ed.* Washington, D.C.: United Supreme Council, P.H.A., 1983.

Web Links on Freemasonry

The web links that follow are to Masonic sites that I used in writing this book. I think you'll find them helpful in your research.

Alexandria-Washington Lodge No. 22, Alexandria, Virginia
www.aw22.org

Anti-Masonry Points of View
www.masonicinfo.com

Canonbury Masonic Research Centre, London
www.canonbury.ac.uk

Cedar Lodge No. 270, A.F.&A.M., Oshawa, Ontario
www.durham.net/~cedar/famous.html

Chancellor Robert R. Livingston Masonic Library of the Grand Lodge of New York
www.nymasoniclibrary.org

DeMolay International
w22.demolay.org

General Grand Chapter, Order of the Eastern Star
www.easternstar.org

George Washington Masonic National Memorial, Alexandria, Virginia
www.msana.com

Grand Lodge of British Columbia and Yukon, Vancouver, British Columbia
www.freemasonry.bcy.ca

Grottoes of North America
www.scgrotto.com

International Order of the Rainbow for Girls
www.iorg.org

Job's Daughters International
www.iojd.org

Masonic Service Association of North America, Silver Spring, Maryland
www.msana.com

The Philalethes Society, the international Masonic research society
www.freemasonry.org/psoc

The Phylaxis Society, the Prince Hall research society
www.freemasonry.org/phylaxis

Pietre-Stones Review of Freemasonry, Italy
www.freemasons-freemasonry.com

Shriners of North America, Tampa, Florida
www.shrinershq.org

Supreme Council, 33°, N.M.J., Lexington, Massachusetts
www.supremecouncil.org

Supreme Council, 33°, S.J., Washington, D.C.
www.srmason-sj.org

Supreme Council, Order of Amaranth
www.amaranth.org

Tall Cedars of Lebanon of North America
www.tallcedars.org

United Grand Lodge of England, London
www.grandlodge-england.org

York Rite Information Site (Royal Arch Masons, Cryptic Masons, Knights Templar, etc.)
www.yorkrite.com

Contact Information for Masonic Philanthropies

These Masonic philanthropies were described in Chapter 12.

Chicota Youth Camp
Prince Hall Grand Lodge, F.&A.M., of Louisiana
Post Office Box 2974
Baton Rouge, LA 70821-2974
www.theplumbline.org

Children's Healthcare of Atlanta
Children's at Scottish Rite
1001 Johnson Ferry Road
Atlanta, GA 30342-1600
404-785-5252
www.choa.org

Humanitarian Foundation
Grottos of North America
1696 Brice Rd.
Reynoldsburg, OH 43068
614-860-0717
www.scgrotto.com

Knights Templar Eye Foundation, Inc.
1000 East State Pkwy., Suite I
Schaumburg, IL 60173-4592
847-490-3838
www.knightstemplar.org/ktef

Masonic Service Association of North America
8120 Fenton St.
Silver Spring, MD 20910-4785
301-588-4010
www.msana.com

RiteCare Childhood Language Program
Supreme Council, 33°, S.J.
1733 16th St., N.W.
Washington, D.C. 20009-3103
202-232-3579
www.srmason-sj.org

Shriners Hospitals for Children
Shriners International Headquarters
2900 Rocky Point Dr.
Tampa, FL 33607-1460
813-281-0300
www.shrinershq.org

Texas Scottish Rite Hospital for Children
2222 Welborn St.
Dallas, Texas 75219
214-559-5000
www.tsrhc.org

32° Masonic Learning Centers for Children, Inc.
Supreme Council, 33°, N.M.J.
33 Marrett Rd.
Lexington, MA 02141-5703
781-862-8518
www.childrenslearningcenters.org

Masonic Rituals

Freemasonry's rituals really separate it from other organizations. Every Mason for centuries has experienced these formal ceremonies designed to teach moral lessons through symbols. The ritual is much more than just custom with origins that stretch back beyond memory; its symbolism is the heart and soul of Masonry. For example, the Volume of Sacred Law (usually a Bible in American lodges) represents God's revealed will to man; a lodge simply cannot meet without an open Bible on the altar in the center of the room.

Ritual is one of those curious human activities that has an impact far greater than its individual parts. Consider the funeral ceremonies where family and friends symbolically drop dirt or flower petals on the coffin, or where a bugler plays Taps. The emotional impact of these two rituals transcends their simple actions. Masonic ritual can be like this.

This appendix has two examples of Masonic rituals to give you a flavor of the ceremonies and language used in Masonic initiations.

The Mystery of Freemasonry, 1730

The Mystery of Freemasonry (or *Grand Whimsy of Masonry*, as it is sometimes known) appeared in the *London Daily Journal*, no. 2998, August 15, 1730. About a dozen exposés of Masonic ritual had been published in London between 1723 and 1730 (some have uncertain dating), and *The Mystery* refers to but does not elaborate on the "Master's Word and Signs" and the "Master's Part." We do not know if this refers to a separate, third degree, or if this is another name for the second degree. Prichard's *Masonry Dissected* of October 1730 is the first publication to clearly present the Third or Master Mason Degree.

The Square Deal

The expression, "Giving someone the third degree," often referring to intense questioning, is thought to have originated from the supposed rigors of initiation into the Third or Master Mason Degree.

Benjamin Franklin reprinted *The Mystery of Free-masonry* in his *Pennsylvania Gazette*, December 5–8, 1730, making it also the first exposé of Masonic ritual in America. What we don't know is how closely these ceremonies come to those used in actual lodges, English or American. The anonymous author of *The Mystery* claimed the rituals came from a deceased Brother who had "committed to Writing, the Form and Manner of his Admission, which he kept among his choicest and most private papers, and in the most secret Part of his Cabinet." Further, the Grand Lodge in London on August 28, 1730, presumably in response to *The Mystery*, adopted some unspecified rules for "preventing any false Brethren being admitted into regular Lodges."

Since no official record of Masonic ritual survives from that time, we are forced to piece together early Masonic ceremonies on the basis of exposés like this that were usually intended to damage the fraternity.

The Mystery of Free-Masonry presents 29 questions and answers summarizing the initiation ceremonies. The new member presumably answers these questions before the lodge to complete his initiation. A similar summary recitation, the symbolic "work" of a degree, is required today before a new member can advance to the next degree.

The Mystery of Free-Masonry

London Daily Journal, no. 2998, August 15, 1730

Q: Are you a Mason?

A: I am.

Q: How shall I know you are a Mason?

A: By Signs, Tokens, and Points of my Enterance.

Q: How was you made?

A: Neither naked nor cloathed, standing or lying, but in due Form.

Q: Give me a Sign.

A: Every Square is a Sign; but the most Solemn is the Right-hand upon the Left-breast, the Arm hanging down, a little extended from the Body.

Q: Give me a Letter.

A: B. O. A. Z.

When this Question is ask'd you are to give the Letter B. The Querist will say O. you A: he Z.

Q: Give me another.

A: J. A. C. H. I. N.

Alternately as Boaz. N.B. Boaz and Jachin were two Pillars in Solomon's Porch, I Kings vii 21.

Q: To what Lodge do you belong?

A: The Holy Lodge of St. John.

Q: How is it seated?

A: East and West, as all other Temples are.

Q: Where was you enter'd?

A: In a Just and Perfect Lodge.

Q: What makes a Just and Perfect Lodge?

A: A Master, two Wardens, and four Fellows, with Square, Compass, and Common Gudge [Judge, a measuring device or template].

N.B.: One of them must be a Working Mason.

Q: Where was you made?

A: In the Valley of Jehosaphat, behind a Rush Bush, where a Dog was never heard to bark, nor a Cock to crow, or elsewhere.

Q: Where was the first Lodge kept?

A: In Solomon's Porch, the Pillars were call'd Jachin and Boaz.

Q: How many Orders be there in Architecture?

A: There be five, Tuscan, Dorick, Ionick, Corinthian, and Composite or Roman.

Q: How many Points be there in the Fellowship?

A: There be five, 1st Foot to Foot, 2d Knee to Knee, 3d Hand to Hand, 4th Heart to Heart, and 5th Ear to Ear.

Q: How do Masons take their Place in Work?

A: The Master's Place East, the Warden's East, and the Fellows the Eastern Passage.

Q: How many precious Jewels be there in Masonry?

A: Three, the Master, Wardens, and Fellows.

Q: Whence comes the Pattern of an Arch?

A: From the Rainbow.

Q: Is there a Key for your Lodge?

A: Yes, there is.

Q: Where is it kept?

A: In an Ivory Box, between my Tongue and my Teeth, or under the Lap of my Liver, where the Secrets of my Heart are.

Q: Is there a Chain to your Key?

A: Yes, there is.

Q: How long is it?

A: As long as from my Tongue to my Heart.

Q: Where does the Key of the Working-Lodge lie?

A: It lies upon the Right-hand, from the Door two Feet and a half, under a Green Turf, or under a Square Ashler.

Q: Where does the Master Mason set his Mark upon the Work?

A: Upon the South-East Corner.

Q: Have you been in the Kitchen?

N.B.: You shall know an Enter'd Apprentice by this Question.

A: Yes, I have.

Q: Did you ever dine in the Hall?

N.B.: A Brother Mason by this Question.

A: Yes, I did.

Q: How old are you?

A: Under 5, or under 7, which you will.

N.B.: When you are first made a Mason, you are only entered Apprentice; and till you are made a Master, or, as they call it, pass'd the Master's Part, you are only an enter'd Apprentice, and consequently must answer under 7; for if you say above, they will expect the Master's Word and Signs.

Note, There is not one Mason in an Hundred that will be at the Expence to pass the Master's Part, except it be for Interest.

Q: How was you admitted?

N.B.: Some will ask what was that Form after the third Question and Answer above.

A: When I came to the first Door, a Man with a drawn Sword asked me, If I had any Weapons? I answer'd. No. Upon which he let me pass by him into a dark Entry; there two Wardens took me under each Arm, and conducted me from Darkness into Light passing thro' two Rows of the Brotherhood, who stood mute, to the upper End of the Room, from whence the Master went down the Outside of one of the Rows, and touching a young Brother on the Shoulder, said, Who have we here? To which he answer'd, A Gentleman who desires to be admitted a Member of the Society. Upon which he came up again, and asked me. If I came there thro' my own Desire, or at the Request or Desire of another? I said, My own. He then told me, If I would become a Brother of their Society, I must take the Oath administered on that Occasion. To which assenting, a Square was laid on the Ground, in which they made me kneel bare-knee'd, and giving a Compass into my Right-Hand, I set the Point to my Left-Breast, and my Left-Arm hanging down. The Words of the Oath I can't remember, but the Purport was as follows:

I Solemnly protest and swear, in the Presence of Almighty God, and this Society, that I will not, by Word of Mouth or Signs, discover any Secrets which shall be communicated to me this Night, or at any time hereafter: That I will not write, carve, engrave, or cause to be written, carved, or engraven the same, either upon Paper, Copper, Brass, Wood, or Stone, or any[thing] Moveable or Immoveable, or any other way discover the same, to any but a Brother or Fellow Craft, under no less Penalty than

Hits and Myths

This part of the ceremonies seems to be entirely accurate as Masons in London today still wear white gloves and aprons to their meetings. All Masons wear aprons to their meetings, and many, especially officers, wear white gloves.

having my Heart plucked thro' the Pap of my Left-Breast, my Tongue by the Roots from the Roof of my Mouth, my Body to be burnt, and my Ashes to be scatter'd abroad in the Wind, whereby I may be lost to the Remembrance of a Brother. After which I was cloathed.

N.B.: The Cloathing is putting on the Apron and Gloves.

Q: How was the Master cloathed?

A: In a Yellow Jacket and Blue Pair of Breeches.*

Q: What was you doing while the Oath was tendering?

A: I was kneeling bare-knee'd betwixt the Bible and the Square, taking the solemn Oath of a Mason.

*N.B.: The Master is not otherwise cloathed than common; the Question and Answer are only emblematical, the Yellow Jacket, the Compasses and the Blue Breeches, the Steel Points.

N.B.: There's a Bible put in the Right-Hand, and the Square under the Right-Elbow.

Disciple Degree, 1826

Robert Benjamin Folger became a Mason in New York City in 1826 at the age of 23 and participated in the fraternity with enthusiasm. In July 1827, he dated a small book in which he had written in cipher the rituals for the degrees of Disciple, Fellow, and Master. The ceremonies, dissimilar to almost all American Masonry, seem to be variants of those of the European Rectified Scottish Rite (no relation to the American-born Ancient & Accepted Scottish Rite). There is circumstantial evidence these rituals were used by Zorobabel Lodge No. 498 of New York City, which was chartered in June 1827 with Folger as Senior Warden. Zorobabel Lodge, along with most New York lodges, closed shortly thereafter as anti-Masonry swept the state. There is no evidence the rituals were ever used thereafter.

Regardless of their use, the rituals represent almost 100 years of evolution of Masonic ceremony. The symbolism is much more sophisticated than that of *The Mystery of Free-Masonry*, and it is also strongly Christian, definitely at odds with the generally accepted universalism of the fraternity. It does, however, give a good flavor of 1826-era Masonic ritual.

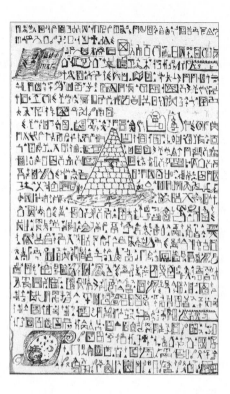

This page is an example of the cipher used by Robert B. Folger in 1826 to protect his ritual. The text talks about the Bible as a guide for moral and ethical behavior. The pyramid seems to be nothing more than decoration.

Note that sometimes stage directions have not been given and that a speaker may refer to something that appears to have happened "off stage." For example, the Master refers to a naked sword pointing to the heart of the candidate, but there is no indication of who carries or points the sword. Also, there may be a symbolic temple with steps painted on the floor as the Master tells the candidate to "ascend the three first mysterious steps leading to the Temple," without any other instructions.

Grade of Discipulus

-First Section-

The candidate is conducted by the Introductor and his Deputy to the Chamber of Preparation, a small, dark room lit by a candle, where he is seated.

Introductor: Hither we have come. Let us now rest for a short time. I beg you to abstract yourself from all worldly thoughts for a short space of time and to devote this time to the consideration of yourself and such things as may here occur to you.

[Shows cross to candidate.] To the place of which this is a symbol we must all sooner or later come. It is dark, black, separated from the world. The rules of our Order have made me bring you here. Let me make you acquainted with these things.

[Shows Hourglass to candidate.] The hourglass, an emblem of time. [Turns it.] Behold how rapidly the particles of sand run. It will soon run out, and then, if no external power set it in motion again, its movements will never be renewed. Forget this not.

Here is water for your refreshment.

[Shows skull to candidate.] Here is an image of death and an emblem of mortality. No human philosophy or thinking can divine what lies on the other side of this veil or what shall happen to us there, yet it is certain we shall all thence, and it is certain that duration beyond the grave, in comparison to the period of human life, is infinite. This subject is interesting then.

[Shows Bible to candidate.] See, here is the only light by which we can learn how to enter the grave so as to enjoy happiness hereafter. It is the book of wisdom and contains a revelation of the Divine will.

Question first: Do you believe in the existence of a God, perfect and good, the creator of all things?

Second: Do you believe in the immortality of the soul?

Third: What do you believe is your duty toward God, your neighbor, and yourself?

Here it is proper for the Deputy to return to the Master the aspirant's answer.

Introductor: The Lodge have commanded me to inform you respecting some of our customs and to prepare you in a proper manner to be brought to the Lodge in order to be accepted a Disciple. Permit me to advise you: I would encourage you to exercise fortitude in the trials you are about to endure and to place confidence in those who shall conduct you on the way in which you have concluded to enter upon. The first sign of your ready determination to join us is to deliver me your hat and sword.

[Speaking to the Deputy.] Brother, please deliver this to the Lodge and return hither to me again.

Sir, will you please to lay from you all money, jewels, metal, and other signs of distinction; uncover your left breast and expose the knee; tread down the left shoe. Now, Sir, you are externally prepared to be presented to the Lodge, and it is pleasing to me to believe that your heart and thoughts correspond with this external preparation, and that you have taken, and will continue to take, all possible pains to eradicate all prejudices and emotions of the mind which militate against your proper duties as a man.

But Sir, you must be convinced that a man who is stripped of all sensual and false decorations and ornaments and coverings of vanity cannot be known and distinguished from others but by righteousness and virtue. It is absolutely necessary that you henceforth be convinced of your own weakness and that it is impossible to go forward toward the Temple of Truth without help and guidance.

In order to give us a plain to know of your want of confidence in yourself, you must permit us to deprive you of the light. It is an emblem of the false views which are the lot of that man who is left to his own guidance.

Bandage is placed over candidate's eyes.

Tell me, can you see any thing? On your honor? Be careful not to use deception with him who shall guide you. You will else presently certainly repent.

You are now in darkness, but fear not. Those who guide you go in light and will not lead you astray. Hold your hands before you and guard against the hindrances that can meet you. You are now left alone. Strive to go forward, but use the utmost prudence in order to avoid surrounding danger.

The candidate takes three steps forward.

I acknowledge you as one who seeks. I mark well your serious desire, but in thick darkness and alone you would undoubtedly go astray.

The Introductor takes his left hand and says:

As such I will bring you to the Lodge. I pray, be constant and confident, learn to suffer with patience and abstinence, and thereby make yourself worthy to obtain in time what at present you ask for. Follow me. Fear not.

Three knocks at the door.

Deacon: Who comes here?

Introductor: One in darkness who seeks light and wishes to be accepted.

Deacon: His name? Age? Father's name? Where born? Profession? Religion? And has he made any vow that forbids his joining the Masonic fraternity?

Enter, Sir.

Introductor: Here I have brought you. My task is now finished. You are in safe hands, even with them who deserve your perfect confidence.

When in the west and the Guide has left him Master says:

Worshipful Master: Thus, Sir, you have sought to be received among us. This your request we have seriously attended to, and from the good opinion we have conceived of your character, and as one of our Brethren has pledged himself for you in a solemn manner, and he who I sent to inquire as to your motives in joining us and your opinion of our institution has reported so favorably of you, we have therefore sent you a Guide who has opened our door to you, and now you are in the midst of us in a state fit for trials which you must endure and which everyone who wishes to be received among us must endure, remembering that the present is a state of trial.

But, Sir, before we can proceed further, I have some questions to ask to you which I must require an audible and unequivocal answer. But first, Sir, I must state to you that there is nothing in our Order which is incompatible with religion or with civil or moral duties. For the truth of this we pledge you our honor.

And I now ask you if you are prompted to join us by a desire of being charitable and useful to your fellow man?

Second, are you prompted to join us by a desire of the knowledge of truth and to be associated with those who profess to promulgate it and encourage virtue and laudable pursuits?

Third, will you conform to the regulations of the Freemasons and do you voluntarily request to be made a Mason?

Well then, your request shall be granted you. God give at some future day it may serve to make you happy. You are about to be going on a mysterious journey, and, although you cannot see the way, yet confiding in him who leads you, go forward with firmness, yet with caution, and rest assured that your guide will not bring you in paths where you should not go.

Three gavel raps

Guide: Sir, the naked sword pointing to your heart is but a weak symbol of the dangers which surround one who wanders in darkness, put your trust in God and fear not. Come with me.

The candidate is conducted around the lodge room three times.

First Round

Man was created in the image of God, but who can know him when he deforms himself?

Second Round

He who is ashamed of religion and of truth is unfit for and unworthy of fraternity.

Third Round

That man whose ear is deaf to the cries and the distresses of his fellow man is a monster in the assembly of the Brethren.

Worshipful Master: Let him now ascend the three first mysterious steps leading to the Temple to try his strength, and then bring him to the East to make his vow.

Sir, your patience has enabled you to reach an altar at which, by the rules of our Order, you are required to make a solemn and irrevocable oath or covenant never unlawfully to reveal any of the secrets, symbols, signs, or ceremonies belonging to the Order of Free and Accepted Masons. You have already been assured that the Order does not contain anything contrary to our duties toward God, our country, our neighbors, or ourselves. This assurance I now repeat to you and ask you if you are willing to make the oath or covenant required? What do you answer?

But, Sir, before you can make a covenant, it is necessary that you be well acquainted with its tenure, we holding it to be wrong to make a covenant with any unless they be well acquainted with its conditions. Therefore, you will please to kneel on the left knee on the square and let your right hand rest upon the Bible, on which lies the square and compasses covered with a sword. Sir, the book on which your hand now rests is the Holy Bible opened at the first chapter of St. John and the fifth verse where there is written, "And the light shineth in darkness; and the darkness comprehended it not."

Do you believe that your hand thus rests upon the Bible? And why do you believe it? Thus you conceive that a man, upon the serious assurance, can believe the thing of which he has no other evidence than this assurance?

Now, I desire you to be attentive to the voice of the Senior Warden who will repeat to you the covenant which you are required to make, even in the presence of the Supreme Architect of the Universe, and which, when made, can not be recalled.

Senior Warden: Disciple's Obligation. I do promise, solemnly and sincerely, in the presence of God and this Lodge of Freemasons, that I will be faithful and true to the holy Christian religion and to the government of the country in which I live, and that I will strive to gain the esteem and love of my fellow man by practicing virtue and shunning vice, and by encouraging others so to do. And I promise that I will, as far as I can, help the distressed, and that I will conceal from everyone who is not a Free and

Accepted Mason all the secrets, signs, symbols, and usages of this Order and every part thereof, and I will not unlawfully reveal any of these things, nor write them on anything, or make them legible so that the secrets of our Order can thereby be unlawfully revealed. And I will strive to cherish and love all worthy and good Brethren Free and Accepted Masons as Brothers, and should I violate this oath, the keeping of which I solemnly promise, I am willing to be looked upon by all honest and good men and all Freemasons as a man without honor and every praiseworthy quality and deserving their contempt and disdain. And I now repeat my wish to be made a Mason. So help me God.

Worshipful Master: Have you heard and rightly understood this solemn covenant? Are you willing to make it and to sanction it according to the customs of our Order? I ask you for the last time.

One gavel rap

In order Brethren, and while this man makes this covenant, let us give a token of our accordance with it.

The candidate repeats the covenant.

You are now bound to us and we to you by this your oath, but the trial of your sincerity, which is the hardest trial, is now at hand. You have said that you would sanction this covenant according to the customs of the Order. Are you willing to sanction it with your blood if it should be required of you?

Then I accept you as a Disciple in Masonry, to the honor of almighty God, in the name of fraternity, and by virtue of the power vested in me, Amen.

Response by the candidate

Worshipful Master: Arise.

This last trial, your being willing to sanction your vows with your blood, is convincing of your sincerity and I now salute you by the name of Brother, but forget not under what conditions you obtained this name. Brother Wardens, bear him to the West, there to come to light.

Senior Warden: He is prepared.

Worshipful Master: One gavel rap.

The new Disciple's blindfold is removed, and in dim light he sees several Brothers apparently threatening him with their drawn swords.

Worshipful Master: However weak the present light that flames before you may be, yet my Brother it is sufficient to show you our weapons turned against you, threatening you with shame and disdain if ever you should unhappily betray the trust we have reposed in you. Let him be veiled again.

One gavel. After the Brethren with swords retire the light is restored, and the blindfold is removed again.

Sic Transit Gloria Mundi! For a moment since, you saw our weapons turned against you, apparently hostile. Look at us now, armed for your defense and welfare. Yes, my Brother, the Order will not and shall not forsake you as long as you are faithfully doing your duty and keeping your covenants.

Brother Master of Ceremonies, let our new Brother be clothed and return with him to the Lodge.

-Second Section-

Deacon: Worshipful Master, one knocks.

Worshipful Master: See who it is, and, if a Brother, let him enter.

Deacon: It is our new made Brother.

Worshipful Master: Bring him to the East by the Northwest.

My Brother, permit me to clothe you with this lambskin, and in the name of the Order I present you with these white gloves. The white clothing you are now decorated with is emblematic of purity and innocence. Worn honorably it is a very honorable badge. Preserve them from stains. Wear them and never appear without them in the Lodge.

The Order of good Masons does not permit women to its assemblies, yet we profess and cherish esteem for the virtues and good among the other sex. In token of this, I present you with these gloves, which you can give to such a one as merits your esteem.

Here is your money. Take them, my Brother. In giving you back these, we would admonish you to bear in mind that it is a most certain truth that the love of gold, silver, and the like has produced more evils than anything else in this world. Yes. Covetousness and avarice have led men much astray, have induced them to commit the meanest acts of cowardice and most atrocious acts of injustice and oppression and violence. Acts so mean and so atrocious as to excite disdain and horror in every honest and feeling man. Acts which cause the sign of sorrow to burst from the breasts of the really pious, and which, alas, it is to be feared, have brought down the thunder of damnation on the heads of the guilty perpetrators. Therefore, respecting the pernicious influence of these things, we should watch.

Here is your hat. In delivering it to you, I must remark that none except they be Masters sit covered in Lodge.

Take your sword, use it carefully when called upon by your country for its defense, but bear in mind that a man of blood is deemed unfit to build a temple to the name of God, and never forget His commandment, who gave law to man in order to make them happy, saying, "Thou shalt not kill."

I will now teach you the tests of this degree.

[The candidate is taught the words, grips, and signs of this degree, unwritten by Folger.]

Go to the Wardens and make yourself known to them and to the Brother who pledged himself in your behalf, as a Mason. Afterwards, the Senior Warden will teach you the symbolic work upon the rough stone.

Senior Warden: My Brother, the rough stone, an emblem of which you here see, is a symbol of man deformed by prejudices and passions. To eradicate and to subdue them is the duty and the work of every Mason.

The gavel is symbolical of power. It is used by hewers of stone to strike off the asperities of the ashlar and to reduce it to the form which the Master has prescribed it should have. And we are reminded by it to strive to subdue our passions and eradicate our prejudices to fit ourselves for that spiritual temple, not made with hands, eternal in the heavens. In token of your willingness to do this work, which the Great Master has ordained we should do, stoop humbly down toward the earth and strike the rough stone as I do.

The Senior Warden and the candidate each strike a rough stone three times with a gavel.

Continue constantly in the work you there began to do, that the Supreme Architect may not be displeased with your labors and that you may strive to merit reward: His approbation. Now, let the first work you do as a Mason be a good work. Do a deed of charity, give a pittance to help the distressed.

Turn around, be attentive to a recitation of the rite of initiation which now is ended.

Worshipful Master: The symbols, usages, and customs of our order are intended to lead the mind to the contemplation of things of the greatest importance to that man who is wishful to learn, and to meditate upon that which may promote his welfare. You was first led into a dark and narrow chamber where you was separated from the world and from your friend who brought you there. Although this separation was but short, yet the things there led you to meditate upon subjects however common, yet of a very serious nature.

Your meditations were disturbed by the coming of a Brother who inquired of you your motives for joining our Order, for none but those actuated by right motives should be admitted among us. He who was deputed to guide you hither in company with your friend caused you to be divested of all money, jewels, and the like, and otherwise prepared you for introduction into our Lodge, that you might know that worldly distinctions can not give rank and must not create differences among Masons. In the Lodge we all meet upon the level. In fact, among the good and impartial, nothing but virtue and mental acquirements can give preeminence among men in the world, and nothing else can distinguish Brethren in the Lodge.

In the Chamber of Preparation, it is hoped you spent the time profitably. You was abstracted from the world and, for a moment perhaps, was engaged in the consideration of yourself and, that external objects might not entirely engage your attention or disturb the impression which you there received and that you should show confidence in your guide, you was deprived of the light and thus led to the door of the Lodge where you was received by the Warden. He demanded your religion, name, age, and other particulars, for none but a professor of religion, and one who is free, and who we know a man arrived at the years of real manhood, can be admitted to our Lodge.

The three blows on the door of the Lodge should remind you that for him who seeks with constancy, who seeks with humility, and who knocks rightly, the door of the Temple of Fraternity and Peace shall be opened. You was conducted to the care of the Warden and stood then upon the threshold of the Lodge, your former guide leaving you with assurances that you were in the hands of those who would not mislead you. But before you could, by the assistance of your new conductor, proceed on your way, the Master addressed you, and your motives for coming here were acknowledged to the Brother by him who best could inform us thereof, by yourself.

Then we, reciprocating the confidence you had hitherto placed in us, believed you, and you commenced a journey on which you learned from the East some truths on which the tenets of our Order in a great measure rest. You then ascended the mysterious steps of the Temple, and was brought to the altar to make a very serious promise.

On the whole of this journey reciprocal confidence supported you. Confidence between you and us, for if you had not had confidence in us you would have refused to follow our directions and, if we had not have believed you to have been upright, we would not have received you among us.

You was joined to us by a solemn tie, and afterwards you saw a blazing and unsteady light which was only sufficient to discover surrounding apparent dangers. Finally, the veil was removed wholly, and you saw the light. You beheld Brethren armed for your defense and welfare. All hostile appearances were done away, and everything bore appearances of love. Those scenes are emblematical of the different states of man.

The unenlightened state, in which man makes sacrifices and oblations for obtaining favors from heaven or for the atonement of atrocious deeds he may have committed. In which state nearly all the objects he perceives were hostile in appearance, and his fellows seemed strangers to him, and their arms appeared to threaten him, their power to place him in danger. He shuns, fears, or even hates them, but, in a more enlightened state, he perceives that heaven rather accepts a sincere and contrite heart than burnt offerings and oblations. He then acknowledges his fellow men as his Brethren, and he looks upon their power as means for his own defense and welfare. He joins them, relies upon them, and loves them. You was invested with the badges of innocence and purity and admonished by good conduct to keep them unsullied.

And then you received the tests of this Degree, by which you can make yourself known to Brother Masons. Do not, my Brother, be among those who strive to publish to the world that they are Masons. Neither countenance anything tending to this end, for the honor and usefulness of the Order are much more extended by concealment and by an intimate acquaintance with the exalted aim of our labors and the probable extent of their influence upon the welfare of the human race. You will be assured that silence and circumspection tend to give our Order force.

The carpet before you [painted with emblems], containing the principle symbols of our Order deserves your attention. The Border, including the whole, is a representation of Mason work, and this is the covering to all the other symbols and should remind us of that concealment of which we have already spoken.

The Rough Stone and Square Stone are symbols. The one of the raw and uncultivated man, the other of him which has subjected himself to the discipline of truth and virtue.

The Trestle Board should admonish us carefully to study and to follow the plans of the Master.

This diagram is reconstructed from a faint pencil sketch. It probably was intended to be painted on carpet or canvas and unrolled on the lodge floor during initiations.

You see the Sun and Moon. They are here represented to remind us of application to our duties day and night, for this is all a man can do without erring.

There are the different instruments used by Masons as Plumb, Level, and Square and so forth. They are adopted as hieroglyphs by us, and therefore are here represented.

And in the center is the Blazing Star, which we view with reverential silence.

And finally, the Cord. It is here in remembrance of the cord which the veil of the tabernacle was drawn aside with, and it is emblematical of the tie which unites all good men and Masons, and we should remember ever that silence is the veil which keeps our sanctuary in safety.

Close before you is the Mosaic Pavement, which in Solomon's Temple covered the courts and on which the sanctuary stood. It is emblematical of the foundation which we seek in those we accept among us. They should be men of a firm and fair character, fit for surrounding and supporting a sanctuary.

On the left you see a Pillar with the initial of the word of your degree. Bear in mind the meaning of the word: "In him is strength." [The word *Boaz* means "In him is strength."] You ascended those three first steps of the Temple, but, as your time was not yet come, the door remained shut and you was led back again, and it is recommended to you to wait with patience and to labor diligently yet with meekness, that when the door of the Temple shall be opened to you, you may hope, yes believe, to enter into the inner apartments with great joy.

Appendix D

Famous Freemasons

Any organization that's been around for over 300 years is bound to pick up a few well-known members (and the occasional black sheep). The list that follows records a few more than 200 Freemasons, mostly American, that I thought were interesting. It provides a nice demonstration of the sort of men who have been attracted to the fraternity and perhaps influenced in some way by its tenets of Brotherly Love, Relief, and Truth.

This list gives you all of the ammunition that you need to "prove" that Masons rule the world, or that civilization as we know it would collapse without Freemasonry. Please resist the urge! The list only proves that the fraternal bonds of Freemasonry are attractive to a broad spectrum of men, many of whom have accomplished a lot in their careers.

Abbott, William "Bud"—Half of the Abbott & Costello comedy team; Daylight Lodge No. 525, Michigan

Acuff, Roy—"King of Country Music"; East Nashville No. 560, Tennessee

Aguinaldo, Emilio—President of the Philippines who declared their independence in 1898; Logia Pilar y Imus, Philippines

Aldrin, Edwin E. "Buzz"—American astronaut and second human to walk on the moon; Montclair Lodge No. 144, New Jersey

Allen, Charles H.—First Governor of Puerto Rico (1800–1802) when it was freed from Spanish rule; William North Lodge, Massachusetts

Allende, Salvador—President of Chile; Lodge Progresso No. 4, Chile

Anderson, Brad—Cartoonist and creator of the Marmaduke comic strip; lodge unknown

Arnold, Benedict—Major General in the Continental Army who defected to the British; Hiram Lodge No. 1, Connecticut

Arnold, Henry "Hap"—Commander, Army Air Force in World War II who helped establish U.S. Air Force; Cassia-Mt. Horeb Lodge No. 273, Pennsylvania

Ataturk, Mustapha Kemal—Founder of the modern Republic of Turkey; Macedonia Resorta e Veritus Lodge, Italy

Austin, Stephen F.—The "Father of Texas" who helped colonize the territory; Louisiana Lodge No. 109, Missouri

Autry, Gene—American actor and singing cowboy; Catoosa Lodge No. 185, Oklahoma

Bartholdi, Frederic A.—French sculptor of the Statue of Liberty; Lodge Alsace-Lorraine, France

Basie, William "Count"—Orchestra leader and composer; Wisdom Lodge No. 102, PHA, Illinois

Bayh, Birch— U.S. Senator from Indiana, 1962–1981; lodge unknown

Baylor, Robert E. B.—Founder of Baylor University, Texas's first Baptist college; Grand Chaplain, Grand Lodge of Texas

Beard, Daniel Carter—Founder of first American Boy Scout organization; Mariners Lodge No. 67, New York

Bellamy, Francis J.—Baptist Minister who wrote the Pledge of Allegiance; Little Falls Lodge No. 181, New York

Benes, Eduard—President of Czechoslovakia who led his government into exile during WWII; Lodge Ian Amos Comensky, Czechoslovakia

Bentsen, Lloyd M.—U.S. Senator from Texas, 1971–1993, and Vice-Presidential candidate; McAllen Lodge No. 1110, Texas

Berlin, Irving—Composer of more than 1,500 songs and several musicals like *Annie Get Your Gun;* Munn Lodge No. 190, New York

Black, Hugo L.—U.S. Senator from Alabama, 1927–1937, and U.S. Supreme Court Justice; Temple Lodge No. 636, Alabama

Blanc, Melvin Jerome "Mel"—The voice of Bugs Bunny, Elmer Fudd, Daffy Duck, Porky Pig, and many more; Mid Day Lodge No.188, Oregon

Bolivar, Simon—"El Libertador"; Bolivia is named after this Freemason; Protectora de la Vertudes Lodge No. 1, Venezuela

Boone, Daniel—Early explorer of Kentucky; said to be a Mason by his son

Borglum, Gutzon & Lincoln—Father and son who carved the presidential busts on Mt. Rushmore; Howard Lodge No. 35, New York and Battle River Lodge No. 92, South Dakota

Borgnine, Ernest—Film and television actor, known for *Marty*, for which he won an Oscar, and *McHale's Navy*; Abingdon Lodge No. 48, Virginia

Bowie, James—American-born Mexican colonist who defended the Alamo; Humble Cottage Lodge No. 19, Louisiana

Bradley, Omar N.—Five-star General in World War II; West Point Lodge No. 877, New York

Brant, Joseph—Chief of the Mohawks, 1742–1807, and British supporter during the American Revolution; Hiram's Cliftonian Lodge No. 417, England

Buchanan, James—Fifteenth President of the United States, 1857–1861; Lancaster Lodge No. 43, Pennsylvania

Burbank, Luther—Horticulturist and naturalist; Santa Rosa Lodge No. 57, California

Burnett, David G.—First President of the Republic of Texas; Holland Lodge No. 1, Texas

Burns, Robert—National poet of Scotland; St. David's Lodge No. 174, Scotland

Butterfield, Daniel—Major General in the Civil War, U.S. Army, credited with composing "Taps"; lodge unknown

Byrd, Richard E.—U.S. Admiral and explorer, the first to fly over the North Pole; Federal Lodge No. 1, District of Columbia

Carson, Christopher "Kit"—Frontiersman and explorer; Montezuma Lodge No. 109, New Mexico

Chrysler, Walter P.—American automobile manufacturer who founded the Chrysler Corporation; Scottish Rite Valley of Salina, Kansas

Churchill, Winston—Prime Minister of England during WWII; Studholme Lodge No. 1591, England

Citroen, Andre—French engineer and motor car manufacturer; La Philosophie Positive Lodge, France

Clark, Roy—Country-Western singer; member of the Grand Ole Opry; Jenks Lodge No. 497, Oklahoma

Clark, William—Explored the Mississippi River with Merriwether Lewis; St. Lewis Lodge No. 111, Pennsylvania

Clemens, Samuel L. "Mark Twain"—Writer and humorist; Polar Star Lodge No. 79, Missouri

Clinton, DeWitt—Mayor of New York City and Governor of New York; Grand Master, Grand Lodge of New York

Cobb, Ty—Baseball player with highest lifetime batting average (.367); Royston Lodge No. 426, Michigan

Cody, William "Buffalo Bill"—Guide, scout, and showman, he founded the "Wild West Show"; Platte Valley Lodge No. 15, Nebraska

Cohan, George M.—Composer and lyricist of such songs as "Yankee Doodle Dandy"; Pacific Lodge No. 223, California

Cole, Nat "King"—Pianist and singer; Thomas Waller Lodge No. 49, PHA, California

Coleman, Frank—Founder of Omega Psi Phi Fraternity; lodge unknown

Cooper, Leroy Gordon—American astronaut; Carbondale Lodge No. 82, Colorado

Crockett, David ("Davy")—Frontiersman and U.S. Representative, 1827–1835, and defender of the Alamo; lodge unknown

Crosby, Norm—Comedian and entertainer; Euclid Lodge, Massachusetts

DeMille, Cecil B.—Film director, known for *The Ten Commandments* and *The Greatest Show on Earth*; Prince Orange Lodge No. 16, New York

Dempsey, Jack—Heavyweight boxing champion; Kenwood Lodge No. 800, Illinois

Dixon, George—Commander of the ill-fated submarine *Hunley* during the U.S. Civil War; Mobile Lodge No. 40, Alabama

Dole, Robert J.—U.S. Senator from Kansas, 1961–1996, and presidential candidate; Russell Lodge No. 177, Kansas

Dow, Herbert Henry—Founded Dow Chemical Co.; lodge unknown

Doyle, Sir Arthur Conan—British physician and writer, creator of Sherlock Holmes; Phoenix Lodge No. 257, England

DuBois, W.E.B.—Educator, scholar, and co-founder of the NAACP; Widow's Son Lodge No. 1, PHA, Connecticut

Edson, Carroll A.—Co-founder of the Order of the Arrow, the Boy Scout honor fraternity; lodge unknown

Ellington, "Duke"—Jazz composer and bandleader; Social Lodge No. 1, PHA, District of Columbia

Elway, John—Denver Bronco quarterback and NFL Hall of Fame; South Denver Lodge No. 93, Colorado

Ervin, Samuel J., Jr.—U.S. Senator from North Carolina, 1954–1974, and chairman of the "Watergate Committee"; Catawba Valley Lodge No. 217, North Carolina

Evans, Bob—Founder of Bob Evans Restaurants; Morning Dawn Lodge No. 7, Ohio

Faber, Eberhard—Founder of the Eberhard Faber Pencil Company; Chancellor Walworth Lodge No. 271, New York

Farragut, David G.—Admiral, U.S. Navy during the Civil War; Visited Naval Lodge No. 87, California

Fields, W. C.—Movie actor and comedian; E. Coppee Mitchell Lodge No. 605, Pennsylvania

Fleming, Sir Alexander—Discovered penicillin and received the Nobel Prize; Grand Officer, England

Ford, Gerald R.—Thirty-eighth President of the United States; Malta Lodge No. 465, Michigan

Ford, Glenn—Movie actor; lodge unknown

Ford, Henry—Founded Ford Motor Company; Palestine Lodge No. 357, Michigan

Franklin, Benjamin—Printer, author, diplomat, philosopher, scientist, and signer of the Constitution of the United States; Grand Master, Grand Lodge of Pennsylvania

Gable, Clark—Movie actor, played Rhett Butler in *Gone with the Wind*; Beverly Hills Lodge No. 528, California

Garfield, James A.—Twentieth President of the United States; Columbus Lodge No. 246, Ohio

Garibaldi, Giuseppe—Italian revolutionary and liberator; Tompkinsville Lodge No. 471, New York

Gatling, Richard J.—Inventor of the Gatling Gun; Center Lodge No. 23, Indiana

George VI—King of England during World War II; Naval Lodge No. 2612, England

Gilbert, William S.—British playwright and lyricist known for comic operas written with composer Sir Arthur Sullivan; St. Machar Lodge No. 54, Scotland

Gillette, King C.—Inventor and manufacturer of the safety razor; Adelphi Lodge, Massachusetts

Glenn, John H., Jr.—First American to orbit the earth, U.S. Senator from Ohio, 1974–1998; Concord Lodge No. 688, Ohio

Goldwater, Barry—U.S. Senator from Arizona, 1953–1965, 1969–1987, and presidential candidate; Arizona Lodge No. 2, Arizona

Gompers, Samuel—Founder of the American Federation of Labor (AFL); Dawson Lodge No. 16, District of Columbia

Goodman, E. Urner—Co-founder of the Order of the Arrow, the Boy Scout honor fraternity; Lamberton Lodge No. 487, Pennsylvania

Goodnow, David—News anchor on CNN News; Lessing Lodge No. 464, Indiana

Grissom, Virgil "Gus"—Astronaut and Command Pilot on the first manned Gemini flight, killed in launch pad explosion; Mitchell Lodge No. 228, Indiana

Guillotin, Joseph Ignace—French physician who developed a more humane method of execution; Lodge of the Nine Sisters, France

Hahnemann, Samuel—German physician and founder of homeopathy; Minerva Lodge, Germany

Hall, Prince —First African American Worshipful Master; African Lodge No. 459, England

Hampton, Lionel—Best known for playing the vibraphones, he is a jazz giant; Boyer Lodge No. 1, PHA, New York

Hancock, John—President of the Continental Congress and first signer of the Declaration of Independence; St. Andrew's Lodge, Massachusetts

Harding, Warren G.—Twenty-ninth President of the United States; Marion Lodge No. 70, Ohio

Hardy, Oliver—Half of the Laurel and Hardy comedy team; Solomon Lodge No. 20, Florida

Haydn, Franz Joseph—Austrian composer; Lodge Zur Wahren Einracht, Austria

Helms, Jesse—U.S. Senator from North Carolina, 1972–2002; Grand Orator, Grand Lodge of North Carolina

Henley, Vernard W. Henley Sr.—President, Consolidated Bank and Trust Co, Richmond, Virginia, the oldest African American owned bank in the United States; Grand Lodge of Virginia, PHA

Henry, Patrick—American patriot known for saying, "Give me liberty or give me death."; Believed to be a member of Tappahannock Lodge, Virginia

Henson, Josiah—Escaped slave who inspired *Uncle Tom's Cabin*; Mount Moriah Lodge No. 4, Ontario

Henson, Matthew—Fellow explorer with Bro. Adm. Robert Peary when he discovered the North Pole; Celestial Lodge No. 3, PHA, New York

Hilton, Charles C.—Founder of Hilton Hotels; William B. Warren Lodge No. 309, Illinois

Hoban, James—Architect of the White House; Federal Lodge No. 1, District of Columbia

Hoover, J. Edgar—Director of the Federal Bureau of Investigation, 1924–1972; Federal Lodge No. 1, District of Columbia

Horton, Frank Reed—Founder of the Alpha Phi Omega college service fraternity; Western Star Lodge No. 37, Connecticut

Houdini, Harry (Ehrich Weiss)—Magician and escape artist; St. Cecile Lodge No. 568, New York

Houston, Sam—First President of the Republic of Texas; Cumberland Lodge No. 8, Tennessee

Humphrey, Hubert H.—Thirty-eighth Vice President of the United States, 1965–1969; lodge unknown

Irwin, James B.—American astronaut and member of the fourth moon-landing team; Lodge Tejon No. 104, Colorado

Ives, Burl—Entertainer and singer; Magnolia Lodge No. 242, California

Jackson, Andrew—Seventh President of the United States; Grand Master, Grand Lodge of Tennessee

Jackson, Reverend Jesse—American civil rights leader and politician; Harmony Lodge No. 8, PHA, Illinois

Jenner, Edward—English physician, discovered small pox vaccine; Faith and Friendship Lodge No. 270, England

Johnson, Andrew—Seventeenth President of the United States; Greenville Lodge No. 19, Tennessee

Johnston, Jack—Heavyweight boxing champion, known as the "Great White Hope"; Lodge Forfar and Kincardine No. 225, Scotland

Jolson, Al—American vaudeville and movie star; St. Cecile Lodge No. 568, New York

Jones, John Paul—"Father of the U.S. Navy"; St. Bernard Lodge No. 122, Scotland

Jones, Melvin—Co-founder of Lions International, the international service organization; Garden City Lodge No. 141, Illinois

Juarez, Benito—First Native-American President of Mexico; apron and regalia on display in Mexico City

Kalakaua, King David—Last monarch of the Hawaiian Kingdom; Progress de l'Oceanie Lodge No. 37, California

Kemp, Jack—Buffalo Bills quarterback, U.S. Congressman from New York, 1971–1989; Fraternal Lodge No. 625, New York

Kipling, Rudyard—British writer and winner of the Nobel Prize for literature; Hope and Esperance Lodge No. 782, India

Kossuth, Lajos (Louis)—Tireless campaigner for Hungarian freedom, he was the first "foreigner" to address the U.S. Congress after Lafayette; Cincinnati Lodge No. 133, Ohio

Kresge, Sebastian S.—Founder of the S. S. Kresge Company, which became K-Mart; Palestine Lodge No. 357, Michigan

Lafayette, Marquis de—French general who supported the American Revolution; Grand Lodge of Tennessee

LaGuardia, Fiorello—Mayor of New York City, 1934–1945; Garibaldi Lodge No. 542, New York

Lewis, Meriwether—Explored the Mississippi River with William Clark; St. Louis Lodge No. 111, Missouri

Lincoln, Elmo—First actor to play Tarzan of the Apes; lodge unknown

Lindbergh, Charles—American aviator who made the first solo transatlantic flight; Keystone Lodge No. 243, Missouri

Lipton, Sir Thomas—British merchant who established tea processing factories in England and the United States; Scotia Lodge No. 178, Scotland

Listz, Franz von—Hungarian composer; Lodge Zur Einigkeit, Germany

Livingston, Robert R.—Chief Justice of the New York Supreme Court who gave George Washington his first oath of office as President; Grand Master, Grand Lodge of New York

Lloyd, Harold C.—Movie star and Imperial Potentate of the Shriners; Alexander Hamilton Lodge No. 535, California

Lott, Trent—U.S. Senator from Mississippi, 1989–; Pascagoula Lodge No. 419, Mississippi

MacArthur, General Douglas—Five-star General during WWII; Manila Lodge No. 1, Philippines

MacDonald, John A.—First Prime Minister of the Dominion of Canada; St. John's Lodge No. 5, Ontario

Macy, Rowland Hussey—Founder of Macy's Department Store; lodge unknown

Marsh, Henry—First Black Mayor of Richmond, Virginia (1977); lodge unknown

Marshall, George C.—Five-star General during WWII, received the Nobel Peace Prize for the "Marshall Plan"; Grand Lodge of the District of Columbia

Marshall, John—Chief Justice of the U.S. Supreme Court, 1801–1835; Grand Master, Grand Lodge of Virginia

Marshall, Thurgood—First African American Justice of the U.S. Supreme Court; Coal Creek Lodge No. 88, PHA, Oklahoma

Mayer, Louis B.—Film producer whose company became part of Metro-Goldwyn-Mayer; St. Cecile Lodge No. 568, New York

Mayo, Charles; William James; and William Worrall—Three brothers who founded the Mayo Clinic; Rochester Lodge No. 21, Minnesota

McCall, Abner V.—President of Baylor University, Texas, and First Vice President of the Southern Baptist Convention; Baylor Lodge No. 1235, Texas

McGovern, George—U.S. Senator from South Dakota, 1963–1981, and presidential candidate; Resurgam Lodge No. 31, South Dakota

McHenry, James—Private secretary to Generals Washington and Lafayette, Fort McHenry, Maryland, is named after him; Spiritual Lodge No. 23, Maryland

McKinley, William—Twenty-fifth President of the United States; Hiram Lodge No. 21, Virginia

Mesmer, Franz Anton—Discovered Mesmerism, the precursor of hypnosis; Les Philadelphes Lodge, France

Mfume, Kweisi—U.S. Congressman from Maryland, 1988–1996; President of the NAACP; Mt. Olive Lodge No. 25, PHA, Maryland

Michelson, Albert Abraham—Measured the speed of light; first American scientist to win a Nobel Prize; Washington Lodge No. 21, New York

Molson, John—Founder of Molson Breweries; St. Paul's Lodge No. 374, England

Monroe, James—The fifth President of the United States; Williamsburg Lodge No. 6, Virginia

Montgolfier, Jacques Etienne; Joseph Michel—Co-developer with his brother of the first practical hot-air balloon; Lodge of the Nine Sisters, France

Mozart, Wolfgang Amadeus—Austrian composer; Lodge Zur Wohltatigkeit, Austria

Murphy, Audie—Most decorated American soldier of WWII and movie actor; Scottish Rite Valley of Dallas, Texas

Nicholas, Samuel—Created the American Marine Corps; Lodge No. 13, Pennsylvania

Nunn, Sam—U.S. Senator from Georgia, 1972–1997; Houston Lodge No. 35, Georgia

O'Higgins, Bernardo—Liberator of Chile; lodge unknown

Oglethorpe, James E.—Founder of Savannah, Georgia; King Solomon's Lodge No. 1, Georgia

Olds, Ransom E.—American automobile inventor and manufacturer of the Oldsmobile; Capitol Lodge No. 66, Michigan

Palmer, Arnold—Professional golfer; Loyalhanna Lodge No. 275, Pennsylvania

Peale, Reverend Norman Vincent—American minister, founder of *Guideposts* magazine; Milwood Lodge No. 1062, New York

Peary, Robert E.—Discovered the North Pole; Kane Lodge No. 454, New York

Penney, J. (James) C.—Founder of J.C. Penney department stores; Wasatch Lodge No. 1, Utah

Pershing, John Joseph—Five-star General during WWI; Lincoln Lodge No. 19, Nebraska

Pickett, George E.—Commanded the Confederate lines at the U.S. Civil War Battle of Gettysburg and led the final assault; Dove Lodge No. 51, Virginia

Pike, Albert—Soldier, lawyer, Grand Commander of the Scottish Rite, S.J.; Western Star Lodge No. 1, Arkansas

Pinchot, Bronson—American actor, played Balki Bartokamous in the TV series *Perfect Strangers;* Harford Lodge No. 445, Pennsylvania

Polk, James Knox—Eleventh President of the United States; Columbia Lodge No. 31, Tennessee

Pryor, Richard—American actor and comedian; Henry Brown Lodge No. 22, PHA, Illinois

Putnam, Israel—General during the Revolutionary War, he is remembered for saying at the Battle of Bunker Hill, "Don't fire until you see the whites of their eyes."; Military Lodge

Revere, Paul—American revolutionary, famous for his ride to warn "The British are coming!"; Grand Master, Grand Lodge of Massachusetts

Richards, Michael—American actor, played "Kramer" in the TV Series *Seinfeld;* Riviera No. 780, California

Richardson, Elliott—Attorney General of the United States, resigned rather than fire Watergate Special Prosecutor Archibald Cox; lodge unknown

Rickenbacker, Eddie—American aviator, the most decorated combat pilot of WWI; Kilwinning Lodge No. 297, Michigan

Ringling, Alfred T.; John Nicholas; Albert Charles; Charles Edward; William H. Otto; August George; Henry William George—Formed the Ringling Brothers Circus; Baraboo Lodge No. 34, Wisconsin

Robinson, "Sugar Ray"—American boxer and six-time world champion; Joppa Lodge No. 55, PHA, New York

Rogers, Roy (Leonard Franklin Slye)—American singer and actor who played a singing cowboy; Hollywood Lodge No. 355, California

Rogers, Will—Actor and humorist; Claremore No. 55, Oklahoma

Roosevelt, Franklin D.—Thirty-second President of the United States; Holland Lodge No. 8, New York

Roosevelt, Theodore—Twenty-sixth President of the United States; Matinecock Lodge No. 806, New York

Sanders, Colonel Harland—Founder of Kentucky Fried Chicken Restaurants; Hugh Harris Lodge No. 938, Kentucky

Sarnoff, David—Organized the National Broadcasting Company; Strict Observance Lodge No. 94, New York

Sax, Antoine Joseph—Belgian inventor of the saxophone; Les Vrais Amis de L'Union Lodge, Belgium

Schirra, Walter M.—American astronaut; Grand Lodge of Florida

Scott, Walter—Novelist and poet famous for *Ivanhoe*; St. David Lodge No. 36, Scotland

Sellers, Peter—English actor and comedian, played Inspector Clouseau in the *Pink Panther* films; Chelsea Lodge No. 3098, England

Sibelius, Jean—Finnish composer famous for *Finlandia*; Suomi Lodge No. 1, Finland

Skelton, Richard B. "Red"—Entertainer and Comedian; Vincennes Lodge No. 1, Indiana

Smith, Joseph—Founder of the Mormon Church; Nauvoo Lodge, Illinois

Sousa, John Philip—U.S. Marine Band leader; Hiram Lodge No. 10, District of Columbia

Stanford, Leland—Railroad builder and founder of Stanford University; Prometheus Lodge No. 17, Wisconsin

Sullivan, Sir Arthur S.—English composer of the tune "Onward Christian Soldiers" and known for comic operas written with lyricist W. S. Gilbert; Grand Organist, United Grand Lodge of England

Swift, Johathan—Author of *Gulliver's Travels;* Lodge No. 16, Ireland

Taft, William Howard—Twenty-seventh President of the United States; Kilwinning Lodge No. 356, Ohio

Thomas, Danny—Entertainer, actor, and founder of St. Jude's Children's Hospital; Grand Lodge of New Jersey

Thomas, Dave—Founder of Wendy's Restaurants; Sol D. Bayliss Lodge No. 359, Indiana

Tillis, Mel—Country-Western singer; Branson Lodge No. 587, Missouri

Truman, Harry S—Thirty-third President of the United States; Belton Lodge No. 450, Missouri

Voltaire, François Marie Arouet—French writer and philosopher; Lodge of the Nine Sisters, France

Wallace, George C.—Four-term governor of Alabama and presidential candidate; Grand Orator, Grand Lodge of Alabama

Wallace, Lewis—U.S. Civil War general and author of *Ben Hur: A Tale of the Christ;* Fountain Lodge No. 60, Indiana

Wanamaker, John—Founder of Wanamaker department stores; Grand Lodge of Pennsylvania

Warner, Jack—Movie producer and founder of Warner Brothers; Mount Olive Lodge No. 506, California

Warren, Earl—Chief Justice of the U.S. Supreme Court, 1953–1974; Grand Master, Grand Lodge of California

Washington, Booker T.—African American educator and author; Grand Lodge of Massachusetts, PHA

Washington, George—First President of the United States; Fredericksburg Lodge No. 4, Virginia

Wayne, John—American movie actor; Marion McDaniel Lodge No. 56, Arizona

Wilder, Lawrence Douglass—First elected black Governor in the United States from the state of Virginia; Grand Lodge of Virginia, PHA

Wozniak, Steve—Co-founder of Apple Computers; Charity Lodge No. 362, California

Young, Andrew—United Nations Ambassador and Mayor of Atlanta, Georgia; St. James Lodge No. 4, PHA, Georgia

Young, Brigham—Founder of the Mormon Church in Utah; Nauvoo Lodge, Illinois

Zanuck, Darryl F.—Movie producer and co-founder of 20th Century Productions; Mount Olive Lodge No. 506, California

References

The Masonic membership of these men has been checked through several sources:

- Anti-Masonry Points of View, www.masonicinfo.com
  (accessed September 3, 2005)

- Cedar Lodge No. 270, Ontario, www.durham.net/~cedar/famous.html
  (accessed September 3, 2005)

- Denslow, William R. *10,000 Famous Freemasons*, 4 vols. Richmond, VA: Macoy Publishing and Masonic Supply Co., 1957.

- Grand Lodge of British Columbia and Yukon, http://freemasonry.bcy.ca
  (accessed September 3, 2005)

- Heaton, Ronald E. *Masonic Membership of the Founding Fathers*. Silver Spring, MD: Masonic Service Association, 1974.

Index